EMERSON'S OPTICS

Biographical Process and the Dawn of Religious Leadership

Richard A. Hutch

UNIVERSITY
PRESS OF
AMERICA

Copyright © 1983 by
University Press of America, Inc.™
P.O. Box 19101, Washington, D.C. 20036

All rights reserved

Printed in the United States of America

ISBN (Perfect): 0-8191-3006-0
ISBN   (Cloth): 0-8191-3005-2

PREFACE

Three general concerns within biographical scholarship serve as the backdrop of the pages to follow. Every biographer must reckon with each in one way or another.

The first concern is for the quantity of biographical information controlled by a life-writer. On the one hand, some biographers include all possible information about the entire span of an individual's life. Often, the span of a life is depicted as including the historical periods preceding and following the birth and death of the individual written about. For our purposes, such an emphasis is represented by Ralph Rusk's, The Life of Ralph Waldo Emerson (1949). It is a treasure-trove of intricately woven information about all aspects of Emerson's life and times from start to finish. On the other hand, some biographers emphasize the opposite tactic. Because of what could appear as an unwieldy mass of information they choose to confine inquiry to events or episodes of a life which can be explored in great depth. Henry Pommer's, Emerson's First Marriage (1967) is an example of this tendency in that it focusses on a period of only two years in Emerson's life. Thus, when compared on the basis of the criterion of quantity, we note that Rusk has given us a "magnum opus," while Pommer has given us a lively look into one particular relationship in a life.

A second concern of biographical scholarship is about the method or approach chosen by a life-writer. Simply put, shall we concern ourselves with the changes undergone by the subject of a biography or with the continuity of enduring personal characteristics of his or her

life?   In the first instance, a chronological approach predominates: A
life is described as a sequence of events extending from birth to death.
In the second instance, depictions of a person's "character", in various
moments of time or across the board of different aspects, takes precedence:
A life is described as a self-regulating series of transformations of a
more-or-less static pattern of personality.   The former tendency is
exemplified not only by Rusk's biography of Emerson, but more recently also
by Joel Porte's, Representative Man: Ralph Waldo Emerson in his Time (1979).
This book describes how Emerson's literary career constituted a record
of a full sequence of life events.   The latter methodological style is
perhaps illustrated by Edward Wagenknecht's, Ralph Waldo Emerson: Portrait
of a Balanced Soul (1974).   This biography avowedly intends a description
of Emerson's "character and personality", not his ideas or writings as
literature which may appear throughout some temporal sequence.
Wagenknecht admits his approach takes seriously the "psychography" of other
biographers, namely, Sainte-Beuve and Gamaliel Bradford.   These biographers
were more concerned with the "being," not the "becoming," of the individuals
they wrote about.

The third and last concern of biographical scholarship which serves
as backdrop for what is to follow has to do with the more psychological
dimensions of the biographical process itself.   This includes not only the
psychological happenings of the subject of a biography.   The psychological
meaning of the process of writing a biography, along with the choice of
an individual to write about, also is of interest.   In short, what

constitutes such psychological dimensions, and how is a biographer to go about describing them in a specific individual and in himself? As one surveys the most important recent studies of Emerson he is struck by the virtual absence of biographical interest in psychological dimensions evident in this nineteenth-century American leader. However, two books by the psychoanalytically-oriented biographer, Erik Erikson - Young Man Luther (1958) and Gandhi's Truth (1968) - pick up on psychological dimensions. Erikson's work also emphasizes the historical dimensions, in terms of which personal psychological events can (and often do) become extended into broadly-based, shared meanings. In effect, Erikson's biographical scholarship can serve to suggest ways in which Emerson studies might possibly benefit by considering the psychobiographical meaning of Emerson's life and writings. This is not to suggest that the psycho-biographer is to aim at "de-bunking" implicit panegyrical understandings of such an American Olympian. Rather, the argument is simply that such psychological probing into Emerson's life could possibly extend our understanding into new dimensions of his humanity and ours. Indeed, unlike persons of the nineteenth century, we living in the contemporary age are very self-consciously "psychological."

In light of these three concerns, how does the biography of Ralph Waldo Emerson to follow stack up? This biography differs from Rusk's by limiting biographical information about Emerson's life to his first thirty-five years. However, it does not go so far as Pommer's study to confine description to only one personal relationship, which is barely considered in the context of a broader vision of Emerson's life. Many relationships will be dealt with, but they will be placed into a sequence of events constituting what are recognized as Emerson's early, formative years. After 1838, his thirty-fifth year, his life becomes less than eventful, as we shall see. The most interesting psychological action takes place when Emerson was in his twenties and early thirties. Thus a middle-road is taken on the issue of the quantity of biographical information coming under control.

In regard to method or approach, a similar course is taken. The biography is organized chronologically around a sequence of events. In this way, it parallels the biography by Porte. However, it differs from Porte's book in two ways: First, it is not primarily concerned with a literary emphasis, though reference is made throughout to various things Emerson wrote. If anything, Emerson's literary output is considered to be a continuous symbolic projection of tacit religious and philosophical reflections. In this general regard, we shall note how for Emerson, as he put it during his twenties, "faith is a telescope". Granted, Porte, too, is concerned for the symbolic fabric of Emerson's life. However, as a biographer, he turns this concern towards literary not psychological inter-pretations of the accretion of the religious and philosophical elements of Emerson's world-view.

A second way in which the biography differs from Porte's makes an even starker contrast. In the pages to follow a deliberate attempt is made to take seriously the spirit of Wagenknecht's "psychographic" approach. A single, architectonic pattern, which is called "expansion within diminishment", is identified as undergirding Emerson's essential character, or personality.

The pattern is visual in quality. However, unlike the "balanced soul" identified by Wagenknecht in aspects of Emerson's experience concerned with topics like "Love," "Politics", "Art" and so on, the pattern evident in the following pages is directly linked to the chronology of Emerson's earlier years. Some may want to argue that Emerson undergoes basic personal change over time. However, although chronology organizes the biography, Emerson is mainly understood as usually unwittingly re-constellating and skillfully deploying his basic world-view in a variety of contexts, from private, baffling idiosyncracies to careful literary output. In this way, pattern becomes process, that is, the process of his ever-unfolding character from event to event.

The most important way in which this biography differs from those already written is in its deliberate attempt to render psychological insight into some of the more anomalous and hitherto unexplored facts of Emerson's life. Not only are psychoanalytic and ego-psychological insights employed to study, for example, the relation between Emerson's early vocational goal, the Unitarian ministry, and the periodic onset of sudden physical ailments, like blindness and diarrhea. Also evident are intimations of some principles of experimental Gestalt psychology neglected in the wake of psychoanalysis and modern behaviorism. In this regard, particular attention is paid to the nature and maintenance of the overall "form-quality" of Emerson's life, a quality which is unique in its practical emphasis on visual perception, occular mechanics, and good eyesight. The purpose in making such attempts is to trace psychological themes without traveling rough-shod over Emerson's genuine creativity and leadership in America. In fact, the tacit argument of the biography is that a personal faith of unique, visionary proportions allowed Emerson to emerge after 1838 as a national religious leader in a broad sense.   A psychology which probes the spirituality of Emerson must by necessity be cautious.   Nonetheless, interpretations are offered which could very well prompt a re-examination of biographical information by more orthodox literary biographers who may feel more at home in the traditions represented by Rusk, Pommer, Porte and Wagenknecht.   While acknowledging a debt to the scholars mentioned so far, others also have been important to this work.

Two mentors stand out from the rest.   James E. Dittes and Donald E. Capps encouraged and guided the training of interests in psychological portraiture and historical manifestations of religious leadership.   For financial support both from the Yale Divinity School and from the University of Chicago, I am grateful.   Lisa Risk and Carol Cox, Secretaries at Southern Illinois University, and Dorothy Bedwell and Sandy Lochhead at the University of Queensland did a good job as typists during the initial stages of preparing a manuscript.   Barbara Bimbi and Bonnie Faddis figure in too.   Dale and Sheila Bengtson and their children helped only indirectly.   However, hardly enough thanks can ever be given to them in return.   I am happy.   Because of them the book will always remain really, a "mythical manuscript," pleasing best when left forgotten on the shelf.   Finally, the book is in memory of Mugs the Cat, who was a steadfast and faithful friend to the end.

R.A.H.,
St. Lucia, Queensland,
Australia.

TABLE OF CONTENTS

INTRODUCTION

Many scholars take for granted that Ralph Waldo Emerson generated his major corpus between the period from 1836, when <u>Nature</u> appeared, and his death in 1882. Beginning in his thirty-third year, so some would have it, Emerson commenced a long career as a lecturer and writer who helped shape limits in which future generations of Americans might broadly define their senses of a shared national identity. For approximately forty-six years he hammered away at themes related to individual heroism, like self-reliance, prudence, nature, wealth, intellect, and love. However, going along with the tendency to focus scholarly attention mostly on Emerson's later years is the implication that one should dissociate himself from the possibility of noting the developmental roots of his genuine and timely creativity. That Emerson's work should not be reduced to his psychosocial development is a maxim that few would argue with. Nonetheless, that so little attention has been paid to Emerson's earlier years, the years constituting his childhood, adolescence, and young adulthood, is at least surprising.[1]

Helpful to the idea of exploring Emerson's earlier years is the fairly recent appearance of a new edition by William H. Gilman and others of Emerson's complete journals and notebooks. With the continuing publication since 1960 of the journals and miscellaneous notebooks of Ralph Waldo Emerson, some scholars have begun to reassess the meaning of the life of this American Olympian. Prior to this recent edition, Emerson scholars were content to rely on a major but limited source, the 1909-14 edition of the journals

---

[1]Two works which probe in this direction are, Richard A. Hutch, "Emerson and Incest," <u>The Psychoanalytic Review</u> (Summer, 1975): 320-332 and Henry Nash Smith, "Emerson's Problem of Vocation," in <u>Emerson: A Collection of Critical Essays</u>, edited by Milton Konvitz and Stephen Whicher (Englewood Cliffs: Prentice-Hall, 1962), pp. 60-71.

edited by Emerson's son, Edward Waldo Emerson, and his grandson, Waldo Emerson Forbes. As James Elliot Cabot had tried to do is his 1887 Memoir, the Emerson-Forbes edition of the journals sought to "fill out and define more closely" for friends and readers of the great man "the image of him they already have."[1] The resulting panegyrical record seems anachronistic today, especially in light of the re-editing of the journals and notebooks by a team of scholars removed from the Emerson family circle. Therefore, it is opportune to launch an inquiry into Emerson's life in this new spirit. This seems particularly so because psychological insights, which purport to be at the bottom of this book, not only are in vogue, but also because they, among all other sorts of possible lines of intellectual inquiry, seem to be those which panegyrical records have obscured most. All in all, the situation invites a psycho-biographical inquiry, especially one suggesting some historical implications that Emerson's life had for nineteenth century Americans.

Yet, because Emerson was a central figure in the vanguard of leadership during the formative period of American culture, it hardly would be appropriate to "debunk" his genuine achievement. Nineteenth-century Americans had a great need to believe in themselves as heroic individuals who were finally free from colonial political and economic strains. In the crucible of his own personal and social struggles with the problem of his vocational identity Emerson supplied a model during the second half of his life of what history would recognize as that peculiarly "American identity". Perhaps we are not immune from the sort of collective fantasizing all peoples share, and by which, through memory and imagination, a sense of identity is created and transmitted. Much of the new American identity, of course, had to do

---

[1]James Elliot Cabot, A Memoir of Ralph Waldo Emerson, 2 Vols., (Boston: Houghton Mifflin and Co., 1887), I: iii.

with imagery associated with that of the so-called "self-made man" who, like Thomas Jefferson, called his countrymen to respond to forces of the Renaissance and urged them by his own exemplary behavior to make a place for themselves in the world in which they lived. This basic social modality of "making" could take novel turns as the instance of Thoreau might suggest. However, regardless of how one was to forge an American identity for himself or herself, a nation of people continually "on the make," as Erikson phrases it in reference to the psychosocial quality of human initiative, could work only to create a new historical and cultural force of considerable signi-ficance to the rest of the world.[1] This new sector of the human species was responding in new ways to the task of survival. In this sense, the history of twentieth-century American life merely dignifies the achievement of the nineteenth-century. Emerson was hardly marginal to this central thrust of culture-building. He asserted effective leadership during the hard work of speciation, that is, the unification of a populace under ever more inclusive canopies of symbolic self-understanding.[2] How did Emerson achieve such a position that would allow him to be remembered as an American Olympian?

It hardly is unfair to say that by 1837 Emerson had learned a major les-son in self-confidence and was taking steps to teach it to others. Both the "American Scholar" address of 1837 and his address on the "Lord's Supper" of 1838 were built upon a solid sense of the importance of self-trust. In

---

[1] The paradigmatic quality of Jefferson's role as a national leader is excitingly documented and depicted in, Fawn M. Brodie, Thomas Jefferson: An Intimate History (New York: W.W. Norton, 1974), and Erik H. Erikson, Dimensions of a New Identity (New York: W.W. Norton, 1974). The social modality of "making" and "being on the make" is specified in Erikson Childhood and Society (New York: W.W. Norton, 1963), p. 247.

[2] For further statements about speciation see Erik H. Erikson, Gandhi's Truth, (New York: W.W. Norton, 1969), pp. 395-448. Collective self-understandings and their symbolic expressions are theoretically delineated in a host of works some of which are Peter Berger and Thomas Luckmann, The Social Construction of Reality (New York: Anchor Books, 1966); and Clifford Geertz, "Religion as a Cultural System," in Anthropological Approaches to the Study of Religion, edited by Michael Banton, (New York: Praeger, 1966), pp. 1-46.

the first address, Emerson asserted that a life of the mind could flourish

in the United States without relying on colonial and English conventions.

In the second address Emerson attacked popular veneration of Jesus, saying

that Jesus was no better and no worse than members of the present audience.

To trust oneself was a central thrust in the overall impact of Emerson's

cultural leadership. However, to teach about self-trust is one thing, and

to win it is another.

The leadership displayed by Emerson in the arena of history and the

history of American letters owes much of its effectiveness to successful

resolutions of personal and social crises of his earlier years. Emerson's

significance, what some would call his "greatness," derives from his decision

to leave old forms of self-understanding behind and to forge new ones.

"Great adults," writes Erik Erikson, the psychologist,

> "are adult and are called great precisely because their sense
> of identity vastly surpasses the roles foisted upon them, their
> vision opens up new realities, and their gift of communication
> revitalizes actuality. In freeing themselves from rigidities
> and inhibitions they create new freedoms for some opposed cate-
> gories of men, find a new leeway for supressed energies, and give
> new scope to followers who, in turn, feel more adult for being
> sanctioned and encouraged. The great, we say, are 'gifted' with
> geni-us; but, of course, they often must destroy too, and will
> seem evil to those whom they endanger, or whom they exclude."[1]

Though this statement may serve as a model according to which any leadership

might come about, it implies that leadership stems from psychological and

social precursors which accrue prior to some occasion when stepping onto the

stage of historical and cultural drama is possible. The assumption here is that

Emerson gradually learned to set such a stage upon which he later would act in

American history in terms of crises of more rudimentary sorts that occurred

---

[1]Erik H. Erikson, "Play and Actuality," in Explorations in Psychohistory, edited by Robert Jay Lifton with Eric Olson (New York: Simon and Schuster, 1974), pp. 132-33.

during his earlier years. What might be recognized as a boy's play was a portent of cultural re-creation. Let us suggest how Emerson learned to play and then say something about the playfulness of his cultural leadership after 1836.

If Emerson was able to master the hard work of supervising culture-building by exhorting countrymen to trust themselves, then his preparation was gained in large measure by having weathered similar tasks in the past, a past which, by necessity, was less historical and, so to speak, much closer to home. During his first thirty-five years of life Emerson learned how to test his strength as a person for whom taking things into his own hands was, at first, a difficult thing to do. During his earlier years, Emerson was a dependent type, owing good fortune only modestly to prowess, but mostly to his heritage and his mother and to his Aunt Mary Emerson.

He learned how to be less at the mercy both of his immediate social world and of the weight of the Unitarian ministry, his tormenting inheritance. Emerson emerged from young adulthood more able to take action in order to alter his attitudes and commitments toward that sense of sameness and continuity which characterizes acceptance of a solid vocational identity--not as a Unitarian minister but as a test of the strength of the new vision and accruing myth of America's national identity. The story of Emerson's earlier years serves as the personal narrative which, in large measure, stood as a symbol of the developing myth-narrative of the heroic individual which so typifies the most inclusive range of available social identities during the nineteenth-century. After the publication of Nature in 1836, Emerson could rest content on laurels won earlier, and for reasons few since then have acknowledged. He forged himself: yet, he was directed in so doing by activating a certain pattern of re-creation or, in other words, a pattern of play which is how a person goes about setting stages for himself and then

acting on them in a host of ways. A word about the meaning of play activity
is in order.

Erik Erikson has written that play and playfulness involve the creation
of a "leeway of mastery" in a set of developments or circumstances in the
life of a child (or an adult). One experiences the possibility of "free
movement within prescribed limits. . .(such that) where the freedom is gone, or
the limits, play ends."[1] Play activity appears in those situations in which
a sense of mastery has not yet been achieved. That is, the ambiguity of
circumstances specifies the "limits" of the unmastered situation, while one
is able to explore possible avenues of mastery with a modicum of "freedom,"
doing so on levels of human response such as with one's thoughts, feelings,
and behavior. To stake out an identity, then, is to master given limits,
converting, one might say, the disappointment of having little leeway of
mastery into the hope of having more expansive leeway. The shift from disappointment to hope develops on the basis of achieved successes in mastering
situational ambiguities with new strength during the past.[2] The structure
of play activity described by Erikson is clearly evident in Emerson's earlier
years. It comes to light in a fairly unique manner by emphasizing a certain
kind of imagery rooted in the imagination of this intellect.

The personal narrative to be told of Emerson's earlier years takes seriously

---

[1]Erik H. Erikson, "Play and Actuality," pp. 111.

[2]Paralleling studies on cognitive development in terms of a principle
of mastery by Jean Piaget, other psychologists have lent theoretical perspective to affective growth. A theory of the role played by situational
ambiguity in affective development is offered in, Erik H. Erikson, "Ritual"
in Gandhi's Truth, pp. 423-436. Those strengths actualized during life-long
affective development have been referred to by tradition as virtues. For a
description of one theory of these probable human strengths emerging from
mastery see, Erik H. Erikson, "Human Strength and the Cycle of Generations,"
in Insight and Responsibility (New York: W.W. Norton, 1964), pp. 109-157.

the play quality of his vocational struggles. Factors of his personal unique-
ness, including his eventual mastery of the legacy of an identity rooted
almost exclusively in New England Unitarianism, as well as the conflict
created by a need to repudiate that identity, appear time and time again
throughout Emerson's life according the structure of play. The structure
of play is expressed throughout Emerson's life as <u>expansion</u> <u>within</u> <u>diminish-</u>
<u>ment</u>, where diminishment suggests inherited "prescribed limits" and where
expansion hints at the "freedom" to resolve situational ambiguities in a
variety of ways. Emerson's playfulness occurs mostly on the level of abstract
reverie. That reverie is expressed symbolically in his journals, letters, notebooks, essays, poems, lectures, and sermons. However, though the pattern of
expansion within diminishment appears in these products of his intellect,
other dimensions of Emerson's presence also evidence this unusual pattern
of play. For example, one might focus attention on Emerson's personal relationship with his classmate, Martin Gay in 1820-22, his social relationship with
what he understood as the orthodox thought of Andrews Norton in 1825, his historical relationship with Christianity and the meaning of Jesus in 1832 when he
resigned from his charge at Second Church, Boston, and his cultural preoccupations with making over a new American identity to replace lingering vestiges
of the old colonial consciousness. On every level of his life, Emerson can
be said to have played through issues of salience for nineteenth-century
Americans, converting disappointment to hope as he comes to master each of
these dimensions of a full life. Yet, Emerson came to resist solitary play.
His early emphasis on personal psychosocial heroics soon was superceded by
care for fostering more inclusive, nationally-oriented play.

To master ambiguous situations according the vicissitudes of play is
tantamount to creating a sense of reality for oneself. However, a personal
reality seeks the authentication brought only by acknowledgement from and

participation by others. While hard at play in 1823, faced with the disappointing routine of teaching school at a time when that was the last thing he wished to do, Emerson hoped to expand his sense of reality beyond its current limitations. One way he sought to do this was to write a letter to his college chum, John Boynton Hill, who , he believed was also a "droning schoolmaster." When considered as an element of his play activity, the letter to Hill becomes a tacit invitation extended by Emerson to another person to share the reality he himself enjoys. In this particular case, for example, Emerson conjures a reverie about his personal sense of having an occult relation of a sort with nature. Emerson's description of his experience moves playfully from disappointment in himself to hope in his capacity to envision nature's presence with enlivened eyes:

> I am seeking to put myself on a footing of old acquaintance with
> Nature, as a poet should,--but the fair divinity is somewhat shy
> of my advances, and I confess I cannot find myself quite as per-
> fectly at home on the rock and in the wood, as my ancient, and I
> may say, infant aspirations led me to expect. . . When I took
> my book therefore to the woods--I found Nature not half poetical,
> not half visionary enough. . . In short, I found that I had only
> transported into the new place my entire personal identity, and
> was grievously disappointed. . . In short, parti-coloured Nature
> makes a man love his eyes. . . what a mutilated mind and existence
> belongs to the blind.[1]

Emerson's attempt to draw Hill into this reverie operates, of course, mainly on the level of intellect. Nonetheless, it reflects similar play activity on the level of affect, which also stems from the ambiguous situation of the school teacher of 1823. At that time Emerson was seeking to mitigate feelings of disappointment about school-teaching. Out of his situation of 1823 blossomed play which operated at a behavioral level, where Emerson takes

---

[1]Ralph Waldo Emerson, The Letters of Ralph Waldo Emerson, edited by Ralph L. Rusk, 6 Vols., (New York: Columbia University Press, 1939), I: 106-108.

steps, in new strength, to close his school at the end of 1824 in order to study at the Harvard Divinity School shortly thereafter.

To seek authentication by John Hill was one thing, but to invite a wider audience into the hard work of his play activity was another. Lest we move to debunk the man's character, let us put to rest any notion that what some might call the eccentricity of his speculative reverie was too idiosyncratic to be of significance to the wider American public. The point is not so much to repeat what Emerson in fact said. Rather, it is important to point to the structural dynamics of his play activity insofar as it contributed to the formation of the symbolic canopy that came to be shared by a rather diverse yet unique nineteenth-century populace. Even though his efforts eventuated in a sense of reality for himself by 1836, he facilitated the creation of a sense of shared reality for a broader population base as well. How was this accomplished?

In this sense, then, Emerson was a ritual actor in the history of American culture.[1] That is, he extended play into the realm of culturally-shared meanings which, themselves, were deeply planted in the fertile soil of some shared sense of collective identity. Not only did he put himself in such a

---

[1]Play is the psychosocial precursor to authentic religious ritual activity. Rituals involve the free affirmation of human virtue but only insofar as that sense of capacity and strength is defined by the limits of some symbolic context. In the Christian ritual of the Lord's Supper, which, of course, precipitated Emerson's refusal to serve as minister of Second Church, in 1832, one affirms the virtue of fidelity to Christ but only after acknowledging one's fundamental sinfulness before the eyes of God. The connection between play and ritual is dealth with by Johan Huizinga, Homo Ludens (Boston, 1955); and and Adolf Jensen, Myth and Cult among Primitive Peoples (Chicago: University of Chicago Press, 1963), pp. 39-79. The specific dimension of "testing one's strength" by means of ritual activity, especially in so-called life or death situations, is given lucid analysis in Erik H. Erikson, "The Development of Ritualization," in The Religious Situation: 1968, edited by Donald Cutler (Boston: Beacon Press, 1968), pp. 695-748 and, by the same author, "Ontogeny of Ritualization," in Psychoanalysis: A General Psychology, edited by R.M. Lowenstein (New York: International Universities Press, 1966), pp. 601-621.

position, he also ritualized his activity by challenging the consciousness or self-understanding of Americans unable to let go of the colonial past. He himself had been challenged in 1832 by what he understood as the "antiquated" Unitarian ministry, no longer in tune with times, and mastered that situation for himself. Now Emerson was prepared to invite others to internalize the new reality for which he was becoming a major architect and high priest. Erikson suggests that the function of rites and rituals is to enable a person to "anchor readiness for loyalty in social reality" and "to attract and to invest that fidelity" over and over again in the history of the human species.[1] The personal narrative of Emerson's earlier years bears a style of ritualization, according to which the American people test their cultural resiliency vis-a-vis other peoples of the world: out of colonial limits burgeoned nineteenth-century freedom to make good on the Puritan hope that the New World would be a "light unto the nations." Emerson was a major ritualizer of this long-standing mythical sensibility, and subsequent myth-makers found him a willing leader of their new literary and cultural movements.

A final note should be mentioned and that pertains to the peculiar character of Emerson's style of play. Perhaps reminescent of the Puritan hope of his forebearers, Emerson's inclination was always to understand the ritual pattern of expansion within diminishment in terms of visual metaphors.[2] One is reminded of the letter to John Hill in which he

---

[1]Erikson, "Play and Actuality," p. 120.

[2]The suggestion that Emerson apprehended his place in the world primarily through his visual sensibility is not a new one. The following works play upon the connection between Emerson and his use of vision, though they do so mainly for the purpose of analyzing his matured literary art: Kenneth Burke, "I, Eye, Aye--Emerson's Early Essay 'Nature': Thoughts on the Machinery of Transcendence," in Transcendentalism and its Legacy, edited by M. Simon and T.H. Parsons (Ann Arbor, Mich.: University of Michigan Press, 1966),

described how he sought hope in Nature but found it "not half visionary enough." Other examples abound throughout the narrative of his earlier years. For instance, Emerson experienced sudden and surprising temporary blindness for about nine months during 1825 due probably to psychogenic factors. Coming out of blindness was equivalent to playing his way from disappointment to hope according to the visual pattern operating at the behavioral level of his life at that time. Emerson always wished to project a "wider horizon," one which would give refreshing perspective to self-disappointment and, lat er, to a citizenry lingering culturally in the colonial past. The reality Emerson offered Americans was rooted in his personal sense of self-trust, which itself was animated by a ritualized process of feeling. To the ideal of heroic individualism he beckoned national fidelity, since he could assert confidently that his own "faith," more than anything else, "is a telescope."[1] Fidelity gets anchored in a national

---

pp. 3-24; Neil Harris, The Artist in American Society (New York: George Braziller, 1966); and Sherman Paul, Emerson's Angle of Vision (Cambridge: Harvard University Press, 1952). An older work, but one that also scratches the surface of the issue of Emerson and vision, is that by Robert Gay, Emerson: A Study of the Poet as Seer (New York: Doubleday, Doran and Co., 1928). Less oriented toward literary criticism and of a more psychological and experimental nature is a monograph useful for understanding how Emerson can perceive his life according to visual patterns, Erich Goldmeier, Similarity in Visually Perceived Forms (New York: International Universities Press, 1972).

[1]Ralph Waldo Emerson, The Journals and Miscellaneous Notebooks of Ralph Waldo Emerson, edited by William H. Gillman, et. al., 16 Vols., (Cambridge: The Belknap Press of the Harvard University Press, 1960 +), II: 308. The ideal of heroic individualism is not without a taint of psychological aggression. While Emerson asserted his self-confidence with the image of a telescope, other Americans asserted themselves by laying tracks westward and by pressing steam locomotives deeper and deeper into the untamed wilderness. Both Emerson and his countrymen relied on aggressive self-assertion by which to take in the widest horizongof anticipated achievement. Psychoanalytic works have suggested a direct connection between a preponderance of visual preoccupations and the desire to vent aggressive impulses. For example, see Phyllis Greenacre, "The Eye Motif in Delusion and Fantasy," in American Journal of Psychiatry 25 (1938): 297-334; and Henry Hart, "The Eye in Symbol and Symptom," in The Psychoanalytic Review 36 (1949): 1-21.

identity only when one has come face-to-face ("eye-to-eye") with the limitations of weakness and the power of strength able to be freely exerted. Emerson was a visionary whose famous phrase of Nature, "transparent eyeball," was an ideological facet of the historical ritual process begun when independence from England was declared two hundred years ago.

Ritualization is grounded in the preverbal experience of infants and reaches its full elaboration in grand public ceremonies, such as in warfare and in the mourning of slain leaders by tribes or nations. Erikson has associated all ritualization with infants' needs to feel that the world into which they have been born is basically trustworthy and that they, in turn, are trusted implicitly by it. Securing this sort of emotional security becomes the first and foremost preoccupation of both infants and mothers during the initial days, weeks, and months of new mother-infant relationships. The task of securing a sense of basic trust sets up patterns of interrelationship which soon become ritualized. The patterns become more-or-less permanent structures of behavior insofar as they are recurrent forms of securing basic trust within the context of the relationship: infant to mother, mother to infant. "Ritualization," writes Erikson, "must consist of an agreed-upon interplay between at least two persons who repeat it at meaningful intervals and in recurring contexts; and that this interplay should have adaptive value for both participants."[1] Erikson submits that these conditions are "already fully met by the way in which a human mother and her baby greet each other in the morning."[2] Therefore, even before a child is able to verbalize the meaning of experience, virtually permanent experiential

[1]Erikson, "The Development of Ritualization," p. 712.

[2]Ibid.

patterns of relating to the world are established.

It is precisely in pursuit of the feeling of basic trust that infants tend to rely predominantly on a visual mode of relating to their new environment, to both the physical and psychosocial constituents of their surroundings. Usually these constituents are embodied in any maternal figure to whom an infant may relate. Within the morning greeting eye-to-eye contact is essential. Mutuality of recognition is the major characteristic of such a ritualized greeting. This involves the mutual assignment of very special meaning to the encounter, and this is punctuated for the infant by the stabilizing force of eye contact. Out of a chaos of sensory stimulation an infant creates and confirms his or her individual distinctiveness to the degree the eyes develop and focus on the face and, more acutely, on the eyes of some maternal figure. Attending to the activity of the greeting ensures a recurring sense of delight. Though a warm reassuring voice may steady an infant's sense of sensory chaos, it is visual centering which permits the infant a reciprocity of response by which separateness from the maternal presence is transcended. In this way the orderly "cosmos" emerges as the giver of basic trust.

Herein lies the groundwork for more elaborate ritual behavior which could very well (and often does) assume historical and cultural magnitude. For example, the child's game, "peek-a-boo," which usually requires some adult participant, not only involves seeing and being seen, not seeing and not being seen. It also has a goal the establishing of a coherent vision of reality through concerted use of a predominant visual sensory modality. At least, on the basis of playing a game involving the breaking and re-establishing of eye contact with an adult a child works toward securing the emotional reality of basic trust. Elaborate religious rituals do no less, especially when they occur at strategic moments of risk or danger during any person's or group's existence. Archaic fertility rites ensured the re-supply of food sources when starvation was imminent; marriage ceremonies grant reassurance to the participants that a life together will be better than lies lived apart, no matter how pleasant being single may have been in each case. In both instances, new horizons are projected and these often are dramatized visually during the staging of the rituals themselves. Therefore, ritualization seeks to re-establish this reality of basic trust over and over again throughout the entire human life cycle, especially on occasions when that reality has vanished or is most easily challenged, as in cases of physical disaster like earthquakes or in cases more psychosocial in nature like the loss of a parent or realizing one is fatally over-committed to some political cause. Ritualized vision can, and often does, work to set things aright.

Therefore, the following study of Emerson at play tells the story of how he learned to master life according a a particular pattern of ritualized vision. His earlier life is organized appropriately in terms of events which he himself understands at first as his immediate present (situation) and, later, as his not so immediate present (reverie). The situational ambiguity necessary to set the prescribed limits in which he freely operated can be recognized in each sense of his phenomenal world. As events transpire, Emerson's reports of their beginnings, middles, and final resolutions move through the ritual pattern of expansion within diminishment, according to visual imagery tied subtley and not infrequently to ancient mythical themes, for example, Plato's allegory of the cave. A good clue alerting one to the onset of a new event, that is, a new ritualization opportunity, is his

intensification of an awareness of overall disappointment with himself.
Difficulties such as his ability to master school-teaching, or complete
Divinity School, or fulfill the required duties of being minister at Second
Church, or whatever his present puts forth, usually are signalled by reports
of expectations unmet. Resolutions of critical events occur when, in fact,
he reports that his life shifts in a new direction, perhaps one in which
a more inclusive ritualization of his vision for a unified American identity
is expressed. Hence, we see him closing his school and going into the
ministry; then we see him leaving the ministry and taking up a place on the
lecture circuit of the Lyceum movement in 1833.

In the prefatory chapter that follows, the ubiquity of Emerson's disappointment is sketched. Disappointment always is the harbinger of his ritualized
vision. Nonetheless, prior to the emergence of his expanded sight he is
locked continually into a sense of being the "dupe of hope" as he put it
then, one not yet able to surmount an overwhelming sense of disappointment
with a new-found sense of wisdom. Emerson starts his vocational identity
struggle as a disappointed, despondent, and discouraged youth. However,
from the time of the death of his father in 1811 to his final renunciation
of the Unitarian ministry of 1838 (after which he felt free to become a
lecturer and writer), disappointment would turn gradually to ubiquitous
hope. At least, he learned how to master disappointment by the use of a
particular sort of intellectual visual ritualization. A more specific outline is called for.

Emerson learned the wisdom of hoping through a ritualized series of
three major clusters of life events, each of which evidences a plateau of
achievement of what Erikson called a "leeway of mastery" of life crises
themselves, whatever intimations of death or renewal each cluster might

afterward spell. The first cluster in which the pattern of expansion within
diminishment allows Emerson a level of mastery extends from 1811 through
1824. From the time between his eighth and twenty-third years, we recognize Emerson negotiating personal crises involving the death of his father
in 1811, his relationship with classmate Martin Gay at Harvard College
from 1820-22, and the creation of a "negative identity" in 1824 when, after
three years of schoolteaching, he rejects that career for a moratorium on
facing self-support by attending Harvard Divinity School and for the wider
horizon of the ministry afterwards. This first cluster of events precipitates
a second major cluster of life events, at the conclusion of which another
"negative identity" arises, whereupon Emerson commences the hard task of
generating symbols fitting not only his new sense of vocation, but also
that of the identity of a broad and diverse populace. He becomes a ministerial candidate and finally a minister in 1839, marries, loses his wife
to tuberculosis in 1831, and resigns from the pastorate of Second Church,
Boston in 1832. Thus, high hopes at the end of the first major period
turn into sour disappointments when he realizes that Unitarian orthodoxy
is for him too narrow an ideology in which to fashion images of American
self-confidence. The last major cluster of life events stretches from
1834 through 1838 and concerns the concrete ways in which Emerson fulfilled
expectations of others that he rise to a position of leadership within
dawning American culture and letters. His new-found wisdom is reflected
by personal moves to make a living on lecturing, to marry for a second
time and to connect these two major moves in symbolic fashion by moving
permanently to Concord, Massachusetts.

Taken together, these three major clusters of life events suggest the
overall development of Emerson's complete ritual process as a collective

understanding of his personal pattern of play and the strength of self-confidence tested therein. First, he inherits the prescribed limits of early nineteenth-century "Brahmin" culture of Boston, along with expectations that sons of ministers, as Emerson's father had been, should follow in the footsteps of their fathers. Second, while trying to fill his father's shoes, so to speak, Emerson's disappointment with the nature of those particular limits thwarted the free expression of deeply felt high hopes for himself, his sense of being not merely a Unitarian minister but being also a man of great destiny. Third and finally, when he rejected the ministry he implied in good measure both a repudiation of his cultural legacy, using only certain elements of it, along with elements of his own experience in order to set new parameters by which future generations of Americans might be instructed anew. By turning Unitarians, for example, from theological debate to a concern for natural, national growth Emerson enlisted them into his cultural cause. Setting new limits for himself as a budding lecturer and writer was also for Emerson to proclaim that his identity was available for others if they, as he, took such matters into their own hands, mastering the task of nation-building by using the new symbolic leeway he offered, that is, learn to trust themselves by taking the initiative to do so. Let us turn to note how Emerson played his way to an expansion of his own consciousness, knowing full-well that in doing so, he supplied his countrymen with a ritualized paradigm by which they might do the same.

Journals and Notebooks as Inklings

Above all, Emerson was a writer, spending most of his mornings practising his art. Writing is an activity which lays great emphasis on visual manipulations of lines on a surface, words and doodlings on paper. In order to establish lines within Emerson's life of all that has been indicated about the man so far, we can turn to the texture of his writings themselves. In doing so we will come to recognize the visual pattern of his play activity clearly evident in his own understanding of keeping his journals and random notebooks, as well as in the manner in which his writing a journal was motivated and proceeded in its initial stages.

On 4 January, 1825, Emerson wrote that he had closed his school and had begun a new year, anticipating studies for the Unitarian ministry which were to begin in one month. With a moment of leisure in hand, his imagination could be set loose. However, when freed, his thoughts settled on rather somber themes: "And this moment of indolence," he wrote, "engendered in me phantasms and feelings that struggled to find vent in rhyme. I thought of the passage of my years, of their even and eventless tenor and of the crisis which is but a little way before one month will determine the dark or bright dye they must assume forever."[1] Rooted reluctantly in an attitude of disappointment, a shift began to capture his imagination. In the very next sentences of his text, the young man's visual drift is clearly marked: "I now turn to my lamp and my tomes. I have nothing to do with society."[2] It is true that Emerson was reading his future in the ministry perhaps as a crisis of identity. Insofar as his personal identity was connected to a vocation, it might result either in a more-or-less "dark" diffusion or in a more-or-less "bright" future of purpose and of calling. However, the symbolic nature of his last lines is even more telling: Sitting in a dark night, hovering over his desk, he is bathed by the light which pours over the pages of his tomes. In effect, Emerson says that he is the one who possesses the "light," and society is, so to speak, "in the dark." It is not difficult to see

---

[1] Emerson, JMN, 2: 309.   [2] Emerson, JMN, 2: 309.

in this scene a structural precursor to those lines in <u>Nature</u> in which
Emerson describes himself as a "transparent eyeball" bathed in the "blithe
air" of nature's lighted woods.

Let us return to the immediate present of Emerson's life and to the
matter of disappointment, in order to lend further credence to the claim that
disappointment lingers like a dark cloud throughout Emerson's sense of
the events of 1811-24. Only when the close horizon of disappointment can
be seen to give rise to a more distant one, that is, the expanded promise
of the future, can one make structural sense out of the details of the
period. Only then will the episodes of Emerson's father's death, his relationship with Martin Gay, and the experience of being a schoolmaster in his School
for Young Ladies in Boston be able to fall together in some sensible or
"eventful" form. Generally, one would want to ask what does Emerson have
to say about his disappointment, its sources and resolutions? To find out
this one would check the record of papers where Emerson dealt directly
with his feelings of disappointment. From the outset, it would seem that
Emerson's journals, at least, lend clear testimony to this point that time-
and-time again Emerson would resort to mitigating disappointment according
to the playful pattern of expansion within diminishment, doing so within
the text and order of journal entries themselves.

Emerson started keeping a journal on 25 January, 1820. His notebooks,
which are included by the most recent editors of the journals and notebooks with the daily record, extend back to about one year before that
date. Four items about the journals and miscellaneous notebooks appear
as inklings of Emerson at play. Noting each item now will make reading
the narrative of Emerson's earlier years according to an inherent visual
pattern tenable later on.

First, Emerson created and then continually seized upon a technique
of personal meditation by writing a journal. Until the end of his junior
year (24 August, 1820) Emerson used a pen-name, "Junio," with which to
sign his journal entries, perhaps as an enblem of self-regard at the time,
but certainly an indication of his reliance on reverie over reason. Though
it may be only of incidental significance, it was the Roman goddess, Juno,
who oversaw all the activities of women. For a young man trained at the
Boston Latin School to respect the ancients, an association and subtle
slip probably occurred between "Junio" and "Juno" in Emerson's mind from
time to time, in a mind rich in reveries. He wrote that he wished to
imprison "all the luckless raggamuffin Ideas" he may have "hereafter in
these pages" of his journals and, more significantly, he wished to "nomi-
nate and appoint 'Imagination' the generalissimo and chief marshall"
over all of them.[1] One can suggest that from the outset of the journals
Emerson raised high within his pantheon of affections "Imagination." Also
implied by doing so is that imagination can either contain or loosen those
prisoners, those "raggamuffin Ideas." Emerson had discovered a technique
whereby he might mitigate overriding feelings of disappointment, namely,
simply by turning to writing tomes by solitary lamplight.

A second item that brings Emerson's character to the fore as one enters
into the journals and notebooks is his tacit wrestling with the question
of his own identity in regard to the meditative products of his imagination.
Undoubtedly, the matter of his sexual identity was involved. His "generalissimo"
of "Imagination" is not devoid of content. The name "Junio" could be a
masculine form of Juno, a kind of hermaphroditic term which associates the

---

[1]Ibid., 1: 5.

the names "Junio," "Junius," and "Julius." Emerson began his first journal

entry playfully on 25 January, 1820, by invoking the assistance of "ye

witches" at first, and then begging the aid of "Fairy Land" as well:

Of the witches, he requested them to "enliven or horrify some midnight

lubrication or dream (whichevery may be found most convenient) to supply

the reservoir" of his "Wide World I" when "other resources fail"; and of

the fairies he begged pardon "for presenting my first petition to your

enemies . . . pardon and favor me!"[1] The point is that by October, 1820,

and with the appearance of "Wide World II," Emerson has bid farewell and

thanks to the "Grim witches from Valhalla, and courteous dames from Faery-

land, whose protection was implored, and whose dreams were invoked to

furnish forth the scroll . . . ."[2] Instead of appointing himself "generalis-

simo," he took charge of the feminine spirits in the journal just as Juno

was believed to have done in Rome. It was Emerson's task to oversee the

witches and fairies, not to rule "Imagination" but merely to be its consort.

His identification with both male and female genders, and his ease of

moving about from one to the other while wrapped in his meditative reverie

is, at least, curious. And, too, such gender confusion is hardly uncharac-

teristic of seventeen-year-old youths prevented from frequent and informal

contact with the opposite sex. Nonetheless, such confusion could be eased

by his technique of vision.

By the time he had bid farewell to these spirits, Emerson had given

up his pen-name, "Junio," forever. This was psychologically significant.

The last time the pen-name was used was on 24 August, 1820. On that day

he had bidden farewell and thanks to Hollis 15, his room during his junior

---

[1] Ibid., p. 4.   [2] Ibid., p. 26.

year at Harvard College. Perhaps it was fitting that as he moved into his senior year at the college, after August of 1820, he was no longer a "junior" and, therefore, no longer felt the need to pen himself as "Junio." As long as he needed it, the playful fantasy world of feminine witches and fairies took him "a little beyond" Hollis 15. Playful fantasy took him also a little beyond his first sighting of and infatuous, initial bewilderment over Martin Gay, "a strange face in the Freshman class" during the 1819-20 school year.[1] It is not insignificant, furthermore, that below the 24 August, 1820, journal entry Emerson watercolored a picture of the inside of his room at Harvard. In this notably visual way he could assert growing distance from fantasy, as well as from the veil of its creation, "Junio." During 1831 and 1832 Emerson would grow distant from similar alterations in his life, having to do with the aftermath of his wife's death, and a growing disaffection over the ministry. During 1820 Emerson began broadening into adulthood by precipitating a protracted crisis of identity, in which themes of mastery would find expression around issues related to the human strengths of hope, will, purpose, competence, fidelity, love, care, and wisdom.[2] Therefore, for him to begin a journal at that time in his life punctuated his growing sense of self. By relegating his "Junior" status to the past after August 24th, he made possible the forging of an individuality for himself by confronting his ideas and feelings head-on. Confronting feelings about Martin Gay, for example, after becoming a "Senior" was a most unwittingly insightful look into himself taken by

---

[1] Ibid., p. 22.

[2] For definitions of these virtues, see Erikson, "Human Strength and the Cycle of Generations."

him in these early journals as we shall suggest in Chapter Two. Wrestling with his feelings about schoolteaching is another lucidly-depicted episode. Thus, these early journals condensed an intellectual's reverie as an expression of the pattern of play upon which Emerson would dwell for the rest of his life, though at increasing levels of national ritual significance.

The third way in which expansion and diminishment seems embedded within the journals concerns Emerson's use of his journals as a "Savings Bank."[1] Much of what he wrote early on in his journals served as the basis for later writings--sermons, lectures, essays, and poems. In this sense even though Emerson did not like what he wrote in his journals, it might be elaborated and developed more to his taste at a later time. Therefore, in this use of the entries diminishment certainly is cued for expansion at a later date. In one way, the "Ideas" imprisoned in the pages are readied for activation by the promise of "Imagination" and, thus, set free.

The fourth and last item depicting an inkling of Emerson at play within the journals is perhaps the most telling of all in spite of the fact of its complexity. Emerson entitled his early journals, "Wide World," and went on to number them in succession. This was a portent of expansion. However, the title was unexplainably dropped after number XIII (the journal numbered XIV is evidently lost). Number XV and all the journals afterwards lack that title, "Wide World," as of 8 October, 1824, or the date of the first entry in number XV. It was with book XV that Emerson was in the final throes of teaching school and about to enter into theological studies and ministerial preparation at the Harvard Divinity School. The last dated entry from number

---

[1]See Bliss Perry, "Emerson's Savings Bank," in The Praise of Folly and Other Papers (Boston: 1923), pp. 114-29.

XIII is 11 August, 1824, accounting for about eight weeks of entries, presumably compiled together in number XIV, the lost book. What might the
significance of this be?

Dropping the title, "Wide World," was emblematic of a new maturity of
mind and heart or, at least, of some degree of personal closure on mastering
his college years and finding himself on the verge of new situational ambiguities by the time the title was dropped. Perhaps this had already been
suggested by the promise of a ministerial vocation which had the matter of
"faith," not facts, at its base. On 8 October, 1824, for example, Emerson
believed it was a "striking feature" in the human condition that "we so
hardly arrive at truth. There are very few things of which we can wisely
be certain tho' we often let unfounded prejudices grow into bigoted faith. .
. . The final cause of this," he believed stoically, "is no doubt found
in the doctrine that we were not sent into this world for the discovery of
truth but for the education of our minds. And our faculties are best exer-
cised by doubts, not by facts."[1] These words sound not like those of a
collegian, eager to learn facts, or like those of a schoolteacher, eager
to put forth facts. Rather, they evidence an awareness that one need not
only fantasize a wide world in writing, but that it is necessary to make
such a world for oneself. Though he could have dwelled upon doing so,
Emerson did not continue to entertain just a reverie about a "Wide World"
in the context of journals and other written work. A future in the ministry
awaited him. He had, at least for the moment, found a calling. Here one
must stop. For at this point in his life began a second major event of
his life, and it is rightfully told in subsequent chapters.

---

[1] Emerson, JMN, 2: 275.

By way of entering into the events of 1811-1824, let us pick up a thread left dangling a while ago, that is, the matter of Emerson's ubiquitous sense of disappointment during those thirteen years and afterward. Once the stage has been set, it will become possible to observe Emerson at play, all by way of setting new limits in which his self-confidence by 1828 might flourish and be on its way to becoming ritualized cultural leadership for others. It is noteworthy within the examples of Emerson's sense of disappointment how that feeling was often coupled as well to a hopeful sense of promise in the future. How, in other words, Emerson experienced the pattern of expansion within diminishment, of which he allows an inkling in his very first attempts to pen journals.

CHAPTER I

DUPED BY HOPE, UNTOUCHED BY WISDOM

Even though disappointment hung like a gray cloud over the whole period
of 1811-24, Emerson expressed it, nonetheless, around several particular
sorts of concerns--education, vocation, his sense of incipient greatness
or "representativeness," and purging national evil. First, the quality of
disappointment will be shown as it coalesced around the first three concerns.
Then, second, the following will be suggested. Namely, that Emerson's expressions of disappointment in terms of human and national "evil" reveal his
assessment of and intimate connection with his times. This was the sense
he bore that Americans were, in effect, exiled souls, capable of being saved
by the knowledge of self-trust. That is, exiled from their destiny of cultural independence and, hence, held by the grip of evil, deep human evil.
Evil could be alleviated insofar as heroic individuals would attain to
greatness as "representative" men and women. Deploying this brief consideration of his disappointment about personal and national evil now will serve
the additional purpose later of illuminating Emerson's decision of 1824-25
to pursue a ministerial career. It appears as a behavioral means to surmount
his deep-seated disappointment and overcome the evil he thought held him
"indolent." One will note later the unusual and psychologically telling
"letter to Plato" which he wrote in his journals and, in effect, to himself
as well as sent afterwards to his Aunt Mary while wrestling with that particular decision. Therefore, weight will be given to a claim later that
Emerson already was locked into the playful pattern of visual expansion
within diminishment which, incidentally, is an analogue of the allegory

of the cave which Plato himself depicts in Book Seven of the Republic.

Of the four particular concerns mentioned above, the first two (education and vocation) capture best Emerson's concerns of his immediate present.
Since the spector of his not so immediate present and its situational ambiguities were ubiquitous to both horizons, immediate and not so immediate,
let us deal with Emerson's disappointment in two corresponding parts. Thus,
we turn first to the immediate problems of the events of 1811-24 as far as
Emerson seems concerned about them. As they are reported in his early journals and letters they can be bound together under the rubrics of learning
and working: How to persist at one's studies and which career to choose?
Or, how to use liberal learning to assume a ministerial career with integrity.
After showing Emerson's disappointment over these two immediate concerns,
one will be able to see through them, so to speak, into the broader, not
so immediate problems of how he strived to achieve greatness and, because
of what his efforts implied, how he hoped to mitigate the force of evil in
America by being a "representative man," free from the evil of a colonial
consciousness. By attempting to differentiate immediate and not so immediate
horizons of Emerson's preoccupation over disappointment, it is hoped the
reader understands the blurred line created between a biographical sketch
of Emerson and a historical narrative explaining his cultural significance.
Both tasks are intended. As Emerson moved toward a greater personal awareness of himself, broader cultural problems of individual greatness and
evil also assumed personal perspective. Already by 1824 he moved closer
to national prominence as a cultural leader. However, it cannot be said
that at that time he was either prominent or charismatically significant
for Americans, just becoming so.

The Disappointing Limits and Freedoms of the Immediate Present

Young Emerson's earliest most disappointing educational experience occurred while he was but a boy of barely three years. By the end of 1805 he was regarded as a "rather dull scholar"; and during the spring of the following year he was going to his remedial teacher, a Mrs. Whitewell, "again."[1] At the same time the lad suffered a most serious illness which was believed to be caused by worms and which, in all likelihood, prompted him to read no better than before. His family thought that for a boy of three years, his skill was meagre at best.

It is also likely that his disappointment over his inability to learn to read well, quickly was accentuated during 1807 when he was four years old and trying his hand at new things in a larger world. During that year a brother was born, Robert Bulkeley Emerson, who was soon noticed by his parents to be mentally retarded, though ambulatory and of some sense. Moreover, eight year old John Clarke Emerson died shortly afterwards. The Rev. William Emerson and his wife, Ruth Haskins, were not unused to such losses. Their first child, Phebe Ripley Emerson, who was born two years after their marriage, had died during 1800 at the age of two years. The death occurred prior to the family's move from rural Harvard, Massachusetts, to Boston. Whatever promise the city held for the Emersons probably was enshrined in their son, John, who was born shortly after their arrival in 1799. During 1801 another son, William Emerson, entered the fold. He was followed by Ralph Waldo Emerson on 25 May, 1803, and Edward Bliss Emerson in 1805. One can only speculate, suggesting that rivalry to succeed

---

[1]Ralph Rusk, The Life of Ralph Waldo Emerson (New York: Columbia University Press, 1949), p. 19.

educationally (and in other ways) was intense among the brothers during
Emerson's first decade. Intellectual competition was taken for granted as
the way in which a Boston Brahmin family sorted out the talents (and every
male child was assumed to have talents!) of their offspring and directed
them toward the professions of Law, Medicine, or Divinity. Rivalry intensified, it would seem, in 1808 with the birth of Charles Chauncy Emerson
and early in 1811 with the birth of the last Emerson, Mary Caroline.

The next evidence of educational disappointment is associated with
Emerson's college days. Source materials are more adequate than those
scant sources for the early years. Jumping to 15 October, 1820, and the
start of his senior year at Harvard, one notes not only the quality of
disappointment, but also Emerson's way of beginning to build a career for
himself which goes beyond that abiding feeling: "My more fortunate neighbors exult in the display of mathematical skill, while I after feeling the
humiliating sense of dependence and inferiority which like the goading
soul-sickening sense of extreme poverty, palsies effort, esteem myself abundantly
compensated, if with my pen, I can marshall whole catalogues of nouns and
verbs, to express to the life the imbecility I felt. . . ."[1] However, to
express felt imbecility is not yet an assertion of a "resource of happiness"
which he will find later in the pen. Taking heart from lessons of his
teacher, Mr. Edward Everett, one reads in the journal that Everett's pupil
was confident that "an all-seeing eye" looked deep into one's heart, and
it saw to it that "obscure struggling" and "unsuccessful virtue" eventually
meet "with reward."[2]

Two months later Emerson still was disappointed about his intellectual

---

[1] Emerson, _JMN_, 1: 37-38.   [2] Ibid.

powers. "How immensely would a scholar enlarge his power," he exclaimed, "could he abstract himself wholly, body and mind from the dinning throng of casual recollections that summon him away, from his useful toil to endless, thankless, reveries."[1] He reported a wish to be "so witched with study" that a "still and rapid and comprehensive course of improvement" would make him forget "self and professions and tasks and the dismal crows of ordinary circumstances" which he felt were all too characteristic of school.[2] But he realized that his life would never be so unencumbered, even if such soliloquies were, as he put it, "sweeter than Chemistry."[3]

Occasionally toward the completion of the events of 1811-24 Emerson was retrospective. His realization of disappointment was clearest after graduating on 29 August, 1821, after looking back at those years when he "was not often highly flattered by success."[4] He continued on 7 February, 1822, that he did not have much cause to wish his Alma Mater well since when he was a student he was mortified daily by his own "ill fate" or "ill conduct": during a trip to Harvard College during that February, however, he recalled fondly and nostalgically the ground where he had "the brightest thoughts" of his "little life" despite his post-graduate experience.[5] However, he took away nothing more that day. Later in a subsequent chapter we shall note that Harvard Divinity School evoked similar thoughts. However, then his reaction would go beyond penning felt imbecility in his journal to the point of decisive action.

As one jumps about topically in an attempt to show Emerson's disappointment, from education one may move to vocation. The crux of disappointment

---

[1]Ibid., pp. 40-41.   [2]Ibid.   [3]Ibid.

[4]Ibid., p. 94.   [5]Ibid.

during the events of 1811-24 that has its focus in Emerson's concern for a suitable vocation swings between school-teaching on the one hand, and projecting a career in the Unitarian ministry on the other hand. His struggle to resolve this issue of vocation occurred after graduation, at a time when family finances and employment required his immediate attention. Readily available to him was the job of being assistant schoolmaster in his brother William's School for Young Ladies in Boston. With reluctance because he had not been appointed an usher at his alma mater, the Boston Latin School, Emerson accepted the position and stayed with it for three years. During the last year he took full charge of the school (from 23 December, 1823 to 31 December, 1824), since William had decided to study for the ministry in Germany and had set sail for Europe on 5 December, 1823.

After the summer of 1821 the wonder of Emerson's "astronomical reveries" in his initial journal entries of just a year or so before worked little magic to lift his opinion and prospects of teaching to an enticing level. Writing to his favorite mentor, his Aunt Mary Moody Emerson, in November, 1821, he confided that he was hardly "tired of the stars" and mourned "the destruction of Astrology," for to "a dull mortal" like himself, whom "the fates have condemned to school-keeping," it was entirely indifferent what planets ruled the heavens.[1] Emerson wished he had been in heaven. Later we shall see how his Aunt Mary provided him with an astrology of sorts during 1817: Late that year he imagined she supplied him with star-like "wakeful eyes" by which the college student's worries could be held in check. The point of the entry of 1821 was not dissimilar to the one in this narrative just alluded to. Emerson turned to his Aunt Mary when he turned from school

---

[1]Ralph Waldo Emerson, Letters, 6 Vols. ed. Ralph Rusk, (New York: Columbia University Press, 1939), I: 102-103.

and childhood to the world of making a living. "I am not yet in the fatal Gehenna," he wrote to her, "and will not alarm you by by [sic] naming the doleful day."[1] Not only is Gehenna to be understood as a place of abomination (see II Kings 23:10), but it is also a place where garbage is dumped. School-keeping was devoid of a poet's wonder and, besides, it was a torment of very little positive meaning to boot. Though he began a temporary career in teaching, he hearkened back to childhood days, days when he benefitted from his aunt's efforts, in order to secure a vestige of that old coveted emotional support. As he attempted to stand on his own two feet he found it necessary to seek encouragement from his father's sister, whose perspicacity suited his own ideal inclinations as a thinker in the field of religion.

Incidentally, though it may not mean anything at all, it is consistent with the context of this particular letter to suggest that the slip of the pen of "by" after "by" is significant.[2] To read "by by" is to hear "bye bye." Hearing this invites the thought that Emerson was putting emotional distance between himself and his aunt. It is possible that Emerson was gradually severing himself from his father and his family's Unitarian heritage, insofar as it bore the expectation that sons would enter the ministry. However, that he wrote to his aunt to begin with was to seek the blessing of the paternal Emerson heritage at the same time. Thus, Aunt Mary, in no mean sense, was something of a "father surrogate" for Emerson. At critical periods of his life Emerson would turn to his Aunt Mary for vocational guidance as

---

[1]Ibid.

[2]For a discussion of the possible psychological significance of phenomena like that of Emerson's slip of the pen see, Sigmund Freud, "Slips of the Pen," in The Psychopathology of Everyday Life, in The Standard Edition of the Complete Works of Sigmund Freud, 24 Vols., edited by James Strachey (London: Hogarth Press, 1960), VI: pp. 116-133.

we shall see later. Usually her suggestions bore the undertow of Emerson's paternal heritage. In any case, it is clear that he was not happy about his new circumstances as the day of his entrance into the "Gehenna" of school-keeping approached late in 1821. To say he was disappointed may very well to be to understate the case. All in all, he hedged to name that "doleful day."

During May, 1922 Emerson commenced to write, as he put it, "amid my diseases and aches and qualms," in order to see, he said, "if my brains are gone."[1] His sense was that something was missing from his life, and that vocational longings had hardly been fulfilled. Expectations and their ful-fillment had persisted as a personal problem involving emotional disaffection. More specifically, he depicted the change in condition and in hope that had come over him since leaving college. During his four years of school he enjoyed some "honours" as well as "traversing in my chamber (Hollis 9) flushed and proud of a poet's fancies; . . . pleased with ambitious prospects and careless because ignorant of the future."[2] Now living beyond memory, he continued clarifying reasons for his gloomy emptiness: "But now I'm a hope-less Schoolmaster just entering upon years of trade to which no distinct limit is placed" . . . though he toils through "this miserable employment . . . with-out the poor satisfaction of discharging it well, for the good suspect me, and the geese dislike me."[3] The thoughts of the "droning schoolmaster," however, seemed to be out ahead of his immediate tasks. Reverie was employed to spur his feelings to new heights of vocational promise. "Nine months" were gone, he feared, and except "some rags of Wide Worlds, half a dozen general notions &c," he thought himself "precisely the same World's humble servant that left the University in August."[4] Some tell Emerson that gloom

---

[1]Emerson, JMN, 1: 129-30.   [2]Ibid.   [3]Ibid.   [4]Ibid.

was good for his character, and that it would make him fitter for the office of the ministry to which he aspired. However, he answered them saying, "if I come out a dispirited, mature, broken hearted miscreant,--how will man or myself be bettered?"[1] Though it may be unfair to call these troubles the work of fate, Emerson thought of himself, nonetheless, as a "disappointed spirit" who found "brooding over castles in the air" his only balm.[2] An architect of nineteenth-century American culture already was at his drawing-board.

Besides brooding as a disappointed spirit, another way in which Emerson soon discovered a ready sense of solace was by writing to his fellow-classmate and also recent graduate, John Boynton Hill who, like himself, became a teacher. Hill was employed at the Garrison Forest Academy in Baltimore. The tonality of his letters to Hill countered the gloomy brooding of the journals. Unlike his more serious epistolary wrestlings to his Aunt Mary, his letters to Hill suggest easy familiarity which is common between peers. "I am (I wish it were otherwise)," he wrote to Hill, "keeping a school and assisting my venerable brother lift the truncheon against the fair-haired daughters of this raw city."[3] Emerson suggested that those "condemned to the 'delightful task'" of school-keeping should have free leave to "waste their wits, if they will, in decrying and abominating the same."[4] Probably with a necessary irony he confessed that, judging from his "own happy feelings" about teaching, his "heart bleeds" for those who teach--"poor, wretched, hungry, starving souls: better tug at the oar, dig the mine, or saw wood; better sow hemp or hang with it, than sow the seeds of instruction."[5] His

---

[1]Ibid.   [2]Ibid.   [3]Emerson, Letters, 1: 106-108.

[4]Ibid.   [5]Ibid.

letter concludes by betraying disappointment over the financial profit of
teachers. He likens himself to the discoverer of a rich silver-mining city
in Bolivia: "Why may not a schoolmaster as well as a slave--strike his weary
foot upon another Potosi."[1] One can readily suspect a cauldron of anger
boiled eruptively behind this reverie of depression.

Solace was one thing, decision another. In 1824, the year of his twenty-
first birthday, the spector of the ministry soon dwarfed whatever prospects
for continued school-teaching lingered in his mind. On 18 April, 1824 Emerson
wrote that in a month he would be "legally a man" and, forsaking the past
and its times of indolence, "I deliberately dedicate my time, my talents,
and my hopes to the church."[2] This was not the deliberateness of inner
conviction, but the resolute setting of ideological issues into which he
might playfully project inner ambiguities, though playing with a sense of
dire seriousness. He continued to use his journal entry as the occasion for
a careful and fairly thorough self-assessment, weighing his readiness to
become a minister in terms of inclination of a negative sort (he is not
inclined to Medicine or Law) and in terms of acquired skills (oratory). For
as he said, "I should be loth to reflect at a remote period that I took so
solemn a step in my existence without some careful examination of my past
and present life."[3] Coming at this particular juncture in his life, this
self-assessment tends to be a deliberate attempt to complete his life up to
that point. That is, he began to draw the events of 1811-24 to closure by
suggesting that a new phase of life was being entered into. Nonetheless,
he also betrayed the ever-present tone of disappointment as it carried over
after 1824 into his future, though he evidences scant awareness of doing

---

[1]Ibid.   [2]Emerson, JMN, 2: 237-42.   [3]Ibid.

so. Emerson's 1824 "self-assessment" should be examined briefly, if only because it is one of the longest and most torturously-written entries into his early journals.

"I cannot dissemble by abilities," he wrote stoically, they "are below my ambition."[1] However, he believed he had a fine "imagination," but that he had not committed very much of what it had produced to paper and, therefore, he hardly gratified his poet's vanity.[2] Socially, Emerson confessed virtual failure. A comparison of himself with his peers of "six or seven, perhaps sixteen or seventeen years" (his age was twenty-one and that he felt somewhat intimidated by his pupils at the School for Young Ladies seems probable), left him feeling "a sore uneasiness" in the company of men and women, a "figid fear" of offending others, a secret "jealousy of disrespect," a bother-some "inability to lead," and a nagging "unwillingness to follow the current conversation."[3] What is called a "warm heart," he said, "I have not."[4] However, and perhaps it served as the wedge driven between a career in the ministry and one as a national lecturer, "I judge that if I devote my nights and days in form, to the service of God and the War against Sin,--I shall soon be prepared to do the same in substance."[5] Closing the door of the School for Young Ladies in December, 1824, however, was not a decision made in a vacuum. Emerson's self-assessment earlier in the year may have been an act of self-delusion as well. Though his ideological rigidity as it related to vocational commitments may have been a delusion, that delusion contributed to his subsequent mastery of self-trust.

At the same time Emerson doubted himself, he also was afforded an occasion

---

[1]Ibid.   [2]Ibid.   [3]Ibid.

[4]Ibid.   [5]Ibid.

in which he was able to test what sense of strength he already possessed. Sometime during the early part of 1824 one William B. Fowle began keeping a school in Washington Court and soon vied for pupils attending other schools in Boston, some of whom were lured away from the School for Young Ladies. This was a direct though reasonable challenge to Emerson's previously unchallenged vocational hopes, insofar as the school-keeper can be said to have sought to be successful, especially after his brother left for Europe. Writing to William on 20 May, 1824 Emerson said first that he needed his brother's guidance: "Pray remember in the quantity of your Communication--that no good seed can be lost on that Cormorant tribe the Schoolmasters; they can glut on all things, yea on garbage, for they devour to give again digested or digested not to their young."[1] He was disappointed not over a raging "War against Sin" but over his "unfruitful hours," perhaps those spent feasting on the garbage of Gehenna or, for that matter, wondering how to arrange for a quick transfer from being a teacher to being one taught: "I blame myself," he said, "for lounging away from school preparation to amuse myself with the dull scrawl.--School is not full and I wait in vain for it to be fuller."[2] If Freud is right by suggesting that jokes--puns included--are unconsciously revised preconscious thoughts related to aggression and hostility, then the next line of the letter lifts the veil of innocence from Emerson's understatement: "Fowle runs afoul of me a little in that particular. . . ."[3]

Closing the school toward the end of the year was an occasion mixed with

---

[1] Emerson, Letters, 1: 141-44.   [2] Ibid.

[3] Jokes such as puns help to criticize one situation in order to create a new organice whole for oneself out of those very same elements. In fact, Freud refers to jokes as "playful judgments" which bear hostile affect. See Sigmund Freud, Jokes and Their Relation to the Unconscious, in The Standard Edition of the Complete Psychological Works of Sigmund Freud, 24 Vols., edited by James Strachey (London: Hogarth Press, 1960), VIII: 14; Emerson, Letters, 1: 141-44.

disappointment. His brother had given up the school in 1823 because he felt called to the ministry. However, Emerson failed his brother as well as himself insofar as he could not succeed with the school without help from William. This will become clearer later. In any case, closing the school also added promise to disappointment as the following summary of Emerson's self-assessment of April, 1824 presents to us:

> I cannot accurately estimate my chances of success, in my profession, and in life. Were it just to judge the future from the past, they would be very low. In my case I think it is not. I have never expected success in my present employment. My scholars are carefully instructed, my money is faithfully earned, but the instructor is little wiser. And the duties were never congenial with my disposition. Thus far the dupe of hope I have trudged on with my bundle at my back, and my eye fixed on the distant hill where my burden would fall. It may be I shall write dupe a long time to come and the end of life shall intervene betwixt me and the release. My trust is that my profession shall be my regeneration of mind, manners, inward and outward estate; or rather my starting-point, for I have hoped to put on eloquence as a robe, and by goodness and zeal and the awefulness of virtue to press and prevail over the false judgments, the rebel passions and corrupt habits of men. We blame the past, we magnify and gild the future and are not wiser for the multitude of days. Spin on, Ye of the adamantine spindle, spin on, my fragile thread.[1]

That Emerson was vocationally disappointed during the events of 1811-24 was portrayed clearly by that last allusion of spinning thread, just as his hope was alluded to in terms of a starting point. Two years after entering Harvard Divinity School Emerson wrote on 5 May, 1827 that his days ran "onward like a weaver's beam."[2] This statement suggests that the Church, like his school, had not been as satisfying as he had hoped it would be in the self-assessment conclusion of 1824 above, even though he would take a parish in 1829 for three years, but largely out of financial necessity. His disappointment would appear to border on despair if a similar Biblical reference to weaving threads together is noted. Job 7:6 reads, "My days are swifter

---

[1] Emerson, JMN, 2: 241-42.   [2] Ibid., 3: 78.

than a weaver's shuttle, and are spent without hope." Even as late as 1827
the fabric of Emerson's life had not warmed the young man's heart to envision
steady expansions of promise and hope within the limitations of his disappointment. The only pattern evident in his sense of his world was one of
disappointment, as far as he could tell. But there was more to Emerson's
immediate present, a hidden dimension which made his disappointment culturally significant in the long run about ten years later.

Therefore, now that the immediate world of educational up's and down's
and his more serious vocational inclinations have been set, a broader dimension of disappointment can be recognized and sketched insofar as Emerson
reports it. That is, Emerson intimated that he had an unusual sense of being
headed for greatness, and that this would intensify his growing sense of
the ominous threat of a widespread national disappointment, that is, evil.
Emerson projects his own feelings into the broader culture in which he lives,
assuming himself (eventually) as a "representative" man in whom all evil-
ness can be purged. His activity in attributing such a dire feature to
the wider world points to a psychohistorical manuever about which he only
later became partially aware. Writing in December of 1834, Emerson likened
the immediate concerns of adolescence to the not so immediate course of human
speciation, thus betraying intimations of his own psychohistorical projections:
"The age of puberty is a crisis in the life of man worth studying. It is
the passage from the Unconscious to the Conscious; from the sleep of their
passions to their rage; from careless receiving to cunning providing; from
beauty to use; from omnivorous curiosity to anxious stewardship; from faith
to doubt; from peaceful (cancelled-out) maternal (inserted) Reason to hard
short-sighted Understanding; from Unity to disunion; the progressive influences
of poetry, eloquence, love, regeneration, character, truth, sorrow, and of

search for an Aim, and the contest for Property."[1] As early as 1824, there-fore, Emerson was an anxious steward in pursuit of a ready career in the ministry; and it is clear that already he sensed the glimmer of the fact that he would have to grapple with the question of how to pass from trust-ing his heritage and his mother's roost to trusting himself.

If Emerson's statement was an ideological overview of his own puberty, then its specific meaning was announced in the lines immediately following it. They imply a literal ability to see beyond the vocational wrestlings with educational and vocational conflict of earlier days and to see beyond the ministry toward greatness and the purgation of human evil: "I look upon every sect as a Claude Lorraine glass through which I see the same sun and the same world and in the same relative places as through my own eyes but one makes them small, another large; one, green; another, blue; another, pink. . . . The dualism is ever present through variously denomi-nated."[2] Emerson continually makes more out of just what he had, namely, his sense of the present world diminished in size and promise by great expectations for the future. Like Thomas Jefferson perhaps, Emerson is a man on the make, soon to become the idealized "self-made-man." At any rate, it is evident from his overview about his puberty that a career in the ministry "in form" would not bring about a change "in substance" as his self-assessment of 1824 projected. At least by 1834, Emerson was discovering the reverse: hope sought the right form or expression, and the Unitarian ministry would not suffice. As an age of crisis, puberty leads to young adulthood. However, young adulthood too is an age of crisis with variations all its own.

---

[1]Ibid., 4: 348.   [2]Ibid.

The Disappointing Limits and Freedoms of the Not so Immediate Present

Having gone into disappointment in Emerson's immediate present as it coalesces around his educational and vocational concerns, let us now turn to Emerson's not so immediate present, to the matters of his sense of destiny or personal greatness characteristic of heroic individuals and to his sense of national evil in need of purging. On 6 April, 1824 he asked, "Does a bold eye never grow impatient of the ill-starred monotony of history nor ask to what end (cui bono) this everlasting recurrence of the same sin and the same sorrow?"[1] After 1824 only time would tell whether his hope would render him as a dupe of hope or not. Before then, however, he remained discontent, asking his broad question of the universe.

That Emerson believed he was headed for greatness is evident throughout the journals and letters. Statements about that particular hope often are linked in the texts to other statements about either educational or vocational disappointment. Emerson forever bemoaned personal "indolence" and literary "nonsense" as he went about trying to place his mark on the world. To his brother William, the college freshman wrote on 29 July, 1818, for example, that to tell the truth, he did not think it "necessary" to understand mathematics and Greek "thoroughly, to be a good, useful, or even great man."[2] Undoubtedly some subjects in college were ruled out for financial reasons, chemistry and the other natural sciences especially.[3] But other reasons seemed to over-ride money. Emerson not only thought disappointment was the fruit of educational and vocational faltering alone, but also that it could occur to one apart from those concerns, as though greatness or

---

[1]Ibid., 2: 378.   [2]Emerson, Letters, 1: 67.

[3]See Rusk, The Life of Ralph Waldo Emerson, p. 62.

being a "representative of virtue" did not depend upon scholarly success or vocational competence at all. Discovering just where, in fact, it did sink roots and draw its vitality was the problem. Some examples of this focus of disappointment can be cited. For the purpose of clarification only, it can be said that the two foci of Emerson's not so immediate present are unlike the other two foci in that concerns for greatness and evil presented him with what today might be called ontological questions, questions about one's existence, which surface especially during the period of a person's late adolescence.

"I find myself often idle, vagrant, stupid, and hollow," he writes during October, 1820,[1] obviously without any muster of inner conviction. Finding his condition "appalling," Emerson believed he must discipline himself in order not to suffer from "remorse" and from a sense of "inferiority" ever afterwards: "All around me are industrious and will be great, I am indolent and shall be insignificant."[2] In order to accentuate the point he pleaded finally, "Avert it heaven! Avert it virtue! I need excitement."[3] Though more will be said about it later on, the fact that this expression of disappointment-inducing anxiety was sandwiched between references in the journal devoted exclusively to thoughts about Martin Gay is relevant. Emerson's statement implied anxiety over his relationship with Gay under the guise of disappointment over a sense of personal insignificance. Perhaps an affinity to merge with Gay, if only visually, required a compensatory assertion of self. More will be said about this in the next chapter. Other examples touch similar chords of disappointment over not having greatness in sight. Besides, Emerson would never find "excitement."

On 1 November, 1820 he admired anyone not obliged as he was to answer

---

[1] Emerson, JMN, 1: 39.   [2] Ibid.   [3] Ibid.

his "idle call." If the young man was to continue pursuing "reveries," then "it will weaken the grasp with which I would cling," he says, "--with which every young man would cling, to 'visions of glory.'"[1] According to his friends as well as according to his own "whispered suggestions of vanity," Emerson's talents were popular and well-fitted to help him claim a place in the "inclinations and sympathy of men."[2] But this was not enough. For if "I would excel and outshine the circle of my peers those talents must be put to the utmost stretch of exertion, must be taught the confidence of their own power."[3] The next entry, 2 November, 1820, began, "What a grand man was Milton!," and it may not have been merely coincidental that it did. Milton was a "great man" and, furthermore, he was devoted to the Church. He was admired by Aunt Mary as well. But Milton's devotion to the Church was the devotion of a blind man. Though Emerson's temporary blindness was but five years in his future, he quoted Milton in 1820 as if the poet were a culture-hero. That is, Milton was quoted to say what Emerson himself had said on 1 November, 1820: "I forsee that should the Church be brought under heavy oppression" . . . let me (Milton) cultivate "those few talents which God hath lent me."[4] Milton was a great man and, thus, one to be imitated. Here, then, was a grain of excitement which a non-literary churchman could hardly provoke in Emerson's young heart.

Approximately one year later and after graduating from college and taking up a vigorous correspondence with his Aunt Mary, Emerson wrote again to her during December 1821, thanking her for her patience: "I wonder how you can ever have linked a hope to the wayward destinies of a thing like me, to my dream-like anticipations of greatness."[5] He was disappointed by not

---

[1]Ibid., pp. 40-41.   [2]Ibid.   [3]Ibid.

[4]Ibid., pp. 41-42   [5]Emerson, Letters, 1: 105.

realizing where such anticipations may lead him but found "this prophecying vein" a necessary one, "which begin here, and nowhere and never end."[1] For purposes at hand, the following line of the entry is most telling inasmuch as it implied that a fulfillment of greatness proceeds only insofar as one (literally) opened his eyes to the future: Emerson's thoughts of personal greatness were like "putting out an arm into the unseen world," and when some have done it they have felt "the reaching and beckoning of somewhat unearthly."[2] Here greatness mitigates the disappointment of being ordinary, insofar as Emerson assumes he does, in fact, see just where his arm is out-stretched in that unseen realm.

The fourth and final focus of disappointment during the events of 1811-24 is the not so immediately recognized problem of evil in America, evil as depicted as exile or, psychologically speaking, as identity diffusion or more generally, as social fragmentation. Here he assumes that a nation conceived in liberty ought not continue to dwell in colonial sensibilities and dependencies. Several examples of Emerson's statements about evil can be cited in order to make the following suggestion. Namely, that it was when he dealt with the problem of evil, especially as he related it to early nineteenth century American life, visual motifs became most apparent. Those visual features suggest how Emerson gradually transposed through a process of projection the personal pattern of expansion within diminishment over into the national arena and into patriotic concerns.[3] For Emerson, to comment on the problem and symbolism of evil in America was for him to initiate the conception which eventuated in the birth of a cultural, ritual leader after 1832 when he

---

[1]Ibid.   [2]Ibid.

[3]See Emerson, JMN, 3: 31-32. The matters of evil and its patriotic linkages are mentioned.

resigned from the church, as suggested in the introduction. At this level of consideration of the not so immediate present Emerson sharpened the cutting edge of his pursuit after wisdom or, in America, after the "awakening" of the eighteenth-century.

"No elaborate argument can remove the fact which strikes the sense, and which is the first and chief difficulty in the way of the belief of an omnipotent good Principle," wrote Emerson on 23 February, 1822, "namely, the existence of evil in the world, and next, the great share it has in the texture of human life, and its successful opposition to virtue and happiness."[1] Disappointment, then, can be taken as an euphemism of ubiquitous evil in Emerson's case. However, it should be pointed out that he himself did not acquiesce in evil just as he did not rest content with the immediacy of disappointment, whatever locus commanded its daily expression. Emerson's ritual and cultural significance rests in the structures he brought to bear on his not so immediate present. He chose to mitigate evil's effects: "This is certain that war is waged in the universe, without truce or end, between Virtue and Vice."[2] These he correlates, as the larger configuration of inquiry into his life offered, with "Light and Darkness, they cannot harmonize."[3] As a symbolical expression implanted within Emerson's journal entry as a visual motif, the battle of light over darkness is "forcibly consorted" on earth, and the "perpetual struggle which they make, separates by a distinct line, Man from Man throughout the world."[4]

However, a year later on 8 April, 1923 the universal panorama of a young schoolmaster had diminished to include American exigencies alone. He

---

[1]Ibid., 1: 92.

[3]Ibid.

[2]Ibid., pp. 117-18.

[4]Ibid.

considered seriously how to rout-out evil from his own country. "Powerful
and concentrated motive . . . is necessary to a man, who would be great . . ."
for ". . . there is a huge and disproportionate abundance of evil on earth,"
Emerson wrote.[1] He suggests, however, that "the good that is here," is but
a little "island of light, amidst the unbounded ocean."[2] Such an island is
subject to being associated with the similar imagery portrayed before pertaining to the young scholar, sitting over his desk and books. The image
presented a picture of another "island of light" in the dark night and in
the shadows of society (see Introduction). Though he penned, "I have nothing
to do with society," early in 1825, he was not fully aware of the implications of pursuing a career in the ministry, let alone concentrating his
preoccupations on the problem of evil. Actually, he had very much to do
with society. For he continued to say that he could not help resolve "to
embark in the cause of God and man" but, after surveying the magnitude of
the problem of evil in the world, he decided it was necessary to re-think
the size of the world--"contract it."[3] Here enters society, young America:
"Let the young American withdraw his eyes from all but his own country,
and try if he can to find employment there, considerable enough to task the
vigorous intellect he brings."[4] For Emerson's "little island of light"
of journal writing is none other than his sense of the United States in this
particular entry. The structure of his vision is the analogue writing his
personality with his budding surmise of his place in national and world
history. His confabulations will eventuate in serving historical demands
for cultural innovations and leadership from 1836 on.

The United States, he wrote, has been "separated from the contamination"
which infects "all other civilized lands"; but America has always "boasted

---

[1]Ibid., 2: 114-16. [2]Ibid.

[3]Ibid. [4]Ibid.

a great comparative purity."[1] In its leap "from infancy to manhood" the
nation has produced "free institutions" which alone have attracted "the
eyes of the world" to that land.[2] Here Emerson seemed aware of his country's
identity crisis, insofar as it was forged by way of allaying national and,
then, global evil. He was concerned that "the vast rapidity" with which
"the desarts and forests of the interior" of the land is peopled "have led
patriots to fear lest the nation grow <u>too fast</u> for its virtue and its peace."[3]
His point was that in their pursuit of nationhood, Americans may very well
fall prey to national diffusion or, in Emerson's own words, become to the
world a people without the kind of virtue that results from strength continually
tested, not merely exerted without the recognition of an opponent's integrity.
Americans, he believed, would become, "an accursed tribe of barborous rob-
bers" or imperialists, national abundance notwithstanding.[4] A concern about
the perils of over-extending oneself and risking possible extinction is a
dominant concern of any crisis of identity. A person or a nation too diffuse
may "fall apart" by allowing its ethical strength to go unchecked or, for
that matter, not checked enough. Ritual, which leads to integrity and the
virtue of wisdom, involves tested strength, not merely supremacy or submission.
Emerson held firmly to the belief that "the reformation of the world would
be to be expected from America" only if individual men learned to speak with
the "voice of wisdom and virtue."[5]

This concern prompts momentary lingering, since it would appear to be
the most explicit connection between the kind of picture painted in the
introduction and Emerson's marked preparation to become a cultural leader.

---

[1]Ibid.   [2]Ibid.   [3]Ibid.

[4]Ibid.   [5]Ibid.

That is, when Emerson talks about America in terms of a visual sort one can rest assured that the pattern of expansion within diminishment is being cued-up for ready use. Emerson's playfulness is readying itself as ritual potency.

Emerson seems to be touching base with Governor Winthrop's "Modelle" whether he was aware of doing so or not. And he proposes that if the United States is to be the "city on a hill," as the Puritan Governor hoped his experiment would be, upon which all eyes are fixed, then that version of Emerson's "little island of light" must become decentralized governmentally. To the degree that this tendency of government is assured will the light of "purity" brighten across the whole nation. "Now the danger is very great," wrote Emerson, "that the Machine of Government acting upon this territory at so great a distance will wax feeble or meet with resistance and that the Oracles of Moral law and Intellectual wisdom in the midst of an ignorant and licentitous people will speak faintly and indistinctly."[1] However, calamity can be reasonably averted only if "the senates that shall meet hereafter in those wilds shall be made to speak a voice of wisdom and vir-tue."[2] Emerson was not only making suggestions for better government, but also making a direct connection between America and the world, between the symbolic images of light and darkness projected on the basis of other major ruminations about himself. His desire to master disappointment pressed him to continue at such lengths.

When he said in that same journal entry of 8 April, 1823, "contract it.--Leave out of sight all those vast barbourous countries and continents. . . . Let the young American withdraw his eyes from all but his own country,"

---

[1]Emerson, JMN, 2: 116.   [2]Ibid.

Emerson should be taken at his literal word.[1] The governmental suggestion simply carries this contraction one step further toward the separate region and toward the ultimate Emersonian reference point, the individual person. The question becomes, will the individual rise to moral "purity" and, therefore, become "representative" or great? At the beginning of this entire journal entry of 8 April, 1823 the movement of the text appears to be one of contraction, or what we recognize as visual diminishment. However, as the passage moves toward a conclusion, Emerson affirmed that the "little island of light" not only commands the "eyes of the world" in this age when "the despots of Europe are engaged in the common cause of tightening the bonds of monarchy . . . [and] the bulk of human society [is] gasping for breath beneath their chains," but also that another movement operates as well.[2] Such a movement begins in the text as Emerson begins to say, "the western frontier population of the United States are rapidly expanding themselves."[3] At this point, the bright purity of America gets projected as the catalyst of "the reformation of the world." Emerson concluded the entry of 8 April, 1823 by assuring himself of not knowing "who he is, that, can complain that motive is lacking in this latter age, whereby men should become great."[4]

The point of drawing attention to this entry of April, 1823 is more than to suggest merely that Emerson was a governmental commentator or a national optimist, though it is evident that these characteristics were like lines in his face. The greater significance of the entry is the psychological movements according to which he construed a linkage between evil,

---

[1]Ibid., p. 115.   [2]Ibid.

[3]Ibid., p. 116.   [4]Ibid.

national identity and consolidation, light, and world reform. By means of contracting the perspective of consideration to America alone at the beginning of the entry, he was able to turn the other way toward the end. That is, Emerson was able to envision new, expanded horizons of "purity" radiating throughout the world starting from the American hub. It is possible to say that the structure of this particular journal entry, itself probably a first and most critical Emersonian reflection on some religious and cultural vicissitudes of American life, is a psychohistorical and textual artifact which is a real find in that it clearly suggests Emerson operated playfully according to the visual pattern of expansion within diminishment. Furthermore, at this particular juncture in his life Emerson may very well have sensed the drift of imminent greatness, insofar as the "little island of light" opened wide the eyes of the oppressed peoples of the world, the "prisoners" gasping for breath beneath their chains. One could easily speculate that Plato's allegory of the cave seems clearly to have been at work in Emerson's imagination on 8 April, 1823, though he mentions nothing of it. Now we can turn to the cluster of events of 1811-1824 itself, knowing some of the details as well as having a sense of the range of Emerson's abiding disappointment.

CHAPTER II

TOWARD WISDOM: THE CONFIGURATION OF 1811-24

There is a taint of despair running through Emerson's feelings of
disappointment. It prompted him toward partaking in personal future prospects
as any young man might. He evidences no lasting "life or death" sense toward
quickly finding a vocational calling. Nonetheless, Emerson was more preoccupied by finding his niche in New England's labor force than by anything
else at that time. Emerson was about as oblivious as anyone else his age
about the consequences of the present, especially as those effects would
linger on into the future. It never occurred to him that the course of his
life during the time between 1811 and 1824 would give rise to the core of
his religious insights later in life, after 1833. His growth in what can
be called the strength or virtue of wisdom or, as Erik Erikson defines it,
"detached concern with life itself, in the face of death itself," went largely
unrecognized by the end of the event of 1811-1824.[1]

For all he knew, Emerson understood himself simply to be putting the
past behind in order to embrace the promise held by the future. Thus, his
horizons were close and evident, distant and faint. He separated them in
his mind, focussing on only what was present, close, and evident. The larger
meaning of that horizon would only later become clear as a personal and
national horizon of native wisdom. However, during 1811-1824 these two
integral horizons of self regard remained split apart and seemingly irrecon-
cilable. It is likely that after 1833, Emerson recognized these two horizons
and joined them together in one new self-trust of wisdom. Then he would sense

---

[1]Erik Erikson, "Human Strength and the Cycle of Generations," p. 133.

possible interminglings between his immediate choice of lecturing and his not so immediate affinity toward assuming a place of leadership within American culture. Nonetheless, during 1811-24 he was unable to see even a glimmer of historical and cultural significance in those years, even though they clearly carried the personal structure of his peculiar vision for Americans.

The Death of his Father in 1811

Recollecting the journal entry of 8 April, 1823 is a good way to begin understanding the way in which the entire event of 1811-24 carried the pattern suggested. As the passage moved from diminishment to expansion, so too moved Emerson's response to his father, from before to after his father's death. The death of Emerson's father in 1811 is the beginning of the cluster of events of 1811-1824, when the young boy's world is quickly diminished in both size and promise.

On 12 May, 1811, just thirteen days before Ralph Waldo's eighth birthday, his father, the Rev. William Emerson of Boston's First Church, died of tuberculosis, which was complicated by tumors of the stomach. He was forty-two years old (b. 1769); not an old man. Prior to his installation as the pastor of the prestigious First Church, William Emerson lived a poor life as a bachelor and country pastor. And before assuming his first ministerial post in March, 1792 he had graduated from Harvard College and had eked-out a living on a slender salary from teaching at the Roxbury grammar school--an evening school during the winter, a girls' school during the summer. Ralph Rusk, a major biographer of Ralph Waldo Emerson, reports that the Rev. William Emerson could recall his own father only faintly but, nonetheless, rose from a condition of a rather "impecunious, if well instructed, country boy."[1]

---

[1]Rusk, The Life of Ralph Waldo Emerson, p. 1.

Though it might have occurred to one already, in many ways the Rev. William Emerson's life was paralleled later in a striking manner by that of his son, Ralph Waldo: from virtually unknown fathers, to Harvard College, to school-keeping (especially girls' schools), and, of course, to the ministry. However, even more striking is the parallel of their ages and the times when their lives took critical turns. During March, 1792, when he was twenty-two years old, the Rev. William Emerson took his first parish, one in Harvard, Massachusetts. When Ralph Waldo was the same age in 1826 he became approbated to preach and supplied various pulpits in Massachusetts and environs where, about three years later, he met and married Ellen Tucker. His father met and married Ruth Haskins about the same time, after taking up his parish in 1792. In 1799 the Rev. William Emerson left his ministerial post in Harvard in order to travel to Boston and to the vocational slot which he had long awaited there, First Church. When Ralph Waldo was the same age, thirty years old, in 1833 he too found his long-sought-after career as a national lecturer. Broadly speaking, Emerson followed in his father's footsteps. Though he turned a corner in 1833, as his father had done earlier by taking the job at First Church, Emerson clearly turned the same sort of corner but in the opposite direction.

In any case, it was necessary from the outset for the Rev. William Emerson to supplement his very meagre income from the Harvard congregation by means of school-keeping. The tiny congregation could afford very little for their pastor, especially since it was torn by religious dissention and since their new pastor was cautious but, nonetheless, reputed to be a liberal. The parishioners probably preferred him more cautious than liberal. In any case, on 25 October, 1796 he married and brought his bride, Ruth Haskins of Boston, to the village where he labored, which was just over the hills from

his own native home of Concord, Massachusetts. Though the marriage served
as temporary relief from the young pastor's embroilments in theological
dissention, the new financial burden which it created, along with the provincial nature of the town, worked to shift his sights toward Boston. A
daughter, Phebe Ripley Emerson, had been born, adding to the family's financial burden late in 1798, and another baby was expected before the end of
1799.

Therefore, it was for solid strategic reasons that he accepted the
invitation to preach the Election Day sermon before the Ancient and Honourable
Artillery Company of Boston in the spring of 1799. For it was soon afterward that he accepted a call to First Church for the specific purpose of
countering the "Alarming attacks that are made on our holy religion by the
Learned, the Witty and the Wicked," sounding very much like his contemporary
in New Haven, Timothy Dwight.[1] Four years to the day that that fateful
Election Day sermon was preached (and the signal of another parallel portent)
the Rev. William Emerson would return from the Governor's mansion to find
a son, Ralph Waldo, had been born late that afternoon, a son who would join
the ranks of the learned, witty, and wicked later in life. Meanwhile, several
weeks after re-locating to Boston, and after settling on Summer Street, a
child was born, John Clarke Emerson, and he was named after the late minister
of his father's new church. However, the small family was rocked by the
death of Phebe Ripley Emerson during September, 1800.

In spite of this disaster, the Emerson household looked toward the
future, and the birth of another son, William, during July, 1801 testifies
to this fact, insofar as it contrasts with the loss of Phebe only ten months

---

[1]Quoted ibid., p. 7.

before. Ruth Haskins found herself back in her native Boston, living once again in the aura of her father's lucrative distillery and cooper business. Her husband's world had been enlarged appreciably by his own move into the more liberal theological climate of the city, as well as into the prestigious world of Boston's financial, political, and literary elite. In fact, William Emerson regarded all of the cultured part of Boston as his parish. It would not be accurate to say that their marriage was a stepping-stone to his new-found success, though it did not hinder it. He soon found himself with less and less time both for his wife and for domestic life in general. While his wife was confident about her own return to Boston, William Emerson was soon in the habit of making his position in the city more demanding, perhaps, than it actually required of him. His calendar was always filled, especially with engagements intended to found or encourage clubs, societies, and institutions intending to aid science, literature, and the arts. As Ralph Rusk mentions, "The school committee required his attention. The singing society met at his house. Across the Charles, in Cambridge, he attended the exhibition at Harvard as a member of the visiting committee; and he was soon due at a meeting of the overseers. He did not neglect the Humane Society or the Agricultural Society. He attended the club at Popkin's. He was driving himself hard and had little privacy for either thought or relaxation."[1] On the day of Ralph Waldo's birth, 25 May, 1803, the Rev. William Emerson, after returning from dining with the Governor, noted simply in his journal that his wife was "in a favorable condition."[2]

Three other brothers were born prior to 1811: Edward Bliss Emerson in 1805, Robert Bulkeley Emerson in 1807, and Charles Chauncy Emerson in 1808.

---

[1]Ibid., p. 42. [2]Ibid., p. 1.

A sister, Mary Caroline Emerson was born in 1811, just one month prior to her father's death. Robert Bulkeley was recognized to be retarded but ambulatory not long after 1807. During that same year John Clarke died at the age of eight years. Up until 1834, the only other loss of a family member from this immediate circle was Mary Caroline, who died at the age of three years in 1814 during a time of dire family financial crisis. Edward Bliss died in 1834 and Charles Chauncy died in 1836. Both died of tuberculosis, while each sought health in the Caribbean. All this is by way of suggesting that the Emerson family was a tightly-knitted one, and that an attitude of vigilance relating to the broad concerns of living and dying prevailed within it. Wisdom, then, appeared disguised as the attitude of shared vigilance as to the state of one's life and limb, one's health, and vigilance as to a hard-won Brahmin status, sustaining which became the obsession of Ruth Emerson after her husband's death. Ralph Waldo, we shall see, took concern for vigilance especially to heart around these two axes later during his life. This will be suggested later in subsequent chapters when the cluster of events of 1825-33 is depicted.

During his first eight years of life Ralph Waldo remained close to the household established by his mother which, in spite of the subtle pressures of his father's upward mobility orientation, remained remarkably warm and secure. However, the most important moments of his life, at this time, it seems, found him deeply immersed in wonder about what appeared to him as mysterious comings-and-goings of his prestigious father. Though he seems to have wanted to count on his father, so to speak, he knew his mother was more self-assured and available to him because she stayed at home. But as he looked out from his small world at home with his mother, the boy would imagine a personal horizon of infinite possibilities which began in his father, that

is, where the small world of domestic security ended and the wide world of cultural challenge began. Emerson's exaggerated sense of the importance of
men-of-letters, for example, probably was not thwarted by the meeting of the
Anthology Society in his home. At these meetings members selected articles
for their magazine. His sense of wonder was also heightened by the rising
tension between the French and the British and the Imminence of the War of
1812 in a city which remembered the Revolution of 1776, as noted before.
So it was the wide world of his father's accomplishments that, in all likelihood, became a focus for young Ralph Waldo's wonder.

Indeed, much of Emerson's early education occurred in this informal
manner. The Emerson family must have heard much around Boston, and with
pride, about the Rev. William Emerson of First Church and high expectations
were reserved for his sons. However, struck more with the pomp and circumstance of the enormous cortege of his father's funeral, than by grief, young
Ralph Waldo thought it all a "grand sight."[1] Despite the fact that it would
remain only a memory thereafter, the grandeur of that sight soon bowed to
the reality of financial distress. The stipend which Ruth Emerson received
from First Church was modest at best--$125.00 per quarter for the next seven
years. Moreover, the family would not be permitted the use of the parsonage
much longer. In fact, only one week after the death of her own father, John
Haskins in October, 1814, Ruth Emerson was obliged to relinguish the house,
moving to Concord, Massachusetts and to her husband's relatives' home.

Financial solutions begat problems over and above those she already
weathered, namely, quelling anxiety over rising threats from British fleets
off the coast of Boston, just as the War of 1812-14 was coming to a jagged

---

[1]Ibid., p. 29.

end. Meanwhile, in 1812 Ralph Waldo had entered the Boston Latin School and
took remedial writing lessons afternoons from Rufus Webb at the South Writing
School. It was not uncommon for his mother to receive news of her son's
truancy. Boarders came and went, alleviating the financial situation somewhat.
But these persons as well as his teachers, Webb and the often intoxicated
William Biglow, were hardly seen through the same awestruck eyes of curiosity
and wonder of just months before by the boy. Indeed, something had been lost,
and one might venture to guess that Emerson began to cling more and more to
whatever strength his mother could muster. The world around him must have
appeared hardly as enticing at this time as the world of grand sights which
he had come to associate with his father, a world of cultural panoramas.
Indeed, young Emerson was growing up and (literally) seeing things differently.
Writing to her sister-in-law for help when the loss of the parsonage seemed
at hand, Ruth Emerson unknowingly articulated well her son's possible source
of bewilderment: ". . . then the last visible connexion will be dissolved
between this family and the society so dear to my departed husband."[1] However, as the world of his father shrank from view, the world of his mother
expanded from within it.

The death of Mary Caroline Emerson occurred just before the oldest
brother, William, entered Harvard College. And her death probably approximated
the "last straw" which fell upon Ruth Emerson's burdened back. She could
have remained in Boston with her own side of the family. Instead, with William
off at Harvard, and her unusual fears of attacks by the British, she took
the remaining children to Concord where their step-grandfather, Ezra Ripley,
was the local minister. Here, then, the patriotic thrust of the ministry was

---

[1]Ibid., p. 35.

taught to Emerson, for such was the meaning of that town of minuteman fame, the harbinger of the family heritage. Mary Caroline's death was followed by the death of the children's robust maternal grandfather, John Haskins (b. 1729), the distiller and cooper. However, Ralph Waldo was beginning to find a certain psychological technique useful in such instances, even though it is clear that he was not aware of it. Despite these two probably emotionally-numbing experiences, Emerson employed his wonderment in the midst of them for the purpose of seeing things differently and for aligning his affective life along less troubled, more congenial lines. In spite of Emerson's perception of a diminished world, he learned to project expanded horizons within it. About his grandfather, for example, he composed an elegy which, as Ralph Rusk mentions, "betrayed no sense of incongruity as he transformed the man who had sailed the seas on a privateer and had more than once been taken captive by foreign ships into a merely conventional angel, singing and soaring, his head 'covered with a crown of gold' and his hands holding a harp."[1] Therefore, his father and the wide world which he represented, long gone, became the idealized object of Emerson's nostalgia time and time again. The limits in which this psychological technique was generated and freely sustained in such a playful manner consisted of the subtle affective embrace of maternal supports.

The way in which Emerson perceived himself in the flickering light of nostalgia becomes patterned: the pattern fluctuates between diminishment and expansion. Emerson's sense of the death of his father, scant though source material about it may be, thus, was the beginning of the events of 1811-24. Now one can jump ahead somewhat to Emerson's college years. For an episode that occured during the last two years of his collegiate experience provides

---

[1]Ibid., p. 42.

a suitable middle for the whole event, one especially visual in nature.

Emerson's Relationship with Martin Gay, 1820-22

References to Martin Gay appear only in the journals and are spotty and, in many instances, quite cryptic. Nonetheless, no references to Gay appear prior to the entry of 8 August, 1820 which, significantly, appears only two weeks prior to Emerson's ascension to the senior class on 24 August, 1820, graduation day at Harvard College. Therefore, it may hardly be a coincidence that the pen-name, "Junio," which Emerson had used since beginning his journals on 25 January, 1820 was dropped after that August date. Emerson's ambivalence over his relationship with Gay was indeed curious: It entailed a continual and psychologically coherent response which, in effect, allowed Emerson the convenience of being at arm's length from the attractive (perhaps "idealized") freshman. Dropping the pen-name, "Junio," did not at all infringe on Emerson's efforts to remain at arm's length. In fact, it may have been a subtle way of further distancing himself from _his_ junior, Gay (though Gay was to move only from the freshman class to the sophomore class at that time). In any case, had Emerson continued to pen "Junio," Gay would have automatically followed symbolic suit and would have moved closer. Emerson nipped in the bud such a consequence, at least in the context of his journals. And, of course, it was in his journals that the arena or stage existed where he implied he felt most free and in control of his life. The journals were Emerson's intellectual and personal playground.

It will be under the same symbolical canopy of meaning of dropping his pen-name explicated above that a narrative account of Emerson's relationship with Martin Gay will proceed. For just as Emerson managed to keep Gay at

arm's length not only in everyday life at Harvard, but also in his journal
accounts (disguising the name of and cancelling-out entries about Gay), he
became involved with his schoolmate according to a ritualized visual modality,
as suggested before. Emerson's relationship with Gay was ostensibly one of
avoidance or distance. Less ostensibly, it was one of vital engagement
and, one might say, of enlivening physiognomic perception.[1] That is, Emerson
learned his skill at intellectual idealizing with little hindrance, and
probably much help, from this strange relationship with Martin Gay. Therefore, the relationship can be understood as critical to the matured writings
of Emerson, most of which depended upon Platonic, Neo-Platonic, and nineteenth-
century idealism.[2] In any case, one will want to pay attention to the curious
manner in which Emerson distances himself from yet persists engaging visually
in Gay. It will be necessary generally to recognize that the process of
distancing occurs hand-in-hand with an accentuation of vision, of "seeing"
Martin Gay and penetrating his character's essence. Emerson entered Harvard
College in the fall of 1817 as a freshman and as President Kirkland's orderly,
but it was not until late in his junior year (1820) that one can reasonably
believe Gay had been sighted or, if he had been seen before that time, that
Emerson reported it in his journals. In order that the dimension of visual

---

[1]See Ernest G. Schachtel, Experiential Foundations of Rorschach's Test
(New York: Basic Books, 1966), pp. 193-242. Empathetic projection is the
basis upon which the psychological process of inner creation may begin to
occur. Emerson seems to be projecting into Gay in this manner. Later in
Emerson's life such a basis of empathetic projection will foster the capacity
for empathy with the "ideals" of Nature. Such inner creations, when conveyed
in his writings, betray Emerson to be laboring according to the structure
of empathetic perception, namely, expansion within diminishment.

[2]For a range of sources of Emerson's propensity toward idealization
see, Anton Ehrenzweig, The Psychoanalysis of Artistic Vision and Hearing (New
York: George Braziller, 1956); John S. Harrison, The Teachers of Emerson
(New York: Haskell House, 1966); and for a sense of the idealism of Emerson's
times, see F.O. Matthiesen, The American Renaissance (New York: Oxford
University Press, 1944).

intimacy of the relationship comes into proper focus as well as the dimension of visual isolation, it is helpful to jump backwards a bit.

Emerson was prepared to find a visual engagement with another person efficacious in some way as early as 1811, noted before by citing and reconstructing facts and processes of a psychological sort that coalesced around the death of his father, the funeral cortege of which was a "grand sight," as Emerson reported the tenor of his grief. In a sense, Emerson grew to embrace his mother after losing his father, and then would project paternal horizons while simultaneously depending upon maternal supports. But much of that episode was necessarily more imaginative than it was an accurate reconstruction of the facts. As primary source materials improve in quality and quantity after 1811, especially with the gradual appearance of a corpus of correspondence, one example can be cited to suggest the nature of Emerson's psychological preparation to place emphasis on seeing. William H. Furness remembered that one of Emerson's favorite pieces for recitation at the Latin School was called, "The Pleasures of Hope."[1] In a similar vein, and carrying the same pleasure and enthusiasm, Emerson wrote a letter in verse on the very same subject on 24 September, 1817 just one month before entering college. A discussion of the nature of this particular letter will serve as a jumping-off point into the meaning in thought, affect, and behavior of the Emerson-Gay relationship.

Of the many things which might be mentioned about the "letter on Hope," two points are more important than others. The first has to do with the social circumstances in which Emerson found himself as he commenced writing. What of his situation may have prompted him to write a letter in the first

[1]See James Elliot Cabot, A Memoir of Ralph Waldo Emerson, 2 Vols., 1 (Boston: Houghton, Mifflin, and Company, 1887): 44.

place? The second point concerns the psychological significance of the subject of hope itself. It was a subject which, notably, was not a new preoccupation for the young man who was waiting then, as he said, with "hope and trust" to enter Harvard College.[1]

One year prior to the appearance of the "letter on Hope" Edward Emerson had broken family precedent and had entered the Phillips Academy in Andover, Massachusetts instead of the Boston Latin School. Distance alone made letter-writing necessary. But other reasons prompted his older brother, Ralph Waldo, to write. William Emerson, their brother, had been working intermitantly in a probate office in Waltham, Massachusetts and was not living at home on any sort of regular basis at all. Moreover, William was about to begin his senior year at Harvard, much to the envy of Ralph Waldo. Emerson had always looked up to and admired his older brother. In fact, when William first entered Harvard in 1814 it was Ralph Waldo who wrote, drew, and colored an elaborate letter "in hieroglyphics" to the freshman on 10 November, 1814, from the family's temporary residence in Concord.[2] By the time Emerson himself was to enter Harvard it was increasingly evident that William felt far fewer family constraints than Ralph Waldo. The record of Emerson's correspondence with his older brother testifies to his disappointment over being somewhat slighted by William. On the other hand, the record also suggests that when this feeling swept over him, Emerson found the pretext he needed for increasing his correspondence with his younger brother Edward, especially after 1816

---

[1]Emerson, Letters, 1: 47.

[2]A facsimilie of this letter is reproduced photostatically as the frontispiece of the first volume of the collected letters. In it Emerson substitutes drawings of human eyes in places where normally written "I's" or "i's" would appear. It would seem that even prior to his relationship with Martin Gay, and prior to beginning journals, Emerson evidenced his visual preoccupations in writings of a sort which were unusually imaginative for a thirteen-year-old boy.

when both William and Edward were away from the tightly-knitted Emerson family fold.

The tone of Emerson's letters to William differed very much from the tone of his letters to Edward. Emerson vied for William's attention: "I was offended as a 'man of honour' as I profess to be, in your writing to Charle the youngest in the family first and omitting to write to me the 'Man of the House' "Generalissimo' &c, &c."[1] Again Emerson asked, "But is there any excuse for you to write a <u>note</u>? when I received it I was so angry I could have torn it to pieces . . . when I first had it in the rage of the moment I was going to run and write on a piece of paper I am much obliged to you for your <u>note</u> but soon expect to receive the <u>letter</u>."[2] He signed-off his letter, "Write a <u>long</u> answer. . . ."[3] This letter of 12 January, 1816, followed by a note of apology on 20 January, 1816, were the last things written by Emerson to William until 13 September, 1817. It is odd that Emerson did not continue corresponding with William, even though the latter's work in the Waltham probate office and schooling continued as it had before. Perhaps going on within Emerson was the need to believe that persons older than himself would eventually serve only to disappoint him. When Edward went to Andover Emerson secured the audience and authority he was unable to secure from William. Unlike William Emerson, Jr., who could disappoint as William, Emerson, Sr.'s death had done in 1811, Edward was a younger brother. Moreover, it seems to have been personally important to Emerson to hold his family together when he sensed that it was becoming too diffuse. This particular inclination, notably, was expressed in our text already when Emerson's reference

---

[1]Emerson, <u>Letters</u>, 1: 13.　　　　　　　　　[2]Ibid., p. 14.

[3]Ibid.

to a "nation" growing "<u>too fast</u> for its virtue and its peace" was given over
to the "Machine of Government" and, he hoped when he wrote those lines during April of 1823, the government would not fail. Like his mother, Emerson
seemed particularly inclined to see to it that the household and its govern-
ing patterns of authority remain intact. The other Emerson brothers hardly
were inclined along these lines, at least to the degree their brother was,
as we shall see later on.

Emerson did two things which tended to unify the impact of these early
letters to Edward. Because "mother says you are likely to be dull during
the first days of your stay in your new abode," Emerson took upon himself
the task of seeing to it that such homesickness was abated by the mail.[1]
This was the first thing he did to hold the family's life together intact.
"Aunt's only message is 'be brave' i.e. Do not be cast down by thoughts of
home. . . ."[2] At this particular time in the history of the Emerson family,
Emerson was obliged to live for a time in a basement in the house of Hancock
Street in Boston. This house held out greater prospects of attracting boarders
than did the house on Beacon Street. Emerson told Edward that he had not
gotten out of "my confinement yet . . . the prospect from the great basement is not the most ample I have nothing great to delight my powers of
vision from this room."[3] Plato's allegory of the cave might be noted as an
obvious intellectual parallel of his feeling and behavior at this point.

However, perhaps more important is that Emerson was comforting himself
more than comforting Edward, because William and Edward had left <u>him</u> alone
and homesick for a complete family life. That Emerson was projecting his own
particular needs is strikingly clear: He comforted Edward by telling him
that "if you are dull remember that I can sympathise a little with you."[4]

---

[1]Ibid., pp. 17-19.　　　[2]Ibid.　　　[3]Ibid.　　　[4]Ibid.

Emerson could do this sympathizing for reasons other than the coincidental fact that he was living in a basement at the time. About a week later he again sought to comfort Edward: "Andover, I fear, with all its attractions in gloomy weather as it has been does not look as pleasant as home to you not accustomed to the voices or house of Strangers."[1] It is ironic that Emerson was living in what amounted to his mother's boarding house when this letter was written. He probably had less of a constant home life than did Edward among his schoolmates: Emerson saw more "Strangers" come and go than his brother did. In fact, that Emerson may have been more "dull" or homesick than Edward seems possible since, writing again to his brother on 3 November, 1816 he thanks him for saying "nothing of having been attacked with a certain disease called by the name 'Homesickness.'"[2]

The second unifying thrust of Emerson's letters to Edward is his tendency to wax poetical, what he hedged doing in letters to William. "I fear as it was so stormy a day when you went up that the People of Andover did not come out to meet your Excellency," he pictured on 7 March, 1817, "and perform the honours due to your highness and to a member of the 'family of Emerson.'"[3] Perhaps with necessary visual fabrication, he continued with the picture: ". ... when you went up first the sky wept rain at your departure but this time (owing to the season of the year) it wept snow."[4] Had Emerson felt a similar chill from the withdrawal of family intimacy, a chill unmitigated by his mother who also served as a father to her sons? Just prior to this letter, and sometime during the previous December, Emerson had been studying astronomy at the Latin School, choosing to write about this particular topic in a lengthy theme. There is a connection between the image of the

---

[1] Ibid., pp. 20-22.   [2] Ibid., pp. 22-24.

[3] Ibid., p. 35.   [4] Ibid.

weeping countenance hanging over Hancock Street and astronomy, which undoubtedly

played in and colored his thoughts at the time. For as one has seen already

in earlier parts of this study, both the image of the face appearing

in fantasies and concerns for sustaining the cosmos and meaning in which one

finds security have a common psychological root.[1] The root is the human

strength of "hope," and Emerson's writing to Edward activated it best at

this time during their lives.

Erikson has defined the virtue of hope as "the enduring belief in the

attainability of fervent wishes, in spite of the dark urges and rages which

mark the beginning of existence."[2] With his family seemingly diminished

to a mother and a younger brother Charles (Bulkeley was farmed-out to

---

[1]See ibid., p. 30. Emerson mentions his friend, R.T. Paine to Edward
by way of securing information about Andover and Phillips Academy for the
boy; and he fails to note that Paine later became an avid student of astronomy,
becoming prominent in the area for his astronomical abilities. For presenta-
tions of the psychological and structural root of the face in imagery and
the sense of basic trust in one's world and outlook, see Erik H. Erikson,
Young Man Luther (New York: W.W. Norton, 1958), p. 259. Luther, who
suffered what Erikson calls a "protracted identity crisis," was not unlike
Emerson, who also found a vocation a long time in coming. If one is to
understand the "deepest nostalgia of lonely youth," writes Erikson, then
one must pay close attention to such youths' "search for mutual recognition,
the meeting face-to-face," which is an aspect of the religious consciousness (p. 115). Like Luther, Emerson was pushed into precocity by high
expectations of his father enforced by his mother after 1811. This thwarted
his reliance on what Erikson refers to as, "the generous breast and the
eyes that care" belonging to the maternal presence of his mother and father
(p. 117). Like Luther, whose "once-bornness" sought completion in a face-
to-face encounter with the Pope's representatives in 1517-23, Emerson's
own vocational completeness was sought in continued encounters with the
religious establishment of his day and of his personal situation. Children's
play activity serves often as the psychological mediator between infantile
adorations of the face, eyes, and eye-like breasts and face-like torsos,
and the "face-to-face" encounters sought during adolescence for the purpose
of testing one's strengths. Play, thus, serves to give one "another chance
at being born," either during infancy or during adulthood (p. 117). In
this regard, see Adah Maurer, "The Game of Peek-a-boo," in Diseases of the
Nervous System, 28 (1967): 118-121.

[2]Erikson, "Human Strength and the Cycle of Generations," p. 118.

relatives), Emerson had cause to feel his own homesickness. Nonetheless,
it was psychologically feasible to concern himself with the whole matter of
hope since, as Erikson correlates it, that particular human strength is
achieved by-and-large during the first affective crisis of life, namely,
"trust versus mistrust." During that time the mother-infant relationship
is one's total arena of play activity. Moreover, during that time (and
ritually thereafter as well) the mutual interplay of "eye-centeredness"
is the primary mode of making affirmative and reciprocal contact with one's
world. By writing to Edward a letter on the topic of hope when he did
(24 September, 1817) Emerson affirmed his own desire to counter personal
inklings of disappointment and imminent despair. That is, the suggestion
that his family was, at least, changing or veering off the Brahmin path walked
by the Rev. William Emerson. Therefore, having touched on the social circumstances in which the letter was written, and having connected the topic of
hope with the underlying psychology of linking "seeing" to "trust" to "home,"
a discussion about the "letter on Hope" itself can be undertaken.

The suggestion here is that the letter on hope is an example of how
Emerson was already prepared to find vision ritually efficacious when he
began his visual engagements with Martin Gay during 1820. Once this point
is recognized and emphasized, then it is possible to understand his relationship with Gay better, especially insofar as the relationship is seen as a
further differentiation of earlier play activity, which would include his
letter-writing to William and Edward. At any rate, the "letter on Hope"
is a ritual expression of Emerson's visual preoccupation, and understanding
this preoccupation is preparation for understanding the meaning of Emerson's
involvement with Martin Gay. Let us turn to an analysis of the letter itself.

"What shall my subject be--Ah, one bright form--/ Comes dancing forth, while gathers round the storm/ Yes t'is sweet Hope--I know her by the smiles/ That banish doubt and each sad fear beguiles . . ."[1] These opening lines connect directly to similar imagery employed in Emerson's letter to Edward of 7 March, 1817 in which the "weeping sky" was portrayed. Under the bright countenance of hope, however, the "storm" is mitigated by hope's "smiles:" "Thither lov'd Hope all fair and fearless flies/ And points her finger upwards to the sky,/ And tells of bliss above the storm's dark mystery" (Edward's middle name was "Bliss").[2] Visual imagery increases, especially the motif of light over darkness, as Emerson assures Edward that ". . . when the clouds of Sorrow and Distress/ The thickest join in Life's dull wilderness,/ Then Hope is strongest--as the stars of Heaven,/ Which brighter grow, as darker grows, the even":[3] Arriving at the middle of the letter, a supreme example of hope is cited: "And in the Christian's breast what hope so strong,/ As that which animates the martyr's song/"[4] In regard to this example of the martyr a significant psychological point can be proposed.

Just prior to citing the Christian martyr as an embodiment of hope, Emerson pointed out that as hope grows "brighter," each "reflecting mind its wisdom sees."[5] The martyr is, by tradition, that person who faces death without despair. Already mentioned was Erikson's understanding of the human strength often associated with "wisdom." That is, a detached concern with life itself, in the face of death itself. This virtue Erikson has attributed to the successful resolution of the last of his psychosocial crises, namely, the crisis of "integrity versus despair."[6] In some ways, then, "wisdom"

---

[1]Emerson, Letters, 1: 42-44.   [2]Ibid.

[3]Ibid.   [4]Ibid.   [5]Ibid.

[6]Erikson, "Human Strength and the Cycle of Generations," p. 133.

is much like "hope," except that wisdom is the virtue or strength of hope tempered and cultivated by the passing of time. At the age of fourteen years Emerson seems remarkably aware of these sorts of connections, if only on the level of intuition. As the letter concludes he salutes the wisdom of hope by relying once again on the unifying image of a smiling face, usually fleshed-out with natural objects: "Then let us hail fair Hope and though Despair/ In placid frenzy tear her demon hair./ Yet hope all kind at distance still appears,/ And bids new joy smile thro' the glistening tears. . . . And Though in clouds still hides his beams, the Sun/ Yet I will sit and hope a better day."[1] If, as Erikson suggests, the central fact of wisdom is death (here, martyrdom), then the central fact of hope is life, or the religious notion of eternality. The thrust of Emerson's vision is stretched out on this cosmic rack, and it seems to be nothing less than numinous in nature. Such inklings were felt, it would appear, when Emerson sought to make sense out of his relationship and responses to Martin Gay. A similar mental world would then be put to the same use again.

William's part-time employment in Waltham and occasional school-teaching lessened family financial anxiety somewhat in the fall of 1817. During winter vacation of that, his last year at Harvard, he taught school in Kennebunk, Maine, where he would later take a full-time position for the last months of 1818 and the first half or so of 1819. When William returned to Boston early in 1819 it was for the express purpose of easing further the family's financial difficulties. Emerson wrote to him on 14 June, 1819, "You know there was one of the Faculty in Boston, one Dr. Kast and family who boarded with mother; well they go today to housekeeping unless they lied last Saturday when I

---

[1]Emerson, Letters, 1: 42-44.

visited the family; this you see puts us out of order again and brings toil
on trouble for us to procure a <u>boarding</u> reinforcement."[1] William's return
probably also was prompted by another letter of 3 July, 1819 from Emerson:
"As to the 'wherewith' to get along in this life with, we are still in the
lurch and rather more so than usual. Mother has only those two boarders
that I told you of and one is in the country a few weeks now which takes
away half the value of even that; So that Mother wishes me to ask you if
possible to take up another quarter's salary to pay our rent August 8th."[2]
Again, it is Ruth Emerson's will which is to prevail. However, knowing
full-well that his brother will be inconvenienced in his own life in Kennebunk
by the request from the Emersons in Boston, Emerson comforted himself more
than he did William by projecting a distant horizon of hope: "In all these
difficulties it is a comfort to remember that we are growing older and I
don't doubt that the good taste of mankind will soon discover the talents
which now like. . . 'Full many a gem of &c.'"[3] Probably with some resignation William pleased his mother by returning to Boston shortly afterward.
He founded a School for Young Ladies, the revenues from which kept the
family and its young Brahmin scholars afloat.

Within this family context Emerson's relationship to Martin Gay takes
on its full meaning. By the fall of 1820 Edward had entered Harvard College
and he and his brother Ralph, of course, roomed together. In a sense, therefore, the Emerson family was no longer scattered late in 1819 and Ralph Waldo
had found the security which only his family seemed able to provide. That
security was required for the purpose of pursuing the fascination not only
of keeping his new journal early in 1820, but also of pursuing his relation-

---

[1]Ibid., p. 84.   [2]Ibid., p. 87.

[3]Ibid., pp. 87-88.

ship with Martin Gay, such as it was. This tightness of filial bonding
was affirmed when, during April, 1820, Ruth Emerson relocated to Franklin
Place (No. 24) in order to have a house large enough to include a room where
William could conduct his school without leaving home.[1] However, across
the Charles River in Cambridge Emerson was beginning to take notice of his
schoolmates.

"There is a strange face in the Freshman class whom I should like to
know very much," he wrote in his journal on 8 August, 1820.[2] Martin Gay
had a "great deal of character in his features" and it was Emerson's belief
that the boy "should be a fast friend or a bitter enemy," and later cancelling-
out the name, "Gay," Junio asserted, "His name is ____."[3] Evidently an
infatuation had begun, for Emerson innocently betrayed a full-blown ambivalence
toward Gay by referring to him as both a possible "friend" or "enemy."
Nonetheless, he said earnestly that he would "endeavor to become acquainted
with him" and hoped if possible that he would "be able to recall at a future
period the singular sensations which his presence produce at this.--"[4] Now
it may not be convincing at this point to single out Emerson's mention of
Gay's "face" as an example of the visual emphasis in references to the
boy from this early entry on. However, about two months later, on 20 October,
1820 an entry of one short phrase, bearing the name, "Gay," is cancelled-out
in the journal. Next to the cancellation, and I shall refrain from the
the attempt to make a great deal out of such scant evidence, Emerson has
penned a sketch of what might be taken as a picture of a lamp with the word,
"DULL," written across it.[5] This cancellation and the one of 8 August, 1820

---

[1]Rusk, The Life of Ralph Waldo Emerson, p. 76.

[2]Emerson, JMN, 1: 22.

[3]Ibid.

[4]Ibid.

[5]Ibid., p. 38.

especially, serve to suggest that Emerson was indeed "turning down the lamp," so to speak. He was "closing his eyes" and preventing others from seeing "Gay."

Presumably Martin Gay was referred to again on 24 October, 1820, and Emerson linked him directly to his own sense of the religious efficacy of "seeing." He said that he was beginning "to believe in the Indian doctrine of eye-fascination. The cold blue eye of ____ has intimately connected him with my thoughts and visions."[1] He was haunted day and night and found himself wrapped-up in "conjectures of his character and inclinations."[2] Emotion mounts in a fashion quite atypical of Emerson's narrative when he reports that "we have had already two or three long profound stares at each other. Be it wise or weak or superstitious I must know him"[3] Odd, it seems, that two months earlier he had made a similar but less frantic commitment to meet Gay and had not yet carried it out by October, and the end of the month to boot. There is evidence to suggest that Emerson was relieved, if not happy, to receive reports that Gay was "proverbially idle."[4] Punctuating his peculiar accentuation of the cancelled references to Gay's name, as usual, Emerson once again sketched a male head in the margin of the entry. It is pointed to by another sketch, a pointing finger, which is inserted in the place where the name would have been written ("My opinion of ____. . . .").[5] If Martin Gay's idleness caused Emerson to hold a low opinion of him, the senior's thoughts were changed by new reports about the heroics of the wily sophomore: his opinion of Gay was "redeemed" by learning Gay was a "superior man."[6] That is, "this week, a little eventful in college, has brought a

---

[1]Ibid., p. 39. [2]Ibid. [3]Ibid.

[4]Ibid., pp. 39-40 [5]Ibid. [6]Ibid.

share of its accidents to him."[1] Emerson referred to the customary riots

staged by sophomores, who would ransack through the dining hall at some

appropriate moment each year. Evidently, Gay was a ringleader in the class

of 1823, because when Emerson paid the event literary tribute in his note-

book during October, 1820, just days after the riot, he lauded Gay's valor:

> You might say what you please of the current rebellion
> Tonight the Conventicle drink to a real one.
> The annals of ages have blazoned its fame
> And Paeans are chanted to hallow its name.
> Derry Down
>
> Alas for the windows the sophs have demolished,
> Alas for the laws that they are not abolished,
> And that Dawes could abide the warm battle's brunt
> And the Government's vote it was Gay Lee and Blunt
> Derry Down
>
> But this shock of the Universe who could control
> Aghast in despair was each Sophomore soul
> Save one who alone in his might could stand forth
> To grapple with elements--Mr. Danforth
>
> Let the Earth and the Nations to havoc go soon
> And the World tumble upward to mix with the moon
> Old Harvard shall smile at the rare conflagration
> The conventicle standing her pledge of salvation.
> Derry Down[2]

It should be noted for the sake of clarification that Rufus Dawes was a

participant but, because he was only a freshman, he was merely admonished

for his activity. Gay, Lee, and Blunt, the ringleaders, were temporarily

suspended and rusticated. In 1823 Gay and Danforth would participate in

another riot and would be dismissed from the college along with thirty-four

others, probably without the good fortune of graduating.

Emerson had good cause to have a "redeemed" opinion of Gay if the

latter was, indeed, recognized as such a "superior man," a man of riotous

valor. The Conventicle was a social club in which Emerson had become a

_____

[1]Ibid.

[2]Ibid., pp. 244-45.

prominent member. The club had been formed with fond memories by the rioters of the class of 1821, Emerson's class, and those fond memories bonded together most members of the Conventicle after their riots of November, 1818. Emerson, one knows, did not participate at all in those 1818 riots, probably out of fear of suspension or the loss of the job which he had at the time of tutoring President's Kirkland's nephew.[1] Therefore, he salutes Martin Gay and thereby lives through in fantasy of a vicarious sort what he missed living through two years before. Through his writing, then, Emerson took his diminished life (financially, socially) and expanded it beyond what it really was. To discover only that he was headed for change, a new career later on.

Though Emerson hailed Gay as something of a local hero, he persisted in remaining at arm's length from him preferring to get information about his hero second-hand. ". . . an anecdote which I incidentally heard of him shows him more like his neighbors than I should wish him to be."[2] Emerson's "ideal friend," he said, he expected "to be different from any individual I had seen. . . . I had vested [Gay] with a solemn cast of mind, full of poetic feeling, and an idolater of friendship and possessing a vein of sober thought."[3] Later Emerson would have cause to rely on his experience with Gay as a model of a fit friend during 1828, though he hardly would recall his college friend had met the bill years earlier. In any case, following these first lines of an entry into the journal on 1 April, 1821, Emerson cancelled-out much of the text which followed them (the cancelled portions are contained within parentheses below): "When I saw (____'s pale but expressive face and large eye, I instantly invested him with the complete

---

[1]See Emerson, Letters, 1: 74.

[2]Emerson, JMN, 1: 52-53.   [3]Ibid.

character of which fancy had formed and) though (entirely unacquainted with him was pleased to observe the notice which he appeared to take of me. For a year I have entertained towards him the same (feelings and should be) worry to lose him altogether (before we have ever exchanged above a dozen words)."[1] The entry was quite meaningless without knowledge of the cancelled passages. However, now and particularly because he inserted meaningless letters and pseudo-letters into the blank space reserved for Gay's name, Emerson's ambivalence stands out clearly, especially its visual dimension. Prying eyes, it seems, were intended to be misled. The short paragraph which follows this entry of 1 April, 1821 was Emerson's suggestion to himself that this book, "Wide World 2," was of such an "inferiour character" and contained "so much doubtful matter" that it should be burned: Oddly, "immediately upon its completion."[2]

There is no other journal entry which is both cancelled-out or so exemplary of Emerson's ambivalence over the relationship than that of 2 May, 1821. "I am more puzzled than ever with ____'s conduct," he writes: "he came out to meet me yesterday and I observing him, just before we met turned another corner and most strangely avoided him."[3] Perhaps puberty prompted his "Unconscious to become Conscious," as he would put it thirteen years later, but now he persisted to maintain visual distance from Gay, yet always as a result of an intense curiosity about him. He did so for a second time as well. When Emerson went out to meet him "in a different direction," he tried stopping and talking to a lounger in order "to be directly in ____'s way."[4] But, alas, Gay turned into a gate and headed for Stoughton Hall,

---

[1] Ibid.

[3] Ibid., pp. 54-55.

[2] Ibid.

[4] Ibid.

evidently as unnerved by the would-be encounter as Emerson had been during the first try. At least, Emerson thought Gay had been unnerved. The senior felt that "all this baby play" went on "without any apparent design."[1] And, almost with habitual occurrence when associated with the Gay references. Emerson affirmed his "most serious expectation of burning this book. . .which Somebody else may light upon" and he added in good Freudian form the paren- thetical remark "(Mr. Somebody, will it please your impertinence to be conscience- struck!)"[2]

This evidence of unconscious conflict over Gay is not necessarily to say that Emerson was either of a homosexual bent or homoerotically involved with the underclassman. This cannot be known for sure. However, the clarity with which Emerson recorded his ambivalence does suggest that this point during his life could very well have been the focus-point of a therapeutic session with a psychologist, had one been available to him at the time. Let us attempt to speculate on reasonably good grounds about this matter as if a psychologist were probing Emerson's mental world. One of the ways in which an analysis of Emerson's report might have proceeded would involve the young man in a battery of so-called "projective tests" (e.g.s., Rorschach's Inkblots, Murray's Thematic Apperception Test). Emerson, of course, cannot be given these tests. However, the next best thing can be done, especially in terms of just what he was getting involved with at this same time of his relationship with Martin Gay. Coincidentally, Emerson's first attempt to write fiction occurred just eight days after the entry about Martin Gay mentioned above, on 10 May, 1821. In effect, therefore, Emerson's short story, "The Magician," can serve as a reasonably adequate semblance of a "projective test" which may tap his mental life at that point in time.

---

[1]Ibid.   [2]Ibid.

The story is a simple one, relying on mythological figures taken from Norse legends, and telling a tale about Uilsa, a witch, and her son, Vahn, a magician.[1] In addition to Uilsa and Vahn, the other major figure in the story, though unacknowledged explicitly in the text, is the narrator, who explains the course of the story's action. For the purpose of analysis later these three characters, then, will be central. The configuration of inter-relationships which Emerson establishes between them will give one insight into his own personal inclinations towards Gay and towards his mother, Ruth Emerson. A summary of the story follows.

Uilsa lived in the woods, "despised and derided" by all the villagers, even though she was proudly descended "from a hundred weird women, fatal and feared daughters of Odin."[2] Her first-born son was borne away from her into slavery by a "gold caravan . . . with galloping horses and tassled elephants from Birmah," but Uilsa called on Odin who thundered a pack of wolves on the caravan, killing all.[3] One of the wolves carried Vahn to a cave and "nourished him from her dugs."[4] Meanwhile, Uilsa waited at the entrance of the cave for years for her son to emerge. The "proud magician"

---

[1]See ibid., pp. 55, 266-68, 284-86, 302-303. Why Emerson chose to employ Norse mythology instead, say, that of Greece, remains an interesting question. One possible suggestion is that Emerson was expressing a sense of personal defeat, at least a personal trial, by using Norse mythology. Valhalla, which he mentioned when he began his journals, was the mythical hall where Odin receives and feasts the souls of heroes fallen bravely in battle. The maidens of Odin whom Emerson invoked for help, the Valkyries, have the job of conducting the souls of those slain heroes to Valhalla and of waiting on them there. By invoking the Valkyries, and then by relying again on similar mythology when he experimented with the story of Uilsa and Vahn, Emerson takes for granted--"projects"--a personal sense of defeat in relating to Martin Gay. He is "slain" by Gay's eyes, and seeks to avert them. However, for Emerson the task takes on "heroic" proportions, and becomes a cosmic struggle not unrelated to his ego-identity formation, especially the sexual dimension of that process.

[2]Ibid., p. 268.   [3]Ibid., p. 285.   [4]Ibid.

did not recognize his own mother when he finally emerged from the cave years later, and he drove her away with the help from a baying pack of dogs "over the snow drift in the cold starless night."[1]

Then the narrator reports that after Uilsa told him her story, it seems as though the villagers take heart and go looking for Uilsa in order to make amends. Meanwhile, she had decided on the course of suicide and had headed for the feared Milboro pits and the "suffocating grip of the serpent" which lived there.[2] Nonetheless, the narrator valiantly assumes the role of a mediator, and he heads out after Uilsa in what would turn out to be a vain attempt to rescue her from her ill-fated course. He discovers that Uilsa was in search of Odin, to join him in death was all she now wished: "I saw Uilsa, remarkable for her majestic gait advancing on the fatal spot, apparently conscious of her proximity to the monster but with her eye unusually bright fixed upon the dark clouds in the north."[3] The story ends with the narrator, powerless, watching as the serpent wraps Uilsa in its grip and casts her into the dark pit, Uilsa crying to Odin as she falls to death. He believes she fell into her lover's waiting arms.

I would like to suggest the following interpretation of this story. What we are playfully assuming is an example of Emerson's less than conscious projections during this particularly emotionally intense and baffling time of his life, 1820-22. In many ways the figure of Uilsa resonates with Ruth Haskins Emerson, Ralph Waldo's mother. She too was without a husband and, because she was forced by financial circumstances to labor as a common house-keeper (and not a very successful one at that), she was an outsider to the lost rich life in which she was raised and which she knew with her late husband. Undoubtedly Emerson wrestled with this matter of his mother, especially in

---

[1]Ibid.   [2]Ibid., p. 303.   [3]Ibid., p. 302.

the light of his up-coming graduation from Harvard. It would mean not only that he would be obliged to forsake the magical fascination over his relationship with Gay, but also begin to labor at school-keeping so that his mother would have bread, and enough of it.

The most dominant image of the story is Vahn's mother at the entrance of the cave. Uilsa appeared able to wait indefinitely at the mouth of the cave for her son to come out. However, her patience was the kind conditioned by circumstances, not the kind which by its inherent power might "draw out" her son. Uilsa appeared to be patient because she could do little else, especially as she was held at bay by the pack of wolves. Therefore, Uilsa's patience resulted from Vahn's regard of this "intruder." By keeping his mother at the mouth of the cave he avoided her completely. When he did come out of the cave he did not recognize her and, hence, added a new dimension to his avoidance of his mother. Vahn (literally) could not see her. His eyes were subject to eye bewilderments, perhaps because he had come out into the bright light of day. This was like Emerson's knowledge of Martin Gay. As he learned too much about him, this new knowledge blotted out his earlier impression of him. Perhaps most significantly, for his mother to be waiting at the mouth of the cave was for Vahn to find coming out quite difficult. He could not come out on his own unless helped by baying, avaricious wolves, perhaps like hungry brothers. Wolves, however, would not be as available to Emerson as they were to the magician in the story he fabricated.

However, a broader consideration seems to be at stake as well, one involving the matter of fidelity. That is to say, he could be faithful, as it were, to Martin Gay. However, this would require him to put aside his duty to his family. To become carried away in the indolence of wondering about Gay and baby play would be to fail to follow one's academic course sufficiently, and this would lead to diminished prospects for greatness.

On the other hand, Emerson could be faithful to his mother and, therefore,

anticipate supporting the family or, at least, doing his share. However,

this would force him into a position where he would be unfaithful to his

own emotions. Emerson's schoolkeeping experience would confirm the devasta-

ting effects of this sort of posture. In any case, the story of the magician,

at least because it appears where it does in the journals and notebooks, is

suggestive of some of the emotional parameters of Emerson's life. What it

suggests generally is a fear of betraying his mother, and an ambivalence

over caring for her and the family's needs while at the same time following-

out the course of his own curiosities and inclinations. In all likelihood

this configuration of meaning was sparked by his relationship with Martin

Gay.

Other references disguise connections with Gay as well as substitute

fictitious names for his. A song, written on 19 November, 1821 seems quite

obviously addressed to Martin Gay. "This song is to one whose unimproved

talents and unattained friendship have interested the writers in his charac-

ter and fate"; Emerson begins. . .

> By the unacknowledged tie
> Which binds us to each other
> By the pride of feeling high
> Which friendship's name can smother
>
> By the cold encountering eyes
> Whose language deeply thrilling
> Rebelled against the prompt surmise
> Which told the heart was willing;
>
> By all which you have felt and feel
> My eager gaze returning
> I offer to this silent zeal
> On youthful altars burning,
> All the classic hours which fill
> The little urn of honour;

> Minerva guide and pay the pen
> Your hand conferred upon her.[1]

It is significant to point out that in the beginning of the eighth line

the phrase, "Which told" was a replacement for "Confessed." Conscience,

and alleviating its pressures, seems to be readily associated with Gay. It

was consistent for conscience to be expressed in terms of "cold encountering

eyes," "eager gaze," and "silent zeal" as the record showed. During 1828 and

again during 1832 conscience will be carried over to other concerns, but

concerns which are of a very similar nature. Then conscience will be likened

to an "umbilical cord" which connects a man with God. Also after resigning

from his charge at Second Church, Boston, Emerson will be relieved that he

has severed the "cord" which bound him to the ministry. In both cases, God

the Father and his own father's ministerial tradition are adorned with

maternal features. Betrayed is Emerson's struggle to overcome not only

paternal legacies, but, and probably of greater importance, the ever-present

directions of his mother. More about this will be said later.

A fictitious name is used as well in a probable reference to Gay in 1821

(since it is so deliberately and so heavily cancelled-out). Emerson pretends

to draw lines from a playwriter who, one knows, did not exist. The play

he calls significantly, "The Friends"--thus, betraying a persistent pre-

occupation which would come to the fore in his life more and more at a later

date. The extracted lines (presumably extracted) are these.

> Malcom, I love thee more than women love
> And pure and warm and equal is the feeling
> Which binds us and our destinies forever
> But these are seasons in the change of times
> When strong excitement kindles up the light of
>   ancient memories.[2]

Again one cannot be certain about how directly this refers to Martin Gay:

---

[1]Ibid., pp. 321-22.   [2]Ibid., pp. 291-92.

Is "Malcom" Gay? If Emerson misspelled "Malcom" (not Malcolm), then it is possible that the name might be some sort of anagram. In this sense, the words of the lines might be addressed, therefore, by Gay to Emerson himself like this: Waldo, Malcom, Ralph. It would seem that this speculation, no matter how interesting, is somewhat far-fetched. However, it is clear from the amount of cancellation of "The Friends" (the first four lines) and from the fact of a drawing of a male head in the margin (which, already noted, is characteristic of Emerson's references to Gay), that the new school-keeper of late 1821 had, indeed, kindled up the light seen in Gay several months before. Almost haunting are the lines in the notebooks of 1821-22, "Why do you look after me? I cannot help looking out as you pass."[1] But we cannot say with certainty that they pertain to Gay, except by inference, on the basis of similar cancellations, disguised words and names, and the similarity of subject matter as well as drawings in the margins. After all, this was the way in which Emerson tried to keep the prying eyes of a "Mr. Somebody" from seeing, especially seeing what he saw in Martin Gay. Inference, moreover, might suggest also that his Latin description of his love for a "man in college" of 28 February, 1822 was a reference to Gay.[2]

The few remaining direct references to Martin Gay can be lumped together as those written by Emerson in the form of a retrospective glance at college days. Only two times after his August, 1821 graduation did Emerson explicitly mention Gay. Never again would any evidence appear anywhere to suggest that Emerson ever met or even knew about Martin Gay during the rest of their lives. This was very unusual in light of Gay's accomplishments, despite Emerson's own ambivalence over reporting his possible knowledge of them. Gay took a M.D. degree at Harvard in 1826 and went on to become a prominent Boston physician and chemist, and a member of the Boston Society of Natural

---

[1]Ibid., p. 353.   [2]Ibid., pp. 94-95

History and Fellow of the American Academy of Arts and Sciences. He died in 1850.[1] However, later during his life Emerson seems to have had a peculiar sort of relationship with physicians in general or, at least, he tended to think more highly of them than his actions would lead us to believe he did later in life, around the time his brother and wife became ill with acute cases of tuberculosis. In one sense, physicians, when they entered his mental world, were kept at arm's length. That he never mentioned Gay, a prominent Boston physician until 1850, was an effective way of sustaining a distance between himself and Gay in a most general way later in life. It is quite unlikely that Emerson was unaware of the Boston physician but it is likely that Emerson's relationship with Gay became a model of how to relate to physicians in general. We shall come to see this more clearly later. At any rate, portraying those remaining direct references to Gay from Emerson's retrospective glance is in order at this time.

In the context of expressing his lack of enthusiasm for school-keeping on 7 May, 1822 Emerson scratched-out Gay's name from the sentence in which he mused, ". . . there was pride in being a collegian, and a poet, and somewhat romantic in my queer acquaintance with (Gay)."[2] Though Martin Gay had come to Harvard more monied than he himself did, Emerson said, "Poverty presented nothing mortifying in the meeting of two young men" with common interests in school.[3] However, his schoolmate was moving into his senior year when this was written, while Emerson was a "droning schoolmaster." Emerson's own senior year was quite memorable, since he fa red well writing prize-winning essays. Should he meet Gay in the future, he said, "the cast of countenance" would be "somewhat altered."[4] Perhaps with deliberate tongue-

---

[1]For a biographical sketch of Martin Gay see ibid., p. 22.

[2]Ibid., pp. 129-30.   [3]Ibid.   [4]Ibid.

in-cheek he continued to say, "Hope, it is true, still hangs out, though

at further distance, her gay banners . . ."[1]

The second and final explicit and direct retrospective glance at Gay

in the journals occurs within the summary entry of 29 November, 1822. Then

Emerson's thoughts were already turning away from his school towards the

prospects of theological studies and a subsequent ministry. Hope, indeed,

was being given a fair chance to push him toward a bright success. The entry

is a lengthy one. Perhaps the length itself indicated how, despite Emerson's

humorous insertion of the exclamation, "Pish," at the end of it, he retained

the pattern of the relationship if not the relationship with Gay itself.

For this reason, as well as for setting the stage for what is to follow,

the entry should be presented in full:

> The ardour of my college friendship for Gay (name is cancelled-
> out) is nearly extinct, and it is with difficulty that I can
> now recall those sensations of vivid pleasure which his presence
> was wont to awaken spontaneously, for a period of more than two
> years. To be so agreeably excited by the features of an indivi-
> dual personally unknown to me, and for so long a time, was surely
> a curious incident in the history of so cold a being, and well
> worth a second thought. At the very beginning of our singular
> acquaintance, I noticed the circumstances in my Wide World, with
> an expression of curiosity with regard to the effect which time
> would have upon those feelings. To this day, our glance at meet-
> ing, is not that of indifferent persons, and were he not so buried
> in his martial cares I might still entertain the hope of departed
> hours. Probably the abandonment of my solitary enthusiasm is
> owing to the discouraging reports which I have gathered of his

---

[1]Ibid. It is striking to recognize in this statement imagery not
dissimilar to that of the American national anthem's ("Star-Spangled Banner")
first verse which, incidentally depicts the strength of the nation's hope for
survival in bright visual terms: "Oh, say, can you see, by the dawn's early
light, what so proudly we hailed at the twilight's last gleaming, whose broad
stripes and bright stars, thro' the perilous fight, o'er ramparts we watched,
were so gallantly streaming? And the rocket's red glare, the bombs burst-
ing in air, gave proof thro' the night that our flag was still there. Oh,
say, does that star-spangled banner yet wave, o'er the land of the free and
the home of the brave." Emerson's budding sense of expanded sight follows
the same structure as the new-born hope of American nationalism after the
War of 1812 during which Francis Scott Key penned this anthem.

pursuits and character, so entirely inconsistent with the indications of his face. But it were much better that our connexion
should stop, and pass off, as it now will, than to have had it
formed, and then broken by the late discovery of insurmountable
barriers to friendship. From the first, I preferred to preserve
the terms which kept alive so much sentiment rather than a more
familiar intercourse which I feared would end in indifference.
. . . Pish."[1]

The point to be made about this last and summary entry about Martin
Gay is that though Emerson seems to have grown beyond it, the pattern of
the relationship depicted in it is retained. In retrospect, therefore,
Emerson construed the relationship as a smaller part of his now wider world,
that is, according to the pattern of expansion within diminishment. Moreover, evident is the dominance of the visual modality, seeing Gay's "features,"
activating "our glance," and observing the "indications of his face." However, going hand-in-hand with the visual engagement, perhaps intimacy,
between "not . . . indifferent persons" was a necessary distance or the
emotional control of isolation. Emerson was loath to breach the "terms
which kept so much sentiment alive" with the "indifference" of a "more familiar intercourse," all by way of lifting high the ideal of "friendship."
Friendship for Emerson was not the fact of intimacy, just the desire for it.
Admiration, or the quality of friendship at a distance, was what Emerson
sought to sustain most of all. Later one will note that both Ellen Tucker
and Thomas Carlyle fill a similar bill. For now, Emerson is noted to have
remained as ambivalent over Gay as the ambiguous nature of that word, "familiar," implied. This experience of two years duration would prove to be
prototypical. The pattern of expansion within diminishment was retained,
and it would continue to become the structure in terms of which Emerson
would decide to pursue theological studies toward the end of 1824.

---

[1]Ibid., 2: 59. Emphasis mine.

Generally, in the first place, Emerson's felt ambivalence toward Gay prompted him to feel indolent and insignificant.[1] Just as he felt these things, so too their opposites were felt awakening within, namely, industry, and a desire for greatness (i.e., becoming representative, the "light" of virtue). In the second place, eyesight was the central mode of contact. That is, Emerson could become a "great man" only insofar as he literally saw beyond his relationship with Martin Gay (and, perhaps, affirmed unconscious fidelity toward his mother).[2] We must turn to the final episode of the period of 1811-24 if we are to see how Emerson transposed the pattern of expansion within diminishment over into his decision to take steps to prepare for a ministerial career. For it is during his three years of school-keeping that oscillation between feelings of indolence and the want of proper industry, insignificance and the want of fame, are most intense. We will note along the way that no longer will it be Martin Gay in whom Emerson is visually engaged, but another figure of a somewhat greater and more meaningful status, at least in Emerson's eyes--namely, his paternal Aunt Mary.

The Schoolmaster of 1821-24

Emerson's muse, about which he wrote to his Aunt Mary in November, 1821, had been awake "ever since the fatal entrance to Gehenna" which occurred when the college graduate joined his brother at the School for Young Ladies.[3] But there was "a pride," he asserted, which was "kindled elsewhere than is supposed," somewhere other than in classroom preparations.[4] As he continued

---

[1]See ibid., 1: 39. The reference is sandwiched in between two references, each about Martin Gay.

[2]See ibid., 2: 59.   [3]Emerson, Letters, 1: 104-105.   [4]Ibid.

his letter to his aunt, mentor, and, now confidante, he believed she would

have a low opinion of her nephew for failing to secure a post as an usher

at the Latin School: "Friend, though thinkest mine hour is passed, the

waters of self-annihilation and contempt are already settling calmly over

me and expanding their muddy sheet between my name, and _light_ forever."[1]

Indeed, his desire for this "Friend" will prompt his aunt to assure him of

her abiding concern for his welfare regardless of how he himself looked upon

his teaching post. Nonetheless, Emerson escalated the importance of visual

imagery in proportion to his pleas for her sanctions when he continued

nostalgically, "The child's dream was blest by some faint glimpses of strange

light and strange world,--but the child looked at his bauble and played

again with his bauble and the light was withdrawn. Now if such light had

been imparted, there was _one_ of whom the boy was taught the nature and

advantage of the visions but when his weak nature and strong fates began

to darken them--will instructor and friend alike forsake him?"[2] Though he

would ask five years later, "who leads the leaders and instructs the instruc-

tor?," for now, Aunt Mary Moody Emerson was a blessing to the young man

on the edge of and about to enter into Gehenna.[3] She was a blessing

in that she represented a feminized paternal heritage.

So it was that the novice school-keeper sustained himself through three

years of that place of abomination, that Gehenna of young ladies. Primarily

by means of encouraging an intellectual correspondence with his Aunt Mary

and a relationship which he seems to have thought more of than all the others

he blazoned with his pen at that time. Other teachers would pass, but his

aunt could be counted on, especially in times of disappointment when he

---

[1]Ibid.   [2]Ibid.   [3]Ibid., p. 167.

needed help pushing his horizons beyond the School for Young Ladies. Thus, Emerson's correspondence brought him a kind of solace which quelled the choppy waters of his disappointment after 1821. He also initiated a lively correspondence with his old classmate, John Boynton Hill of Baltimore for a similar purpose. However, during the years of school-mastering (some may say he was never a "master" at all) corresponding with his aunt was the most significant avenue he found into the future. For example, she introduced him to Oriental thought sometime early in 1822, and his cognition was laden then with the structure of expansion within diminishment as a result: As he lay contemplating on the possible contents of the Gita-- "pages, as dark to me as the Seal of Solomon," he consoled himself by regarding them together as "learning's El Dorado," that is, "Every man has a Fairy land just beyond the compass of his horizon."[1] In this sense, Aunt Mary supplied the "Fairy land" which Emerson himself had dropped out of his journal during 1820. Evidently, it was still required and no less a fascination. Moreover, the "Indian doctrine of eye-fascination" permeating the Bhagavad-gita, once associated with Gay, was now undoubtedly influencing thoughts and feelings associated with his aunt.

As his correspondence increased its intellectual pitch, Emerson gradually focused upon patently theological issues. The issue about which counsel was sought most was the problem of evil. Emerson has been noted to struggle with this problem in the context of the journals (See 8 April, 1823). We have noted a connection between that struggle and American national prospects for world reformation, as far as Emerson viewed them. On 16 October, 1823 he turned to his aunt with "a catalogue of curious questions," the most important of which is "What is the Origin of Evil?"[2] Again Emerson relied

---

[1]Ibid., pp. 116-17. [2]Ibid., pp. 137-39.

on the image of men imprisoned in shadows, perhaps unknowingly expressing the allegory of the cave in more contemporary and personally meaningful terms, as he had done in the story of "The Magician" and prior to that while writing to Edward from the basement on Hancock Street. "And what," he asks auspiciously, "becomes of the poor Slave born in chains living in stripes and toil, who has never heard of Virtue and never practised it and dies cursing God and man? . . . Must he die," the would-be seer asks, "in Eternal Darkness because it has been his lot to live in the Shadow of death?"[1] Indeed, to bring exiles home would be to include the Black population of America as well in his embrace. Nonetheless, Emerson hardly realized that by linking together national identity, slavery, and theological ideas about evil that he signalled the portent of his future as a cultural and ritual leader.

Emerson's more immediate prison, however, placed him on the bottom of the barrel, so to speak, along with slaves. When he attempted to give John Hill "an insight into our city-politics" he clearly betrayed his self-image: three great classes of people constitute the city's population, he began--first, "the aristocracy of wealth and talents; next, the great multitude of mechanics and merchants and the good sort of people who are for the most part content to be governed without aspiring to have a share of power; lastly, the lowest order of day labourours and outcasts of every description, including schoolmasters."[2] Though Emerson had tasted briefly the spoils of aristocratic life in Boston during the early part of the nineteenth century, that he considered himself aspiring to the "great multitude" of the middle class was clear. Even without the humorous note, he would later tell his

---

[1] Ibid.

[2] Ibid., pp. 110-11.

brother Edward during 1827 that "the way is clear to the Temple of fame," not in aristocratic circles but "thro' the Mechanics Institutes" which welcomed itinerant lecturers.[1] However, being a captive schoolmaster implied other valences of push and pull as well.

Most biographers of Emerson make little out of a possible connection between two clearly defined episodes in Emerson's life during the winter months of 1824-25. Instead of following their lead of keeping them separated, one might link them together. The purpose of doing so is, on the one hand, to further explicate the nature of Emerson's experience as a school-master and, on the other hand, to prepare for what is to come in subsequent chapters. Reference is made here first to the episode of Emerson's decision to close his "School for Young Ladies" in Boston by 31 December, 1824, and second, to the episode of his decision to begin theological studies with the faculty at Harvard, commencing on 11 February, 1825. The point intended by drawing attention to a possible connection between these distinguishable occurrences is to suggest that even though Emerson seemed set on theological studies as early as February, 1818,[2] his decision to go to Harvard once

---

[1]Ibid., p. 219. Besides Mechanics Institutes, other avenues for social and economic mobility were open to a budding lecturer. See major studies on the Lyceum movement, which was begun by Josiah Holbrook in 1826, and the Chautauqua movement, which emerged later on in the nineteenth-century during the 1880's: Carl Bode, The American Lyceum Movement: Town Meeting of the Mind (New York: Oxford University Press, 1956), Theodore Morrison, Chautauqua: A Center for Education, Religion, and the Arts in America (Chicago: University of Chicago Press, 1974). Both movements are set within that phase of American national development during which time Americans were learning distinct ways of communicating with each other, that is, building a shared cultural consciousness. On this point of the broader cultural meaning of Emerson's aspiration to be as one historian has put it, the "foremost example of the declamatory character of American literature," see, Daniel J. Boorstin, The Americans: The National Experience (New York: Vintage Books, 1965), pp. 314-318.

[2]See ibid., p. 57: This letter to William was written on 6 February, 1818.

again must be understood as prompted, at least in part, by his experience
of school-keeping and nostalgia associated with his undergraduate days,
including his less than conscious preoccupation with Martin Gay. Though
to say so now would be to anticipate the substance of the second major cluster of
events, that of 1825-33, the first facet of Emerson's temporary blindness
during 1825 can be said to concern his experiences as a teacher, and it is
to this facet that we turn here. In the next chapter this facet will be
dealt with only insofar as it illuminates Emerson's experiences during the
first months of theological studies.

Ever since graduating from Harvard College Emerson had joined his
brother William as a teacher in William's School for Young Ladies in Boston.
Sessions convened in the Emerson house at this time and, later, they convened
in a room in the back of Trinity Church, after William journeyed to Europe
in December of 1823. Interesting is the fact that in less than a year
after Emerson moved the school out of the Emerson house his thoughts started
turning with new seriousness in a different direction, toward theological
study. Though espousing Unitarian moral philosophy to his pupils, Emerson's
day-to-day encounters with them bewildered the shy novice. When a teacher's
decisiveness seemed required, "Mr. Waldo," as his students called him,
usually shrank from such tests, suffering from what he called a "vexation
of spirit" which occurred when "the will of the pupils was a little too
strong for the will of the teacher."[1]

Not only did experiences of teaching test Emerson's will, they also
brought on other unsettlings which struck to the core of what little self-
confidence he had at the time. He soon found himself troubled by "the

---

[1]Rusk, The Life of Ralph Waldo Emerson, p. 90.

infirmities of my cheek" (blushing) and "occasional admirations of some of my pupils."[1] An early habit spared him somewhat from these kinds of catastrophes: refractory pupils would be sent to his mother's room for a "minor sort of rustication."[2] We are led to assume that when the school was moved into Trinity Church and away from his mother's presiding presence Emerson was cast even more deeply into a quandry. Just prior to William's departure for Europe, however, he managed to find a minor but fairly supportive remedy. In the early part of 1822 Emerson resumed his journals after a period of silence. One of the major reasons for doing so was in order to continue to experiment with fantastically imaginative literature, continuing to completion the short story, "The Magician."[3] When, moreover, that story is seen in the context of Emerson's life as a teacher of "Young Ladies," a new slant of meaning rises to its surface. It would not be far-fetched to suggest that just as the "hundred weird women fatal and feared daughters of Odin" gave rise to Uilsa, and just as she ended in a serpent's grip, so too did the girls in Emerson's school make him all too aware of his own struggles to assert himself in the presence of his mother as well as in front of them. We can speculate that through the experience of teaching young ladies, Emerson was haunted by feelings of being destroyed by the Brahmin legacy he faced, a legacy expressed in the image of the Norse father-god, Odin. His balm, curiously, swells from an identification with Uilsa, a mother-goddess.

At any rate, just prior to taking full charge of the school and less

---

[1]Ibid.   [2]Ibid.

[3]On 18 April, 1824, however, Emerson assessed his literary experiment as a failure, replacing it instead with ponderings on the juxtaposition of his "love of eloquence" and his dislike of school-keeping. Emerson, JMN, 2: 238-39.

than one week after his twentieth birthday, Emerson joined his brother William at the end of May, 1823 in signing the "Declaration of Faith" subscribed to by the members of First Church in Boston, the church now led by Nathaniel Langdon Frothingham.[1] Emerson would help fill the small family coffers as long as possible, but his real curiosity was leading him, like William, with more and more certain hope towards theological studies and the ministry, towards the profession of "Divinity."

William's sights aimed at theological study at Gottingen University in Germany when his ship set sail on 5 December, 1823. Emerson's own hopes focused on his brother's venture as well, in spite of the fact that he probably had some intimations that William's religious doubts already invited the traveler to consider a career in law. That other members of the Emerson household would doubt the significance of following in their father's footsteps and refuse to take up their ministerial heritage, is clear from Emerson's report of July, 1824: "Neither of the boys who eat custards and strawberries with me today have determined their profession," Emerson wrote of Edward and Charles.[2] Charles was only sixteen years old. But Edward, Emerson said, "thinks he is too good for a lawyer and too bad for a divine."[3] The question which William took to his younger brother's foreign idol, Goethe, on 19 September, 1824 was this: Should a minister confess his doubts to his parishioners or, simply, tell them "what they wanted to hear?" When Goethe affirmed the latter, any indecision which William had about entering the ministry vanished. Goethe was not a minister, but he did have legal training. While his words may have sounded hypocritical,

---

[1]See Rusk, The Life of Ralph Waldo Emerson, p. 100: A text of the declaration is printed in Rusk's biography of Emerson.

[2]Emerson, Letters, 1: 147.   [3]Ibid.

this German of extraordinarily high regard in the Emersons' eyes exemplified moral truth. Goethe was minister-like, but hardly a Unitarian. William returned to America during September, 1825 and began to prepare to study for a career in law in New York City, disappointed by what appeared to him to be Goethe's lack of conscience.[1]

Knowledge of the immediacy of his older brother's experience doubtlessly contributed to Emerson's increasing solemnity about his own future. His set intention of 1824 was identical to that of his brother of one year before, namely, to pursue the Unitarian ministry. In a manner strikingly similar to his disciplinary habits as a teacher, Emerson appeared undaunted, however, just days before closing his school. On 15 December, 1824, contemplating the ways in which Providence relieved man's "deplorable poverty" of "virtue, affection, knowledge, and passion," the unwilling schoolmaster placed his trust in the real presence of Providence: Providence could "furnish amusement to many hours of idleness in him that once thought life wearisome, to detect beauty and simplicity of the means whereby it is done."[2]

Rare and perhaps auspicious remarks appear in Emerson's journal on 4 January, 1825, four days after closing his school and just one month before registering with the theological faculty at Harvard. His thoughts turned to the passage of his years, of their "even and eventless tenor" and of the "crisis which is but a little way before when a month will determine the dark or bright dye they must assume forever."[3] Though he will continue to prepare for the ministry, his fundamental preoccupation with numinosity, that is, with concurrent "distancing" feelings of isolation yet "seeing"

---

[1] Rusk, _The Life of Ralph Waldo Emerson_, p. 107.

[2] Emerson, _JMN_, 2: 304-308.   [3] Ibid., p. 309.

feelings of intimacy (viz. Martin Gay), will prevent him from being an avid aspirant. There is more in Emerson's remarks than meets the eye of this interpretation, however. Hints are given which seem to bear seeds later to bloom into a new vocational identity and into the cultural innovation of Boston Unitarianism known as Transcendentalism. The auspiciousness of Emerson's remarks is suggested by means of his use of visual imagery, in particular, the "dark" or "bright" color which his future might assume because of what may await him at Harvard Divinity School. This has been mentioned before. Nonetheless, an extremely unusual insertion appeared after his thoughts on Providence which developed further that some visual imagery: "Faith is a telescope."[1] It was his faith in the promise of the ministry which made the profession itself appear at hand, though far off in fact, indeed. Later, during 1829, identical terms about a telescopic faith would be reiterated in an altered but, nonetheless, similar situation, namely, Emerson on the verge of being ordained at Second Church in Boston. To rely on such a faith was to imply that he never would be able to become a faithful minister, since his faith necessitated looking beyond present circumstances. During late 1824 and early 1829 this meant hedging on ministerial commitments. But during the early part of 1825, Emerson

---

[1]Ibid., p. 308. This metaphor suggests Emerson's already-occurring transformation of "eye-centeredness" into a legitimate creative inner experience or religious intuition (see note 1, p. 61). Hence, a groundwork was constructed upon an intuitive epistemology. This would come to clash with the empirical epistemology upon which Unitarian Biblical theology was founded as early as 1825 when Emerson went to Harvard Divinity School and began feigning blindness in light of that fact. Moreover, using the image of a telescope also suggests that Emerson was finding a symbolic expression for growing decisiveness. The tradition of associating the eye with aggression is a long-standing one. See e.g.s., Edward S. Gifford, Jr., The Evil Eye: Studies in the Folklore of Vision (New York: Macmillan, 1958); Henry Hart, "The Eye in Symbol and Symptom," The Psychoanalytic Review 36 (1949): 1-21; and Phyllis Greenacre, "The Eye Motif in Delusion and Fantasy," American Journal Psychiatry 25 (1938): 297-334.

believed that man was "an animal that looks before and after" so that such
a "solemn step has solid ground."[1] By 1829 his ground would be much less
solid. All this, however, may be getting beyond the limits of the period
of 1811-24, and it is not intended that we go very far beyond it here.

Other grounds than those which pertained to vocation alone contributed
to Emerson's sense of solemnity. These stretched into his past and into
the tradition to which he fell heir. These grounds are two in number.
The first has to do with the aura about the Unitarian ministry which was
recognized as what we might recognize as a local virtue, it seems, of the
good citizenry of Boston. The second ground, one of a more sanguine note,
concerns a very strange but, nonetheless, significant "letter" which Emerson
wrote first into the text of his journal and then sent, copied, to his Aunt
Mary while wrestling with the theological implications (as well as those
closer to his warm heart!) of entering the ministry. The first ground can
be considered now. It has to do with what might be referred to as a prevail-
ing rule of frailty under which Boston clergymen especially labored.

The first ground of Emerson's solemnity about his immediate future
suggests that cautiousness on the part of the school-keeper was well-founded,
and that the step he was about to take was a very serious one indeed. Not
only had he lost his father, grandfather, and baby sister years before during a single, relatively short period of time. But the impact of their
deaths lingered as a shadow over family calamities during the early part
of 1825 as it would several years later. Without going too far beyond the parameters of 1811-24, during 1825 Emerson's brother Bulkeley, retarded since
his birth in 1807, became absolutely deranged and it fell upon Emerson to

---

[1]Emerson, JMN, 2: 237.

care for him. Furthermore, their brilliant younger brother Edward suffered

a nervous breakdown resulting from over-work at college, where, later,

he would graduate first in his class. About a decade later both Edward

(1834) and Charles (1836) would be dead from tuberculosis. If as the historian

of Unitarian life and thought in nineteenth-century Boston, Daniel Howe,

suggests, "vicarious suffering" was often a means by which nineteenth-century

Yankees sought "refinement of character" and reaped "moral benefits" by

so doing, then Emerson's character was on its way to being a highly polished

piece of moral crystal during those first months of 1825 when he was trying

to study Biblical theology.[1] His 1821-24 teaching experience, therefore,

can be understood to have prepared him extraordinarily well for such vicarious

reapings of moral benefit. His own suffering in Gehenna was great indeed.

Hence, there appeared to be a fine line between whether a weak and delicate

physical constitution formed a necessary prerequisite, so to speak, for a

career in the Unitarian ministry or not. Of course, the Rev. William Emerson

and other colleagues of his offered young Emerson no clear exception to

this rule of frailty. If the ministry was conducive to physical demise, it

would not be difficult to understand that some persons may have thought

that signs of a failing physical constitution confirmed one's ministry.

A major theme of the period of 1825-33 will be that the plethora of physical

ailments Emerson reported to suffer was a clever way in which he broadly

---

[1]See Howe, The Unitarian Conscience, (Cambridge: Harvard University Press, 1970), p. 160. An astonishing number of Boston's Unitarian leaders either died young or suffered weak and delicate constitutions as semi-invalids all their lives: John Abbot, Joseph Buckminster, Levi Frisbie (died in 1822), Henry Ware Jr., William Emerson, Sr., William Ellery Channing, and Francis Bowen. Emerson himself would suffer many ailments before he was thirty years old, including his unusual experience with blindness early during 1825. Identifying with sickness was a means by which character was thought to develop itself, though most Brahmins were unaware of this tacit "rule of frailty."

affirmed a ministerial course, while at the same time stalled to commit himself to any one particular ministry. In short, Emerson seemed to have followed suit and was obedient to the rule of frailty, but he was also shrewd in his use of its socially approved logical implications. So much for this line of thought until the next chapter.

Even though Emerson himself was unconsciously locked into the rule of frailty, and even though he would soon rely on it to a degree, it is clear that he felt stronger than his younger brothers, his father, and Boston clergymen in general. Just as William may have had the courage to turn away from the ministry in 1825, Emerson showed strength of a similar sort when he pursued the ministerial course, knowing that that course might not hold forever. He knew that he might be so taxed by it that he would die young. However, the whole issue was avowedly superfluous by July of 1828 when Edward suffered another breakdown: then, when he considered the "constitutional calamity" of his family as it fell on Edward Emerson, he would feel such a "mixture of 'silliness'" in his frame that he would believe Providence had tempered him against a similar fate.[1] That Emerson had overlooked his own episode with the calamity of blindness by 1828, let alone his own tubercular signs, rheumatism, and lameness afterwards about three years earlier, suggests that the psychological legacy of constitutional frailty played on his mind, and remained operative to a very significant degree. However, this was to a lesser degree than his conditioning pressed upon him. As we will see, at least he was strong enough to make good use of his ills in the end.

If the cautiousness of the school-keeper to enter the ministry was well-founded, the second ground upon which his solemnity was based during 1824

---

[1] Emerson, JMN, 3: 137.

was expressed in a most odd entry into his journal of 2 May, 1824. Emerson wrote a "Letter to Plato," of all people![1] The letter seems meaningfully situated in the journals, since it follows almost immediately after his "self-assessment" entry of 18 April, 1824 in which he stated his intention and qualifications for the study of Divinity.

At this same point in time, one would do well to recall that Emerson was a fairly regular listener and disciple of William Ellery Channing to which the journals testify.[2] Though Channing showed that one could be nominally a minister and yet be free of creeds, even that of First Church's "Declaration," he nonetheless espoused a fairly orthodox Unitarian line. Specifically, he upheld the unique importance of Jesus, the historicity of the gospel story, including the miracles, and the conviction that the Bible, at least, was a record of inspiration.[3] However, these kinds of issues seem not to have been the roughest grist in Emerson's intellectual mill. What was probably no mean inducement for the would-be divinity student to walk from Roxbury to the Federal Street Church was Channing's demeanor and style: Channing led the Unitarians of Boston in spite of "his frail body, his dislike of controversy, and his horror of any kind of orthodoxy, even the Unitarian kind."[4] This probably included the orthodoxy of Andrews Norton, soon to be Emerson's teacher during a short term at the Harvard Divinity School. Such a demeanor and a style in a prestigious and admired preacher undoubtedly caught the eye of the theological novice more than once, the journals intimated. Therefore, we may ask, what is the meaning

---

[1]Ibid., 2: 246-49.   [2]Ibid., pp. 160, 238.

[3]See Rusk, The Life of Ralph Waldo Emerson, p. 101.

[4]Ibid.

of the "Letter to Plato," especially coming where it did in such a biographical context, or, at least, in terms of the biographical evidence of Emerson's life? To the letter one may now turn.

Appearing where and when it does, the letter to Plato parallels the entry on "self-assessment" of several entries before in terms of the letter's meaning. That is, if the entry on "self-assessment" served as an apt personal completion of the events of 1811-24 in Emerson's own eyes, the letter to Plato is equally an apt symbolical completion of the same period. Emerson was attempting to bring his life to a point of closure on the past, by way of preparing a plateau of psycho-social mastery from which he could envision expanded vocational promise. Emerson's letter to Plato was an attempt to reconcile a system of Unitarian theology with something more akin to a felt sense of a greater meaning in his life, generally, the moral thrust signalled in his mind by the name, "Plato." It has been suggested that Platonic notions tap the psychological core of Emerson's preoccupation with numinosity best insofar as that curiosity has to do with "eye-centeredness" and visual processes not unrelated, for example, to the structure of Plato's allegory of the cave. The presentation of the letter, therefore, is offered as the most poignant and direct confirmation of this specific claim. We may ask, why did Emerson choose to reconcile his personal circumstances with Plato?

Emerson chooses Plato as an intellectual hero or as a "representative man" of virtue when he opens his letter by saying, "The voice of antiquity has proclaimed, most venerable Shade, that if the Father of the Gods should converse with men he would speak in the language of Plato."[1] However, that language, once spoken by all, has grown outdated: "Philosophy discourses in another language and though the messages of Deity are brought to men in

---

[1]Emerson, JMN, 2: 246.

terms as well as on topics to which you, illustrious Athenian, were a stranger"--
"In this old age of the world," Emerson assures Plato, "I shall therefore
speak to the Spirit of Plato in a new language but in one whereinto has long
been transfused all the wealth of ancient thought, enriched and perchance
out weighted by productions of modern genius."[1] What should be apparent
already in these salutary remarks is the structure of expansion within
diminishment of Emerson's intellectual playfulness. Again, as he takes
glances toward antiquity, Emerson speaks of it as having diminished. However, from that ancient dialect a new language has expanded beyond it.
That is, with the aging of mankind or, one might say, with the accretion of
"wisdom" Plato's medium has been developed. Emerson's precise claims may
or may not be significant. But the pattern by which those claims are made
is very important for structural reasons.

Though "you have now dwelled in the land of souls upward of twenty
centuries" and have seen a plethora of things, Emerson continued to write
to Plato of "higher revolutions and vaster communities. I write of the
moral and religious condition of man."[2] As far as he is able to tell or,
at least, the way Emerson construed it for himself, "As the world has grown
older the theory of life has grown better, while a correspondent improvement in practice, has not been observed."[3] Eighteen centuries ago, however,
a "Revelation came down from heaven" he says, which was so clear and simple
that it became a "Rule of life."[4] The general upshot of the meeting between
the forces of Plato and those of Jesus has been that the Bible, "which contains this divine message," has done more than any other expression of virtue
to sap the authority of "the Athenian. . . I might say, to sweep away the

---

[1]Ibid.

[2]Ibid.

[3]Ibid.

[4]Ibid.

influences of Socrates and his disciple."[1] However, as far as Emerson believed, "Men still commend your wisdom; . . . for indeed Plato thou reasonest well but Christ and his apostles infinitely better not through thy fault but through their inspiration."[2] Once again, the structure of Emerson's character comes into play. Here he is not dismissing or casting Plato aside. Instead, he is literally "telescoping" through the ages, Plato being the first but smallest glimmer of light in regard to the "moral and religious condition of man" from which Emerson derives his sense of faith.

Several of the lines following these appear to get even closer to the heart of Emerson's biographical circumstances during 1824. He points out that "the priesthood find riddles hard to solve, wonders not easy to digest."[3] The reason for this is because the skeptical ministers of his day do not believe it possible that men, now "living under the influence of such men and puissant principles as our Gospel hath erected," ever before could have "obtained of thought or action" any high standard of virtue "under the patronage of your gaudy and indecent idolatry."[4] Then, with a portent of his journal entry of 4 January, 1825 which was more telling than he realized, Emerson suggests that there were maverick scholars about, "whose midnight lamp is regularly lit to unfold your spirit" and who appeal "from the long mythology with the poets forged, to your own lofty speculations on the nature of the Gods and the obligations to virtue."[5] He tacks to this the remark, ". . . which Christianity hath rather out-stripped than contradicted."[6] Such comments struck at the core of Emerson's hopes. How he came to realize that Plato may not have been out-stripped by the Biblical theology of Andrews Norton is the concern of the next chapter.

---

[1]Ibid.   [2]Ibid.   [3]Ibid.

[4]Ibid.   [5]Ibid.   [6]Ibid.

Underlying Emerson's struggle to reconcile his innermost psychological drift with Christianity is a subtler, but more significant urge. The
desire to rank among the "representative men" of the world, among whom,
to be sure, Emerson noticed Plato. For great men of virtue need not
tolerate the "strong excitement of religions and its thrilling motives,"
since they customarily renounce the "constant pressure of their yoke" and,
unlike most other people, find religions not "indispensible."[1] In fact,
Emerson says that it is very possible that religion may be "illusory,"
since men see only "particulars" while what really ought to matter for virtue's sake was "the aggregate which we call character."[2] Seeing what he
did placed playing Emerson in a special position where cosmological insight
became possible: "If the law of the universe admitted exception and it
were allowed to me to depart," he mused, "to your refulgent shores and commune
with Plato this is the information I should seek at your hands."[3] Emerson
then states the problem he has in mind, a problem of great significance,
and even a portent of his later years: "How could those parts of the social
machine whose consistency and just action depend entirely upon the morality
and religion sown and grown in the community, how could these be kept in
safe and efficient arrangement under a system which besides being frivolous
was the butt of vulgar ridicule?"[4] With this statement Emerson committed
himself to a religious vocation, or one which needed not necessarily take
an ecclesiastical form in the future. In the long run, it would not. However, in the short run Emerson's problematical vocational identity would toy
in churchly affairs.

Thus ends Emerson's "Letter to Plato." Though he signed the Unitarian

[1]Ibid.

[3]Ibid.

[2]Ibid.

[4]Ibid.

declaration in 1823, Emerson showed strength in 1824 when he composed this letter. Significantly, instead of turning to his Aunt Mary as was usually the case when he entertained theological questions, he turned to Plato, notably, when he faced deeper, more pressing religious doubts striking deeply into the central fiber of his character. Yet, he harbored ambivalence towards Plato. He might have been able to accept Christianity whole, so to speak, had it not been for the prior legacy of Plato. Thus, the Athenian also serves to personify Emerson's self-doubts. Deep-seated ambivalence notwithstanding, one can say that Emerson's first vocational turnabout was his decision during 1824 to close the School for Young Ladies and to start out in the Harvard Divinity School early in 1825. It ran a full course, from head to heart, so to speak. Little did he realize that a second vocational turnabout, perhaps it is more accurate to say revolution, was less than a decade in his future. In any case, late during 1824 he must have felt that, indeed, he had expanded beyond the diminished world of 1811 as he looked back from his vantage point. Nonetheless, he would continue to be plagued by psychological ambivalence related to a vocation in the Unitarian ministry.

The cluster of events of 1811-24 reached only a first major plateau in the total protracted growth of Emerson's wisdom. The entire period of his accomplishment might be understood as an artifact, the structure of which was one of expansion within diminishment, from beginning, to middle, and finally to the closure of the end. But personal closure also is a beginning. As such, the accomplishment of an expanded sense of vocation which Emerson seems aware of in 1824 must be understood broadly as the sense of diminishment in its own right. That is, Emerson's psychological accomplishments on the levels of thoughts, feelings, and behavior should be set within the larger picture constituted by his first thirty-five years of life. Hence, a psychosocial

depiction of the second major cluster of events of Emerson's life will be undertaken, the event which prepared him for assuming his place as a national cultural
and ritual leader after 1833. It too bears the imprint of his character,
but does so at a more differentiated and critical level.

Emerson may have been quite aware that he was entering into a new
or, at least, a different stage of his life during 1824. The reason for
suggesting this is the noticeable absence of the title, "Wide World," in
the journals after the entry for 11 August, 1824. The last book of the
journals to bear that title is number XIII. Number XIV, evidently, has been
irretrieveably lost, and would account for that period of time between
11 August, 1824 and 8 October, 1824, the first dated entry on number XV.
The title, "Wide World," does not appear attached to number XV or to any
other subsequent number or section of the entire corpus of Emerson's
journals. Indeed, as Emerson himself said, his decision to pursue theological
studies and a ministerial career was a very "solemn step." Possibly, Emerson
destroyed book number XIV, but one cannot be certain of this. However,
the loss of that particular book serves simply to substantiate further the
claim that a new stage of life was carrying the young man beyond himself.

CHAPTER III

BOSTON, THE FIRST CIRCLE OF PLAY

In going from (expanding) and returning to (diminishing) Boston during 1825, Emerson enjoyed one of his first major successful experiences trusting himself when the stakes of not doing so were high indeed: the mysterious onset of failing eyesight might very well jeopardize fulfilling the promise which the ministry presented him. He had found few grounds for self-confidence during the previous four years which he spent teaching school (1821-24), as has been seen. The young ladies whom "Mr. Waldo" taught required frequent disciplining, and the schoolmaster (who would advocate the continued use of harsh corporal punishment in 1831, when other so-called liberals were urging permissiveness) shrivelled in the face of such necessities, relying on the convenient presence of his mother's firm hand. He often found himself troubled by the "infirmities of my cheek" (blushing) and "occasional admirations of some of my pupils," as has been seen. Perhaps it was the fact that he now followed in his older brother's footsteps which, when added to his dependence upon his mother's presiding expectation that her sons follow in their father's footsteps, impelled him to feel disheartened as a teacher. However, that the arena of his formative play activity was expanding in 1825 was beyond doubt.

Emerson decided to close the school by the end of December of 1824. More importantly, he decided to enter Harvard Divinity School in preparation for the Unitarian ministry, commencing on 11 Febrary, 1825. In a journal entry of 4 January, 1825 he reported, "I have closed my school, I have begun a new year. I begin my studies."[1] If a moment of personal transition

---

[1] Emerson, JMN, 2: 309.

engendered "phantasms and feelings" which struggled to find a vent in rhyme,
Emerson was writing primarily of days gone by. Now his thoughts turned to
the passage of his years, "of their even and eventless tenor and of the crisis
which is but a little way before when a month will determine the dark or
bright dye they must assume forever."[1] As he turned to his "lamp and tomes,"
believing he had nothing to do with "society," he thought his "unpleasing
boyhood" was behind him. A "solemn voice" commanded him to retire. He
was set upon a course of great expectations at this auspicious moment, and
could hardly entertain any thought about not being born "to fill the eye of
great expectation," resolving, "I will not quite despair nor quench my flambeau
in the dust of Easy, live and quiet die."[2] Emerson trusted Providence because
he believed it relieved human failings, or the "deplorable poverty" of
"virtue, affection, knowledge and passion." For Providence could "furnish
amusement to many hours of Idleness in him that once thought life wearisome,
to detect beauty and simplicity of the means whereby it is done."[3] Such
trust in Providence, and the telescopic faith by which it operated, strengthened
his resolve for the ministry because it implied that "man is an animal that
looks before and after" so that such a "solemn step has solid ground."[4]
It was at this juncture that Emerson concluded, "Faith is a telescope."[5]

By giving up the school Emerson cut himself free from the immediate
heritage of his older brother and from the abiding physical presence of his
mother in the course of his everyday life. On the one hand, he now stood
more on his own two feet than ever before. On the other hand, however, by
cutting that cord to his mother's physical presence, Emerson stood amenable

---

[1] Ibid.

[2] Ibid.

[3] Ibid., pp. 304-308.

[4] Ibid., p. 237.

[5] Ibid., p. 308.

to affirming and incorporating a more fundamental Emersonian heritage. The path trod by his father lay before him. Six generations of Emersons had been clergymen, and most of them called Concord, Massachusetts and environs their parish. After 1833 and a parish of his own, Emerson would take up residence in this town for the rest of his life. Perhaps, this fact alone testified to his subtle affirmation of this thread of the family heritage. In any case, even though Emerson was on the verge of seeking the prized "gown and band," one notices in his reports some degree of discontent with that broad sweep of the past, especially as it bore down upon the young man's incipient vocational crisis even at this early date of 1824. "It is my own humour to despise a pedigree," he said early in January of 1825.[1] Though he was educated by the cares of his "kind Aunt" to prize it, and learned that his forefathers had all been clergymen in New England, he felt that this past was not worth such reverence. "The dead sleep in their moonless night," he wrote in his visual way, "my business is with the living."[2] Emerson's more pressing concern was not fathers in the past, but himself in the present. That is, how to trust himself, not merely live up to the model of his predecessors. But he hardly was one to screen-out the older generation completely. By the end of January, 1825 he had received a "letter from Plato" from his Aunt Mary which, unfortunately, has not yet been made readily available to scholars.[3] If he did not take his aunt's intended message to heart, what she said was easily modified to suit his own needs. Also, reading through a college teacher's orations, he was quick to convert what was said into the motif of light over darkness: "I have been reading

---

[1]Ibid., p. 316.   [2]Ibid.

[3]See Emerson, Letters, 1: 160.

Everett's rich strains at Plymouth,--gazing at the Sun till my eyes blurred . . .
I mourn at the skepticism of prosperity the skepticism of knowledge, the
darkness of light."[1]

His decision to give up the school and to enter study for the ministry
severed much of his connection with his heritage. Having lived in Roxbury,
south of Boston, he went to Cambridge, somewhat west of the city. "It is
the evening of February eighth. . . 'tis the last evening I spend in Canterbury.
I go to my college chamber tomorrow a little changed for better or worse
since I left it in 1821."[2] So the litany of Emerson's ubiquitous disappointment went, already seen before. However, striking out toward a career in
Divinity was not merely a dropping back or merely an anticipation of more
undergraduate days. "I have grown older," he continued to say, "and have
seen something of the vanity and something of the value of existence have
seen what shallow things men are and how independent of external circumstances
may be the states of mind called good and ill."[3] Perhaps it was because the
Haskins family had completed building their hotel and stable in Boston the
year before that made it financially possible for Emerson to attend divinity
school. When William left for Gottingen late in 1823 Emerson thought his
own turn at professional studies would have to wait until his brother's
return. William would not return until September, 1825. That family finances
did not stand in Emerson's way early in 1825 seems evident. By turning from
the School for Young Ladies to the ministry Emerson was free to look after
himself, especially to find out how to achieve a modicum of greatness according to his own wiles.

------

[1]Emerson, JMN, 2: 318-319   [2]Ibid., p. 332.

[3]Ibid.

Registered at Harvard on 11 February, 1825 in the Middle Class, Emerson
studied Biblical theology with Andrews Norton, the "Unitarian Pope."[1] However, just as he had removed himself from his mother's presence and just
as the limited domestic world of home and school intermingled together had
appeared to project him into the wider world of a ministerial career, a
decisive event occurred. Emerson wrote in March of 1825, "Lost the use of
my eye for study." (It is believed that it was sometime after the actual
loss of his eyesight when Emerson wrote this line.)[1] No physiological factor
was noted to have caused this sudden partial blindness. However, there is
significance in the fact that the promise implicit in the geographical move
from Roxbury's limitations to Cambridge's vast horizons, especially as
they pertained to intellect, was transmuted into the modality of visual
perception. At the moment Emerson verged on a career in the ministry, he
literally shut his eyes to the possibility of the ministry, at least as
that profession was being defined for him by Andrews Norton. He received
permission from Norton to attend classes but to forego the usually required
daily recitations. We shall attempt to make sense out of this occurrence
of partial and temporary blindness, and to flesh-out its bare bones.

If it was true that in leaving his school behind he was looking inwardly
at his life, hoping to learn how to trust himself, then when he did so during the first few months of 1825 Emerson saw more darkness than light. On
25 January, 1825, for example, he seemed preoccupied with death. As far as

---

[1]See Emerson, Letters, 1: 152-159. Emerson hopes to be admitted into
the "middle" class and later reports his success in having such an offer
in hand.

[2]Rusk, The Life of Ralph Waldo Emerson, p. 111.

he was concerned, life was a process during which "every honest and natural virtue" was "festered and eaten out" of the person who made it his business to maintain a "fair outside" above all else, at least more so than to culti- vate inner purity and virtue.[1] When one does this, as Emerson phrased it, he goes down to death and his eyes are decently closed by his kin. In spite of such lives, Emerson implied somewhat symbolically for himself, but ostensibly for all men, that this process of decadence can be stood on its head. Dying can be living: ". . . here the curtain falls," Emerson says of decadent people, "and hides from the eyes of mortals the unalter- able history of the following hour."[2] He would soon be able to understand that if his eyes were decently closed by a cleric like those he knew among his own kin, then he too might be able to see the curtain rise on a life of personal virtue and pure calling.

Death comes in many forms, and Emerson intimated that death from within also can eventuate from an illness more devastating than the illness of moral lapse, that is, an illness whose signs would later give him a good scare, tuberculosis. During February he suggested that his own creative output was intimately connected to environmental factors. "I have a mind," he said, "to try if my muse hath not lost a whit of her nimbleness; if the damps of this new region its proscribed and formal study haven't chilled a little her prurient and prolific heat."[3] Three years in the future he would be unable to pen even one sermon because of the "mouse" in his chest, referring to symptoms of tuberculosis.[4] As if he were walking fate's tight- rope, he suggested that he would allow his muse to run freely: "I would boldly take down a topic and enter the lists"; . . ."were there not reason to remember and fear the old orthodoxy concerning fortune. . . . that when

---

[1]Emerson, JMN, 2: 330. [2]Ibid.

[3]Ibid., p. 335. [4]Emerson, Letters, 1: 233.

the humoursome jealous Coquet is presumed on she withdraweth straight her smiles and leaves audacious votary to curse his self-conceit in the dark,"[1] Emerson allows a reader of his last journal entry before they lapse until January of 1826 to see a symbolic connection between what he said there, and what one knows he may have been experiencing at the time he wrote it. Therefore, good reason exists to suggest that on the edge of sudden blindness he referred to how and to what he was being taught at Harvard when he wrote, late in February, that it was difficult to preserve "bold and true conceptions of this life as altogether a relative condition."[2] As merely "an introduction to the Enlarged life," the world, he continued, will be "sadly changed" when these sorts of "novelties" have grown old and dull and disgusting . . ."when your eyes are quenched and the Eye of your understanding is dim."[3] Strange that he should go partially blind during the first days of the next month, less than one month into theological studies with Boston's "Unitarian Pope," Andrews Norton.

Thus, as Emerson was writing about things like the "unalterable history of the following hour," the "states of mind called good and ill" which are "independent of external circumstances," the "damp of this new region its prescribed and formal study," and the dimmed "Eye of understanding," he was cutting a personal path through the dense thicket of theological studies. If all these statements can be classified generally as having to do with the theme of dying, then, indeed, Emerson was leaving the past behind. That is, he was designating the start of a period in his life during which nascent new life was sensed. Following, like an embryo, Emerson had to assume a similar posture: he closed his eyes, so to speak, to the world around him and formed a protective shell against it. Only when the time

---

[1]Emerson, JMN, 2: 335. [2]Ibid., pp. 335-36. [3]Ibid.

was right would he be able to regain his sight late in 1825 and, more importantly, project a national vision for Americans on that personal basis of achievement after 1833. How, one might ask, was it possible for Emerson to talk himself into blindness, especially insofar as it was associated with themes in his journals about dying and being re-born? Little evidence is contained in either the journals or the letters. The former lapses entirely between February, 1825 and 8 January, 1826, while the latter lapses between March and August, 1825. However, with the coming of spring and new journal entries in 1826, Emerson began his first significant journey beyond Boston's diminished confines.

A multitude of factors probably were involved in Emerson's blindness which invite some degree of "psychological artifacting," or trying to piece together a rather unusual episode by means of reasonable psychological conjecture. Not the least important of such factors was Emerson's possible identification with his first "great teacher" at Harvard College (not Divinity School), Levi Frisbie. Frisbie was a tutor in Latin, ancient and English literature, and composition at Harvard since 1805 and, beginning in the year of Emerson's arrival at College (1817), he was the first person to be installed as the Alford Professor of Moral Philosophy and Civil Polity. Frisbie's stature hardly lessened that same year with his marriage to Catherine Saltonstall Mellen, a fact about which Emerson probably was aware. William had been supported in part by her family's financial legacy to Harvard, and since his second year at the College some of Emerson's own financial support would come from the same legacy given to the College by the wealthy Saltonstall family. Moreover, by 13 April, 1825 Ruth Emerson had moved from Federal Street to the old Mellen house on North Avenue, near Jarvis Field, thus punctuating all that Levi Frisbie meant and still was meaning to the faltering theological student. In short, Levi Frisbie set a commanding example of success within the context of Boston culture at first sight. Other reasons as well suggest the probability of Emerson's special notice of and later nostalgia for Frisbie.

Emerson's chief biographer, Ralph Rusk, believes that Emerson "idolized" his teacher.[1] However, Rusk failed to plumb Emerson's attitude more deeply than merely to say that the young student thought highly of Frisbie's "sound doctrines." It is possible to suggest that such a tenor of respect and admiration for his teacher derived from or, at least, was associated with three aspects of Emerson's identification with Frisbie, the last of which connects Emerson's undergraduate days directly to his experience in Andrews Norton's Biblical theology classes early in 1825. We might have cause to wonder just how it happened that Emerson's conflict found expression in the symptom of blindness had it not been for several characteristics of Frisbie's own life and his own ambivalences which hint at the viability of that particular symptom.

To be installed as the "first" professor of any new chair in the College usually meant that such a person bore not only superb intellectual talent, but also displayed a well-developed sense of moral integrity. One was considered mature in mind, body, and spirit--to have a pure character. That this was especially true for a man filling a chair of moral philosophy and civil polity can be assumed. After all, at other colleges teaching in this area usually was reserved for the President of the institution.[2] However,

[1]Rusk, The Life of Ralph Waldo Emerson, p. 118.

[2]See Howe, The Unitarian Conscience, p. 2.

almost everyone admired Frisbie for this success in this regard. Why, one might ask, did Emerson in particular accentuate his regard of Frisbie to the degree of "idolizing" him?

The first possible reason for Emerson's "idolization" of Frisbie had to do with Frisbie's early career aspirations. He wanted to become a lawyer, not a college teacher. For, by this time, the importance of the clergyman in Boston existed not in itself but in what such a role eventually could lead to. The New England intellegentsia gradually gave rise to other professions, mainly in law and in literature.[1] A crumbling theological hegenomy required these new arms of social control. It is quite right to say that the erosion of the role of the minister was precisely the stage upon which rose Emerson's bewilderment when his brother resolved to leave all hopes for a ministerial career behind and to take up legal studies in 1825-26. If it can be assumed that Emerson was aware of his brother's personal style (one which inclined William to legal studies, a spirit of contentiousness and decisiveness) as early as 1817, then it is possible to suggest that both his older brother and Frisbie were strikingly similar in Emerson's eyes. Both older men appeared to be on the right course toward greatness, being men with purpose and strength who were able to weather tides of personal disappointment.

However, Frisbie's failure to become a lawyer invites consideration of a second possible reason for Emerson's attitude toward him. Frisbie found legal aspirations too strenuous for his constitution. As a consequence, not only did he settle for a career teaching in the field of literature eventually, but he also suffered from "eye disorders" which, incidentally,

---

[1] Ibid., pp. 174-175.

brought on periods of severe depression.[1] Such moods blunted the edge of
systematic thinking which was so necessary in a legal career. As a college
teacher Frisbie found such strain lessened, even though his thinking in the
classroom was markedly systematic. What can be surmised from all this is
that Emerson sensed his teacher's plight deeply. For in front of each class
session sat his idol, Frisbie, lecturing on moral philosophy and shading
his aching eyes with a handerkerchief.[2] In the example of nearly blind
Frisbie, then, the pain and suffering of what Emerson perceived to be heightened
systematic thinking was clearly and literally "before his eyes," as was
Martin Gay at the very same time.

No doubt Emerson's college years served to activate his abiding preoccupation with visual numinosity, that is, with the task of furthering
his ritualization of vision. One example of the influence he experienced
during those undergraduate years which moves one towards the sense of the
episode with blindness and travel during 1825 was his verse-like letter to
his Aunt Mary. Emerson wrote it while on vacation with friends and several
of his brothers during the winter of 1817-18. Though deliberately light-
hearted in appearance, his whimsy betrays a more solemn dimension of the
letter: "This petition humbly sheweth--that we the signers undersigned/
Sound both in body and in mind/ Write this petition unto you/ And may it
meet your kind review./ And first beg leave the case to state/ And Lawer-like
[sic] the facts relate . . ." In a footnote the editor of Emerson's letters
says, "the misspelling (of lawyer) is surprising in a letter obviously composed with more than common effort."[3] It is possible to suggest, therefore,

---

[1]Ibid., p. 312.

[2]Rusk, The Life of Ralph Waldo Emerson, p. 81.

[3]Emerson, Letters, 1: 52-53. The portion of the letter and the editor's
footnote are found on page 53.

that in a literal fashion, just as Frisbie was "unable to see" a legal career for himself, so too his pupil, Emerson, was "unable to see" his spelling error. This, however, is only half of the matter.

Though Emerson was quite unaware of it at the time, he betrayed even more clearly the already well-formed connection he was making between "seeing" and numinosity as his letter continued. It hearkened back to infantile reveries: "Then, first, we find your keen survey/ Is wanting to begin the day/ For much we need your wakeful eyes/ To see that we by seven rise/ And when well up we need your care/ To take the Moderator's chair/ And with your peace-commanding voice/ To still the child's morning noise/ But needless it would be to tell/ These reasons which you know so well/ In short your presence much we need/ Our whole concerns and things to speed...."[1] By visualizing the "keen survey" of his aunt's "wakeful eyes," Emerson conjured-up an abiding maternal presence in his life. Therefore, it was no accident that the entire letter was constructed on the foundation of the mother-child or, more generally, the maternal-infantile relationship. Moreover, the accompanying numinosity of this hallowed presence set Emerson's understanding of the tenor of a "true calling," a right vocation. He is asking his aunt to call him to greater industry while he is on vacation, feeling that if he were blessed by her presence he would "by seven rise" and be impelled his "whole concerns and things to speed." The letter which he composed was itself an unrecognized product of the industry he requested, as well as a portent of his future vocation as a man of letters. In any case, the letter suggests that seeing and numinosity have already begun giving rise to vocational expressions. This connection appears to be a step beyond the significance of his relationship with Martin Gay, a relationship upon which the question of vocation was not explicitly stated.

---

[1]Ibid., p. 53.

The third and final reason for Emerson's attitude toward Frisbie takes one out of Emerson's possible personal meanings and places one squarely in the middle of a nascent ideological battle. During the 1830's this battle became a major pivot upon which Emerson's final renunciation of the ministry turned. Figuratively speaking, it was the distinction between "literary eloquence" and "unitarian systematic thinking" which initiated the debate. Ralph Rusk presents the issues: "According to George Ripley, a sophomore during Ralph's senior year, both Frisbie and his contemporary and successor, Levi Hedge, followed Dugald Stewart and Thomas Brown in protesting against Locke and Paley, and thus opposed Andrews Norton, a Harvard Professor who had to be reckoned with by his colleagues. So as Frisbie and Hedge represented the college, its teaching was an endorsement of the Edinburgh brand of Scottish philosophy and pointed slightly in the direction of Transcendentalism."[1] This brand of philosophy held that knowledge was not a string of associated empirical sensations but resulted from intuitions of self-evident principles or, in other words, by means of "common sense." It was according to her own common sense that Ruth Emerson moved from the Mellen house into a room in the house of Professor Levi Hedge early in 1826 so that she might free the funds necessary for securing Ralph Waldo a dormitory suite at Divinity Hall. Emerson was returning to Harvard then.

The theological implication of this non-associational point of view of Frisbie and Hedge, of course, was that Norton's method of empirical scholarship in Biblical theology, which intended to prove the legitimacy of Biblical miracles as confirmations of the divine and Christian nature of the Bible, suffered neglect as well as open attack by the intuitionists.

_____

[1] Rusk, The Life of Ralph Waldo Emerson, p. 82.

They believed that they could discern "divinity" within every person's
soul and, thus, they also believed that divine revelation did not depend
upon taking the Bible off the shelf, so to speak. Thus the Frisbie-Norton
fissure eventuated in the controversy over the "miracles question" several
years later.[1] What does all this mean for Emerson? Just as Frisbie's eye
disorders prevented him from entering into a legal career, Emerson employed
blindness as a buffer against Norton's brand of Biblical theology. However, Emerson's strategy merely made this ideological conflict into the
tip of an iceberg, so to speak. Not only did Emerson feel uneasy intellectually. A deeper source of uneasiness was the plaguing professional
problem which hung in the balance, namely, whether to become a clergyman
or not and, beyond that, how to be "great." During March of 1825, as mentioned already, Emerson was unable to read or write very well because of
his eye. It was at this time that he received permission from Andrews Norton
to attend class and to forego the required recitations. This suggests not
only that Emerson inclined away from Norton's Biblical views, but also that
the student had difficulty facing the person of this particular teacher.
Recitation would require contact face-to-face, but only being in the room
would not. Emerson's blindness made it possible for him to do one without
doing the other, that is, to be in the room without having to face Norton.
Not all contact was broken off, just eye-to-eye contact. Moreover, that

---

[1]The "miracles question" spawned round after round of debate, parti-
cularly between Andrews Norton and both George Ripley and the erudite Theodore
Parker during the 1830's and the 1840's. Norton represented the position
of Lockean empiricism known as Supernatural Rationalism; and Ripley and
Parker upheld Scottish Intuitionism and, therefore, marked themselves as
members of the new movement known as American Transcendentalism. See Clarence
H. Faust, "The Background of Unitarian Opposition to Transcendentalism,"
Modern Philology 25 (1938): 297-334; and William Hutchison, The Transcen-
dental Ministers (New Haven: Yale University Press, 1959).

Norton agreed to Emerson's request implied that an element of the teacher
who could be manipulated may have been involved. Perhaps Emerson learned
this lesson of manipulating his teacher from the girls in his own school,
girls who had manipulated him. But this temporary solution did not last
long. Other measures seemed called for as well.

Not until 8 January, 1826 did Emerson resume writing in his journal.
Prior to the new year, and at the critical point of losing the use of his
eye for study, he decided to leave Cambridge, his mother, and his studies
in theology temporarily behind. He went on his first journey from the
area of Boston and Cambridge, now literally diminished in his sight, to the
rural environs of Newton and Chelmsford. His ostensible reason for doing
so was to try "the experiment of hard work for the benefit of health."[1]
He remained there for the rest of the year. In Newton, he became acquainted
with some field workers, one of whom was a Methodist. In a memo from
St. Augustine, Florida on 1 March, 1827 Emerson would describe being told
the story of the "monstrous absurdities" of the Methodists, ". . . fanatics
jumping about on all fours, imitating the barking of dogs and surrounding
a tree in which they pretended they had 'treed Jesus'!"[2] But in Newton
two years prior to being told this story Emerson was not as jocular. "Though
ignorant and rude," he said that the Methodist field laborer "had some
deep thoughts."[3] The man said that "men were always praying, and that all
prayers were granted. I meditated much on this saying," said Emerson,
and "wrote my first sermon therefrom."[4] Even if this narrative about the

[1]Cabot, A Memoir of Ralph Waldo Emerson, I: 111.

[2]Emerson, JMN, 3: 115.

[3]Cabot, A Memoir of Ralph Waldo Emerson, 1: 111-12.

[4]Ibid.

wisdom of people from rural parts of the country smacks of an anecdote,
it communicates a sense of personal closure on parts of Emerson's life which,
as it were, had long awaited the laborers' confirmations. That first sermon,
"Pray Without Ceasing" (1826), will be mentioned later in connection with
a second significant journey. For now it is sufficient to know that by
September of 1825 Emerson's "experiment" at removal from Boston proper
gradually worked to restore his eyesight so that he was then able to open
a small school in Chelmsford by the end of September. It helped pay the
bills.

By January of 1826 his rural experience made it easy for him to suggest that "it would be good if a minister should institute weekly lectures
for the discussion of collateral subjects for the illustration of his Sabbath
discourses." For example," he went on to say, "if Paley would call his congregation together on secular days to hear his Natural theology."[1] The
point is that Emerson, though he may have been as skeptical of Paley as he
was of Norton, was learning to trust his own inclinations more and more.
The advice of the laborers was taken it seems, for Emerson did open his
eyes upon scenes of pastoral beauty during his stay in Chelmsford: ". . .
where the chestnut first spread its brown harvest on a frosty morning for
the boys; where the apples covered the ground with white fruit."[2] Indeed,
the old sights of Boston where being diminished while at the same time a
curtain was rising on the expansive scenes of country life, scenes of nature.
In short, Emerson grew more and more eye-centered as he became a master
at the intuitive incorporation of nature. He began in earnest taking in

---

[1]Emerson, JMN, 2: 346.

[2]Rusk, The Life of Ralph Waldo Emerson, p. 113.

the world with his eyes.

It would be fair to say that the rural environment and the wisdom of the field laborers symbolically replaced his teachers at Harvard. Emerson hardly could have said his inspiration for sermon-making derived from the lessons of Andrews Norton or, for that matter, from Levi Frisbie or Edward Everett alone. The laborers' example may have brought to mind his own earlier reflections on the gospel of Matthew, that prayer is answered by the utterance of spiritual truth.[1] Nevertheless, it would be fair to suggest that people like the laborers gradually replaced Emerson's teachers at school, and they subtly encouraged him to awaken to the vast world of nature and national horizons around him.

Now as he opened his eyes upon the world late in 1825 he learned that his older brother had abandoned his own plans to enter the Unitarian ministry and had taken up an interest in law. On 19 September, 1825 William had visited with Goethe, a highlight anticipated all during his two-year-long European tour. Goethe told William that in order to be a good minister in America it was necessary to tell the people what they wanted to hear, the gospel, instead of confessing to them one's own religious doubts, which William was inclined to do. At least, this is what Emerson thought William inclined to do. By encountering the man Goethe, William was carried beyond the constraints to follow in his father's footsteps, footsteps which led to the Unitarian ministry. Goethe checked William's despair by giving him

---

[1]Ibid., p. 111. Emerson decided that "faith is the perception of spiritual truth" and that prayer consisted in its utterance. Implicit was the assumption that the numinous element of life equalled religious truth and that such truth was perceived from within a supersensory mode of awareness. Also, see Hutchinson, The Transcendental Ministers (New Haven: Yale University, 1959), p. 54.

a viable "out," a model of a man of character who was not a minister.
Evidently, Emerson's search for an alternative of his own had not become
as critical a problem as William's had been at that same time. It was possible for Emerson not only to hold out longer than his older brother,
but also to give the pulpit a try. Only later, during 1833, would Emerson
meet his own "Goethe" in the person of Thomas Carlyle.

Meanwhile, however, Emerson was amenable to ancestral influence during
this time of his recovery from blindness. He was continually supported
in the belief that "they also serve who stand and wait" by his Aunt Mary,
a staunch Calvinist, and by another blind man, John Milton. In his note-
book, for example, Emerson recorded, "Imagination will always revolt at the
(sight) loss of the butterfly's beauty, and the rude waste of rich dew on
the welkin from its own azure cups--but be patient . . . then you will
find not necessary sacredness in the country. Nor did Milton but his mind
and his spirits were their own place and come when he called them in the
solitude of darkness."[1] The interesting fact about this entry is that the
word, "sight," was crossed-out and replaced by the word, "loss." By doing
this Emerson invites one to assume that he considered blindness something
on the order of a disappointing but necessary prelude to a vision comparable
to that of Milton, a man devoted to the Church as well as a literary cultural leader in his own right. At any rate, patient waiting was not only
service to the Christian ministry. It also was a moratorium during which
service to America was portended.

Other adversities of 1825 gave Emerson even more concern for worry.
During October Edward departed for Europe in order to ease the impact of a

---

[1]Emerson, JMN 2: 380.

nervous breakdown. He closed his school in Roxbury and put a temporary
hold on plans to study law with the great Daniel Webster. On top of this,
retarded brother Bulkeley became "perfectly deranged" during the early part
of December.[1] Emerson himself, though able to "use my eyes to write,"
realized that he was becoming even more infirm as the prospect that he would
have to assume a larger role in supporting his family became clear: "That
lame hip of mine which I have been magnifying into a sacrecrow, maugre
Dr. Dalton's opinions who nicknames it rheumatism."[2] Since September, however, Emerson managed to conduct a small school in Chelmsford and he carried
it through the end of December. For he believed that a ministerial career,
at least the subject of Divinity (as opposed to Law and Medicine), was
still his calling. To get his feet on the ground again would be his best
remedy.

Therefore, Emerson began 1826 by registering in the Divinity School
as a "graduate resident."[3] Just prior to and slightly over-lapping with
his registering as a graduate resident, he took a small school in Roxbury
from January, 1826 to 28 March, 1826. Probably, because at this juncture
he and his mother were trying to take up financial slackening. It had been
brought on, on the one hand, by Edward's European trip and, on the other
hand, by William's failure to support the family in a manner they considered
respectable, he becoming situated as a poverty-stricken legal apprentice
in New York City by August of 1826. If William's religious doubts prompted
his swift and certain move to law and to New York, Emerson's own bewilderment initiated no despair let alone any thought of any such action: instead,
Emerson could muse readily that "doubt darkened every light spot in the

---

[1]Emerson, Letters, 1: 163.　　　　[2]Ibid., pp. 163-64.

[3]Ibid., p. 166.

landscape" during January, 1826, almost with an eye back to Newton and Chelmsford and the laborers.[1] But in spite of family financial strain, Emerson was more doubtful about other matters at the same time, matters of a more personal and more intellectually bewildering sort.

His preoccupation with dying was seen expressed in his journals during the first three months of 1825. This same theme is picked-up again in 1826. However, by this time Emerson realized he was not permanently blind, and he came "with mended eyes" to his journals on 8 January, 1826.[2] Therefore, his journey carried him from blindness to new sight, broadly speaking. Psychologically speaking, it is possible to suggest that infirmities and their alleviation would be a means of achieving a "higher ideal." Several entries in his journals and in his letters during March, 1826 appear to play upon this sort of transformation, that is, "illness" and "commitments" both mitigated by "travel." They bear-out the rule of frailty: "My external condition," he wrote, "may to many seem comfortable, to some enviable but I think that few men ever suffered more genuine misery than I have suffered."[3] As he assumed the status of a graduate resident of Harvard Divinity School once again, he was "confined by a lameness" to his chamber in Divinity Hall and had had good cause to feel miserable.[4] Approximately one or two weeks earlier he thought once again about Providence, how it required "that great objects must be purchased at great sacrifices."[5] Then he believed that that particular lesson was exemplified above all by two documents, of all things, specifically, the New Testament, and "the next best thing in human possession," the American Constitution, which "hundreds and thousands of

---

[1] Emerson, JMN, 3: 10.   [2] Ibid., 2: 340.   [3] Ibid., 3: 13.

[4] Emerson, Letters, 1: 167.   [5] Emerson, JMN, 3: 14.

valiant patriots perished to obtain."[1]

Misery was not without its rewards, though they were of an "ideal sort" and, as he said during July, 1826, it was our duty "to be discontented" with what measure of them we have.[2] Emerson wrote to his Aunt Mary on 6 April, 1826, reporting that "my eyes are well comparatively, my limbs are diseased with rheumatism."[3] In the same stroke of the quill he asked her, "who leads the leaders and instructs the instructor? . . . Is there no venerable tradition whose genuineness and authority we can establish, or must we too hurry onward inglorious in ignorance and misery we know not whence, we know not whither."[4] Perhaps it was the fact that Emerson had opened another school in Cambridge during March, 1826 that he anticipated closing it in his letter to his aunt. The school would continue as a partial Gehenna, adding to his "ignorance and misery" until the end of October, 1826. There was little about teaching he found "venerable," but to be taught was a different matter. He was still lauding his aunt's "letter from Plato" in August, perhaps having considered himself a teacher of this particular relative, his ancestral instructor.[5] However, as early as 12 March, 1826 there is clear evidence that the meaning of physical ailments pointed him in the direction of a tradition which was not, at first sight, readily available to his aunt. "My years are passing away. Infirmities are already stealing on me that may be the deadly enemies that are to dissolve me to dirt," he said, "and little is yet done to establish my consideration among my contemporaries and less to get a memory when I am gone."[6] As one might describe it, Emerson

---

[1]Ibid.

[2]Ibid., p. 26.

[3]Emerson, Letters, 1: 167-68.

[4]Ibid.

[5]Ibid., p. 169.

[6]Emerson, JMN, 3: pp. 15-16.

was unable at this point to call his life complete.

However the only terms upon which Emerson believed he would move toward greater life-closure were if he disclaimed "the vulgar hunger to be known, to have one's name hawked in the great capitals in the streets like a Murdered Man's dismal renown or a naval victor or Erostratus the Ephesian incendiary."[1] If one's suffering was to reap benefit, then one would do well, as Emerson says of himself, to engender "a refined appetite" pleased with a "calm and limited glory," that is, "satisfied with the respect of one Plato . . ."[2] Emerson was anxious to have the glory of obscurity, so to speak, so that "absolutely nothing is known by the rest" of humanity.[3] It was Demosthenes' (also a man as eloquent as Emerson aspired to be) gratification, he said, "to hear the Oyster woman" whose stall he daily passed on his way to the agora say "this is Demosthenes!"[4] Therefore, from the time of the "Letter to Plato" Emerson wrote during 1824, to this 17 March, 1826 journal entry and to the two instances of his mention of his aunt's "letter from Plato" (18 January and 1 August, 1826), the high tides of his vision were given shape by intimations of the Platonic mythos; viz., the allegory of the cave. At least, these unusual references to Plato serve as emblems of the under-lying playful preoccupations with visual numinosity which commanded Emerson's most fascinated and hesitant embraces. The whole period embracing the journey of 1825, from January, 1825 to August, 1826, was Emerson's first experiment at finding illness and commitments mitigated by travel. That he found his vision restored late in 1825, and that his rheumatism kept him at arm's length, so to speak, from an enthusiastic embrace of the Harvard

---

[1] Ibid.

[3] Ibid.

[2] Ibid.

[4] Ibid.

Divinity School thereafter, were concrete examples of a prisoner of infir-
mity who could, as the Platonic allegory describes the seeker after ideal
knowledge, turn round his head and see the light of a wider horizon. Generally,
Emerson was laying-down the first circle of limits for his playful yet
ritualized ascendancy to cultural leadership: The diminishment of blindness gave rise to restored and expanded sight in the country, while the
diminishment of the sedentariness of a rheumatoid condition gave rise to
an expanded sense of being respected by "one Plato." This first plateau
of the growth of Emerson's wisdom during the events of 1825-33 was prefigured
by some of the first remarks he made during 1826. Since those remarks accentuated his identification with Plato, it is worthwhile to make note of
them.

The first journal entry of 1826 was a case in point. Embedded within
the first journal entry is a welding together in very objective form Emerson's
immediate present (i.e., the fact that he wrote about his restored vision)
and his not so immediate present (i.e., the motif of light over darkness,
and the overall structure of expansion within diminishment). After a discussion of this first journal entry of 1826, two other points about the
significance of the first circle of Emerson's play activity will follow.
All of them were tied to the meaning presented in the journal entry in
nascent form. The first concerns an explicit reference that links together
the figure of Plato with other admired friends from Emerson's past. The
second pertains to a curious mention of the "cave of Trophonius." Both
items occur within the same letter to his brother William of 23 September,
1826, a letter, incidentally, in which Emerson first mentions to anyone
that symptoms of tuberculosis have him poised in their suffocating grip.
In a nutshell, Emerson was to talk about friendship in his first journal

entry of 1826. Not among mortals, but friendship among those like himself, those who could see beyond corporeal infirmities. On 28 May, 1826 he would say without qualms that the friends that occupied his thoughts were not men, but "certain phantoms . . . the gods gave life to Prometheus' ivory statue and the revolution of events may one day give me the men for the prototypes."[1]

When Emerson resumed his journals on 8 January, 1826 "with mended eyes," he referred to comrades of Plato when he suggested that restored eyesight made him a "more cheerful philosopher" who was rather anxious "to thank Oromasdes for his boon than to fear Ahriman."[2] It is no mere coincidence that he referred to the dialectical opposites of the Zoroastrian pantheon, the ethical dualism of Oromasdes, the spirit of good, and Ahriman, the spirit of evil. Usually associated with forces of light (good) and forces of darkness (evil), the radical disjunction between light and darkness implicit in this Persian religious tradition sets the parameters of Emerson's own awareness of his seer-like inclinations. But, even more significantly, he made certain textual alterations in his reference to these Zoroastrian spirits, alterations which suggest that an important and characteristic psychological dynamic was at work in his life on the evening of his journal entry.

Having expressed his anxiety to thank Oromasdes for his boon, Emerson proceeded to cancel-out the phrase, "for his boon" (that of Oromasdes), and to insert the infinitive, "to fear," in reference to Ahriman. Perhaps these textual alterations reveal a dynamic which was represented by the recovery of his eyesight and, moreover, by the consummnation of his charismatic incubation at this first level of visual capacity: Emerson is "less

---

[1]Ibid., p. 25.   [2]Ibid., 2: 340.

willing to thank" Oromasdes and "more willing to assert" his lack of fear of Ahriman. The opposite side of "lack of fear" is "discovery of strength." The reader of the entry could very well be led to assume that Ahriman stood for Emerson's subtle dependencies on his brother, his mother, his ministerial heritage, Norton, and the field laborers. Moreover, when the dependent quality of this phase of his life is recognized in this way, Emerson's discovery was a discovery of his own autonomy and strength. These boons thrusted Emerson into the cultural pantheon of "Representative Men," peers including Oromasdes, Ahriman, Plato, and the like. As he would urge upon his brother Charles during May of 1827, "aim to raise your rank not among your compeers alone but in that great scale of moral beings which embraces the invisible and the visible."[1] It would be an understatement to say that Emerson not only had a need to think in terms of great men, but also had a pressing need to identify with them, to think of himself as one of them, a representative "moral being."

By August William had ventured to New York City and Emerson struck-up a lively correspondence with him almost immediately. Evidently, he could count on the friendship of his older brother in spite of the fact that William was often too busy to write back. In any case, as of September of 1826 the chair occupied by Levi Frisbie would be vacant for four years. This gave Emerson the occasion for making a telling comment. In his letter of 29 September, 1826 to William, Emerson reported that one Sampson Reed had printed in Boston and perhaps in New York "a noble pamphlet after my own heart" called "Observations on the Growth of the Mind."[2] Emerson understated himself when he said that in his "poor judgment" the piece is the "best thing since Plato of Plato's kind, for novelty and wealth of truth."[3]

---

[1]Ibid., 2: 340.   [2]Ibid., pp. 176-77.   [3]Ibid.

Emerson's conclusion is most significant because it directly implicates him in an identification with the Athenian: Because of Reed's piece, Emerson believed that "it ought to give him Frisbies chair."[1] If Emerson's identification with Frisbie is, at least, a reasonable assumption, then here is confirmation of the presence in Emerson's mind of a closely-knitted fraternity of men of great character, of which he felt a part.

As the letter of 29 September, 1826 continued, it sandwiched between this reference to Reed-Frisbie-Plato and the upcoming one about the cave of Trophonius, mention about new physical ailments other than persistent rheumatism. Among his many "scarecrows," he wrote, "are my lung complaints."[2] The full passage should be quoted because of the distinctive tenor it conveys, namely, the sense of a child on the verge of tears when faced with unfriendly eyes:

> You must know in my vehement desire to preach I have recently taken into my bosom certain terrors not for my hip which does valiantly, nor for my eyes which deserve all commendation, but for my lungs without whose aid I cannot speak, and which scare me and thro me scare out poor mother's sympathies with strictures and jenesais-quosities. But we must not cry before we are hurt, and any suffering of this sort are so few and small that tho' they may fill a paragraph of my letter such has got to be my desire to call out sympathy they may not give you or me any farther distress.[3]

Emerson's distress would be prolonged and the meaning of these symptoms would be set in a broader cultural context by another tactic of traveling not unlike that employed in 1825 when blindness struck. A journal entry of 23 September, 1816 suggests the particular direction Emerson's thoughts took on this matter of tuberculosis. He anticipated the return from Europe of his brother who had been there since the time Emerson had commenced his Chelmsford school. Edward's return would mark the close of Emerson's Cambridge

---

[1]Ibid. [2]Ibid. [3]Ibid.

school by the end of the month of October of 1826 and the end of teaching ever afterward.

"Health, action, happiness. How they ebb from me!" Emerson exclaimed.[1] Poor Sisyphus had the good fortune of seeing his stone stop at least once when Orpheus, chanted, but "I must roll mine up and up and up how high a hill."[2] However, Edward's return on the "eastern wind" sounded the "harp of my coming Orpheus," said Emerson late in 1826.[3] What this meant was that Edward's return would supply the financial means for Emerson to leave the vicinity of New England in search of his own health and inspiration. Though he expanded his horizons beyond his blindness of 1825, he sensed that if his tubercular symptoms were to be alleviated by traveling, then they would be eased only insofar as he literally could get beyond his immediate present. Specifically, that present had the question of vocation, vocation in the Unitarian ministry, as its abiding backdrop. Nonetheless, he kept on projecting past those sorts of questions: It is "mournful the expectation," he wrote on that same 23 September, 1826, "of ceasing to be an object of hope that we may become objects of compassion, and then go gloomily to nothing in the eye of this world before we have had one opportunity of turning to the sun what we know is our best side."[4] "Turning to the sun" is not unlike

---

[1] Emerson, JMN, 3: 45-46.   [2] Ibid.

[3] Ibid. It also is interesting to note that physical infirmities, always associated with death and dying, appeared eased when Emerson contemplated the return of his brother from Europe on the "eastern wind." At a time when territorial expansion to the west was being advocated by many Americans, Emerson's intuitions responded to the east, not the west, as a source of physical rejuvenation and personal promise. On the psychological and religious symbolism involved in such regard and correlated with Freud's dynamics of eros (east) and thanatos (west), see Leon Altman, "'West' as a Symbol of Death," Psychoanalytic Quarterly, 28 (1959): 236-241.

[4] Ibid.

turning round one's head to the light from within the mouth of a cave. When one returns to the letter to William, Emerson is noted making a similar reference specifically along these lines.

"It is plain," he apologized to William, "I took up my pen in wrong time from the texture of my narrative. But you must let a schoolmaster fresh from his cave of Trophonius be garrulous and silly. He will be the better for it afterward."[1] Emerson's deliberate identification with one who has emerged fresh from the "cave of Trophonius" serves as the basis upon which the meaning of his chest strictures becomes clear. The suggestion is that by identifying himself with one emerging from the cave of Trophonius, he was expressing his willingness to resign himself to his ministerial heritage once again, perhaps as he did when he closed his school in 1824 and entered Harvard in 1825. The cave of Trophonius was an oracular cave in Boetia which was so awesome that no one who visited it ever smiled again. On the other hand, the ocular structure of expansion within diminishment would lead one to conclude that there was more than mere resignation in a ministerial propensity. If he could not emerge from the cave of Trophonius smiling, he could claim nonetheless that a new wisdom had so exalted him that he was able to see beyond resigning himself to the Unitarian ministry. As he turned away from the shadows of the caves, Emerson believed that benefit, in any case, would be his.[2]

---

[1] Emerson, Letters, 1: 176-77.

[2] Emerson's only other reference to the cave of Trophonius in his essay, "Plato; Or, the Philosopher," is as equally ambiguous as his use of the cave here. That Emerson made reference to the cave of Trophonius in this essay as well as in his letter to his brother suggests the necessary unification of resignation to the ministry and, at the same time, growing wisdom to see beyond it, resignation from the ministry. For the reference to the cave of Trophonius in his essay on Plato see Emerson, Nature, p. 494.

Shortly after this important letter to his older brother Emerson suggested in his journals that an "Analogy between Health and Virtue" was
clearly the "design of God."[1] God leads men to assume that the "choice they
should make in this life between good and evil" will make or break their
belief in the immortality of the soul.[2] That Emerson should worry about
his own soul at a time when he was vexed with disease was hardly coincidental. That he assessed health in terms of choices of virtue placed him
squarely in the camp of philosophical idealists. Though he tried to be
"garrulous and silly," he was more of a stoic without a smile on his face
than a man content in the meaning of mortality. "Die? What should you
die for? Maladies? What Maladies?" he wondered passionately in his entry
of 23 September, 1826.[3] He concluded by inciting himself to physical strength:
"Dost not know that Nature has her course as well as Disease? that Nature
has not only helps and facilities for all beneficial operations but fangs
and weapons for her enemies also? Die?" challenged Emerson rhetorically,
"pale face, lily liver! go about your business and when it comes to the
point then die like a gentleman."[4] Little did he know on 23 September, 1826
that in three years as his ordination approached he would refer to it as
his "execution day."[5] Then he would be forced by the pressures of heritage
and marriage to "die like a gentleman," in the Unitarian ministry. However,
with the termination of this stage his play activity, Emerson would be
born again afterwards.

Here during October of 1826 the first circle of Emerson's play can

[1]Emerson, JMN, 3: 49.   [2]Ibid.

[3]Ibid., pp. 45-46.   [4]Ibid.

[5]See Emerson, Letters, 1: 264.

be brought to a conclusion. For during that October he seemed to be concerned mainly with his depressing ailments. Later Emerson's concern was
with more professional matters related to his progress toward the "prized
gown and band" of the ministry. During October, 1826 Emerson preached
his first sermon and became approbated to preach as a pulpit supply by the
Middlesex Association of Unitarians. The matter of physical maladies and
the relation it may have to Emerson's professional development can be submerged a bit for the time being so that we may place the matter of the
ministry itself in the foreground of our considerations. However, it is
hardly the case that these two matters were clearly distinguished in Emerson's
eyes. Quite the contrary: each was held together intimately by the central
importance Emerson gave to traveling, and his trip to Newton and Chelmsford
was exemplary. Then he withdrew from the spector of the person of Andrews
Norton and, more generally, the lecture room of Divinity Hall. Both had
been troublesome eye-to-eye encounters in which Emerson, as it were, "lost
face." He could face neither Norton nor the traditions of ministry and
theology represented by Harvard's hallowed halls. The trip to the country
was Emerson's high water mark in attempting to restore his lost eyesight.
Not even sitting quietly in Norton's presence sufficed. However, traveling
took Emerson far enough beyond Boston that the occasion for eye mending
became psychologically possible. Therefore, the journey of 1825 was central
not only to alleviating a physical woe, but also to postponing further
commitments to the Unitarians for about nine months, from March to December
of 1825. Besides, traveling was a tactful way of avoiding disappointing
his mother. She measured her sons according to her memory of her deceased
husband, and expected Emerson to get on with the arduous business of making
a place of prestige for himself in the ministry as the late minister of

Boston's First Church had done during 1799-1811. To all outward appearances, her son's moratorium of traveling seemed consistent with caring for precarious health, a delicate balance which was assumed a necessary concommitant of the ministerial profession.

Nonetheless, it is possible to suggest in closing that though blindness was relieved and ministerial study postponed by the journey of 1825, during the next several years Emerson's greater torment was the Unitarian ministry itself or, at least, the prospect of it. In a sense, like 1825, similar relief was at hand as Emerson sensed a renewed personal meaning in travel. His realization that the geographical pattern of "going out" (expanding) and "returning home" (diminishing) followed his earlier statement about faith as a telescope would be partially exposed for his own view during his second journey. During the second journey, unlike during the first, he sought escape not from classroom recitations under the guise of blindness, but a delay in his commitments to a ministerial vocation and to any one particular ministry itself. Traveling would relieve him of the ministry completely after his third journey of 1833.

Therefore, this can be said about the first circle of Emerson's vocational play activity. As his gaze fixed on the pastoral delights of rural Newton and Chelmsford his eyes gradually opened. When he returned to Boston he knew that the shadows of pale Unitarianism could not command his final allegiances, though his heritage pressed him further and further into trying on the "prized gown and band." He turned away from Boston and by so doing literally experienced expanded sight as his eyesight was restored. Diminished seeing had given rise to expanded sight: and his returning to Boston began taking on the character of a return by a man with a secret to tell. By January of 1826 Emerson achieved the dawn of a new plateau of personal formation and an invigorated sense of creative inclination. By October of 1826 he was prepared to respond similarly when again he came face-to-face with the possibility and fact of new and greater professional commitments, commitments which would escalate the critical interrelation between his free play at ministry and the prescribed vocational limits of his paternal legacy.

CHAPTER IV

NEW ENGLAND, THE SECOND CIRCLE OF PLAY

Emerson's second significant journey occurred from 25 November, 1826 to June of 1827, and took him from Boston to St. Augustine, Florida. He returned by passing through Charleston, South Carolina; Alexandria, Virginia; Philadelphia, Pennsylvania; New York City; and finally back to Boston, which he viewed anew then in terms of the inclusive region of New England. If a temporary resolution of the problem of trusting himself occurred after his country trip of 1825, then the trip of 1826-27 expressed uncertainty similar to that which aided Emerson earlier to make what he did out of his blindness. The uncertainty which worked to erode his enthusiastic embrace of a career in the ministry turned around the question of whether or not such a vocational identity would become a personal cul-de-sac, thwarting his allegiance to an inner conviction of spiritual truth rather than to formal Unitarianism. As his horizons broadened beyond Boston his return home further diminished the significance which he attached to his ministerial heritage, at least the promise borne by the possibility of a career as a minister of Second Church, Boston. The congregation of that church offered him the position for life if he wanted it. However, it is clear that Emerson understood the job merely as a trial ministry, not one to which a lasting commitment could be at all pledged. But only after 1833 would he realize this. Nonetheless, the journey of 1826-27, carried him beyond the achievement of the journey of 1825.

One way of approaching this new plateau of uncertainty about the ministry and his imminent resolution of the ambivalence it created is to recognize the lack of congruence between his earnest desire to become an eloquent pulpit orator, and his growing apprehension as the day of his official ordination approached. The characteristic lack of congruence of this period is suggested by comparing two pieces of biographical evidence. On the one hand, how whole-heartedly Emerson preached his first sermon, "Pray Without Ceasing," on 15 October, 1826, five days after being approbated to preach and, on the other hand, how, after returning to New England from the South, he feared his coming ordination, set for 11 March, 1829 by the council which offered him a call to Second Church. Therefore, these concerns will serve to frame discussion of this second circle of Emerson's expanding style of play activity. When completed, the stage of his emergence as a cultural ritual actor will have been set.

Evidently Emerson's lungs did not fail him two weeks or so after he mentioned that particular "scarecrow" to William in the letter of 29 September, 1826. Emerson preached his first sermon and was licensed to preach on 10 October 1826. Planning on closing his Cambridge school shortly afterward, and anticipating the return of his "Orpheus," Edward, who arrived home from Europe on 19 October, 1826, were inspirations that gave Emerson strength and hope which facilitated his day in the pulpit and gratified his "vehement desire to preach." His lungs even held up five days after approbation when he preached the same sermon in Waltham for his Uncle Ripley's congregation. In spite of his temporary success preaching, a deeper intention sought fulfillment. When Edward came home, Emerson was free to sail southward in search of his own health and inspiration, and he did so on 25 November, 1826. He arrived in Charleston, South Carolina on 7 December, 1826.

It is important to note that Emerson's first sermon grew out of his "experiment at hard work" as he regained his eyesight in Chelmsford late in 1825. The source of his message was not the empirical theology of Andrews

Norton, but the intuitive lessons of the fields, the down home sayings of the laborers whom he had met there. This first sermon was developed around the central and Platonic preoccupation with envisioning the Ideal, seeing it and being seen by it. The text of the sermon was First Thessalonians 5:17, "Pray without ceasing." Before going on to examine the sermon itself, however, one should note the location of the Biblical text itself. It is situated in the fifth chapter of First Thessalonians and this fact is significant for reasons other than the simple fact that the seventeenth verse coincidentally matched the utterance of the field laborer. Verse seventeen has its meaning in terms of visual imagery, in terms of which the whole of chapter five is recorded in the New Testament. The chapter begins with the notion that "the day of the Lord will come like a thief in the night" (vs. 2). It continues by employing the theme of light and darkness: "But you are not in darkness, bretheren, for that day to surprise you like a thief. For you are all sons of light and sons of the day; we are not of the night or of darkness" (vs. 4-5). Prior to the final benedictory remarks the idiom of light and darkness of the earlier verses shifts into the moral categories of good and evil: "See that none of you repays evil for evil, but always seek to do good to one another and to all . . . hold fast to what is good, abstain from every form of evil" (vs. 15 and 21-22). This shift of idiom is reminescent of Emerson's mention of the meaning of the Zoroastrian pantheon during January, 1826, namely, that good and evil have visual counterparts in light and darkness. What, then, of the sermon itself? How is it developed around the idea of "seeing and being seen" in regard to the expanded horizon of the Platonic Ideal?

In the sermon Emerson suggested that "every thoughtful man has felt that there was a more awful reality to thought and feeling, than to the infinite panorama of nature around him."[1] Indeed, the "prejudice" that

assigns "greater fixture and certainty to the material world" is a source

of "great practical error." Only by the "strong feeling of the reality

of things unseen" might such error be corrected. If the "inward is more

valuable" than the "outward," then retreating from "the public eye" in order

not to be seen, in order to hide one's guilty recollections" and "guilty

wishes," can bring merely exposure and only benefit to such persons, since

the Son of God and the everlasting Father "open their eyes upon them" and

speculate on their "clandestine meditations."[2] After this rather definitive

introduction his message is carried through three sections: first, it is

not only "when we audibly and in form address our petitions to the Deity,

that we pray," but also "every secret wish is a prayer"; second, "our prayers

are granted"; and third, our prayers are written in heaven and require that

one "cleanse his thoughts." For "the heart is pure or impure, and out of

it are issues of life and DEATH."[3]

As early as the previous 11 June, 1826 Emerson began writing this first

sermon.[4] Rheumatism racked his body and Edward was still struggling in

Europe to regain his sanity. Emerson could tell his aunt late during July

and early during August that the poverty he felt and the "prodigious expenses"

of being the major supporter of his family invited him to turn his "little

---

[1]Ralph Waldo Emerson, "Pray Without Ceasing," in Young Emerson Speaks, Arthur C. McGiffert, Jr., ed. (Port Washington, New York: Kennikat Press, Inc., 1938), p. 2; Biblical quotations have been taken from the Revised Standard Version (RSV) of the Bible.

[2]Emerson, Young Emerson Speaks, p. 2.

[3]Ibid., pp. 4-12.

[4]Emerson, JMN, 3: 28.

pennyworths" account in "the preparation of sermons."[1] It would seem money, and his need of more of it, turned Emerson toward the pulpit. At least, financial pressure was a predominant factor in his decision to cultivate his "pulpit way." However, he held views about preaching which he realized were unorthodox. He said that he found in himself no "objections" to preaching at intervals: "tis a queer life, and the only humour proper to it seems quiet astonishment," he reported; that is, "others laugh, weep, sell or proselyte. I admire."[2] Emerson seems to have walked the tightrope over commitment to the ministry on the one hand, and commitment to a personal re-definition of the ministry in terms of his views on preaching on the other hand. If he prayed silently, then his heart bespoke that out of the former alternative issued "DEATH," but out of the latter alternative issued "life." However, the fissure which separated these alternatives had not been opened wide enough for him to have been aware of it, let alone to have taken deliberate action on it. Nonetheless, he responded in terms of more immediate needs and circumstances, his tuberculosis and the promise of modest financial backing from his Uncle Samuel Ripley of Waltham.[3] A journey seemed in order. The fissure would grow wide as a result.

Emerson removed himself from the darkness of physical suffering and the lack of steady work on 25 November, 1826, placing himself in the direction of the bright horizons which fanned-out beyond New England. Ruth Emerson herself moved out of the Hedge house in Cambridge and re-joined the Ezra Ripley family in the Old Manse in Concord as she had done during the tense times of 1814. No doubt finances were a strain, but they were less a cause

---

[1]Emerson, Letters, 1: 170.   [2]Ibid.

[3]Ibid., pp. 180, 183.

for concern than Emerson's new but all too familiar illness. "The true account of the scarecrows is this," he reported early during December, 1826: at sea "a fortnight elapses" in which he remembers himself to have been "a channel thro' which flowed bright and lofty thought."[1] However, he found in himself no desire to recreate "the same brilliant entertainment" he enjoyed before he grew ill, because during those "days of eclipse" to notice their "loss of light" was for the would-be pilgrim to feel an "apprehension lest it might not return."[2] By 30 December, 1826 he contemplated "going to the W. Indies for greater heat," since the "bitter cold eye" of the new year was about to open upon him in Charleston where he "sought warm weather" but found very little of it.[3] If Emerson got off to a difficult and discouraging start, then the remainder of the journey to the South proved easier and brigher.

The first days of January invited back his lost muse. In some comments upon religious ritual, for example, he provided himself with some impressive "brilliant entertainment" and allayed some apprehension to boot. He said that a new year had found him "no more fit to live and no more fit to die than the last. But the eye of the mind has at least grown richer in its hoard of observations."[4] His own insight was that "morals do not change but the science of morals does advance."[5] He had no way of knowing it at the time, but this conviction of 1827 would have personal and institutional implications during 1832. Then he would refuse to administer the sacrament of the Lord's Supper at Second Church, on the grounds that the moral basis

[1]Emerson, JMN, 2: 389.   [2]Ibid.

[3]Emerson, Letters, 1: 183; Emerson, JMN, 3: 60-61.

[4]Emerson, JMN, 3: 60-61.   [5]Ibid.

of this ritual did not change. For if the science of morals does change
even if the morals themselves do not, then it is important that "exercises
of public worship" adapt to the "changing exigencies of society."[1] Though
concerned about the Church's formal nature and about his commitment to a
ministry within it, Emerson was more concerned about the other side of the
tightrope he walked, and about walking above the mundane world itself.
He said, "On the other hand, we see that we are standing on a higher stage. . .
we leave ritual . . . (and) superstition . . . we already discern the broader
light blazing before us."[2] Then, he affirmed, the "true character" of God
and man's relation to him "shall fall upon the soul like the light of the
sun."[3]

However, the issue at hand was what to make out of looking down upon
a commitment to the Unitarian ministry on the one hand, and upon a commitment to a redefinition of the ministry for himself on the other hand. Not
only was the issue rendered symbolically in the less immediate terms of
"light over darkness". But sustaining the issue itself also became a cross
to bear. Emerson's "quiet astonishment" over his preaching can be tied
to a journal entry of 6 January, 1827, one which strikes closer to his
immediate present in Charleston, South Carolina. There Emerson suggested
that "quiet natures suffer most in the apprehension of pain."[4] More significantly, he admitted Jesus into the circle of his "great men" by identifying
himself with the Christ: "I am anxious to sketch out the form of a sermon
I have long had in my head upon the events of the Crucifixion."[5] At Charleston,
aboard the sloop "William," he wrote to his brother William on 6 January,

---

[1] Ibid. [2] Ibid. [3] Ibid.

[4] Ibid., pp. 62-63. [5] Ibid.

1827 beseeching him to take no alarm over his health: "I am not sick; I am not well: but luke-sick--and as in my other complaints, so in this, have no symptom that any physician extant can recognize or understand. I have my maladies all to myself."[1] There was a note of autonomy in this, that is, the autonomy of having his maladies all to himself just as Jesus alone bore the sin of the world on his cross. On a deeper level, the voyage enabled him to have the decision for or against the ministry all to himself as well. However, Emerson, like Jesus, would have to wait about three days before he could sail to St. Augustine, Florida, toward the prospect of more heat, more life. On 10 January, 1827 when he sailed southward, further and further from home, he probably was thinking that it was the "rare fortune" of one born in "these times and this country" to be "born" for the "blessing of the world."[2] Emerson himself felt the portentiousness of his personal times in terms of American identity.

However, at the end of January his geographical isolation in Florida triggered intimacy needs and prompted yearnings for home: "In these remote outskirts of civilization," he wrote to his younger brother Charles on 23 January, 1827, "the idea of home grows vivid."[3] Without the intimacy of home, Emerson was left high and dry, so to speak. For "whosoever is in St. Augustine resembles what may be also seen in St. A. (--) the barnacles on a ledge of rocks which the tide has deserted; move they cannot; very uncomfortable they surely are,--but they can hear from afar the roaring waters and imagine the joy of the barnacles that are bathed thereby."[4] The paragraph of this part of Emerson's letter literally goes on to describe

---

[1]Emerson, Letters, 1: 184.   [2]Emerson, JMN, 3: 65.

[3]Emerson, Letters, 1: 187.   [4]Ibid.

a reverie about barnacles, depicting his "brother barnacles" in the North
while he is in the midst of his own monotonous isolation in the South.
The visual mode of his reverie stands forth clearly: "Thus you see the
poorest of us hath his ideal," he wrote, "and we who walk on the beach are
seers of prodigious events. . . ."[1] Only from afar could Emerson begin
assessing the meaning of his return home. Only from the mastery of a wider
angle of vision could he begin putting the diminished life of the past into
perspective.

While ruminating on the prodigiousness of his own situation, Emerson
was aware of a greater personal destiny ahead of him than the limiting circumstances in St. Augustine appeared to have offered him, should he remain
there. Two days after writing to Charles he described his boredom in a
letter to William. It can be referred to as Emerson's "Turkey Passage":
"Here then in Turkey I enact turkey too. I stroll on the sea beach, and
drive a green orange over the sand with a stick. Sometimes I sail in a
boat, sometimes I sit in a chair."[2] While the image of a ball, the orange
on the beach, may prefigure his dream of 1840 in which he saw himself swal-
lowing the earth as if it were an apple floating in the great Ether, it is
Emerson's boredom which carries the most significance here. The boredom
expressed in his letter was nothing short of the waiting for mastery inherent
in serious play activity: He continued to say, "I read and write a little,
moulding sermons and sentences for an hour which may never arrive. For tho'
there may be much preaching in the world to come yet as it will hardly be
after the written fashion of this pragmatic world, if I go to the grave
without finding vent for my gift, the universe I fear will afford it no

---

[1]Ibid., pp. 187-88.   [2]Ibid., p. 189.

scope beside."[1]

Though he may not have realized it, his regard of Charles, a "brother barnacle," in the letter of 27 January, 1827 carried the idea of how a geographically distant Emerson could shrink geography visually in terms of the structure of expansion within diminishment and thus, put an end to his boredom by playfully making more out of it than it actually was. He said, "I see (Charles) conscious of the dignity of the vows that are on him, measuring with impatient eye the sin and ignorance of the world and hailing the tokens that glimmer in the horizon, of a better era to come."[2] Though he paints a picture of Charles gazing at the distant horizon, it is Emerson himself, "in these remote outskirts" of St. Augustine, who actually was viewing his brother in precisely that same manner, as a "glimmer in the horizon" to the north, to New England. He departed for northern ports on 28 March, 1817. And his horizon became less distant.

On his way home to New England, Emerson's vocational ambivalence, or his "quiet astonishment" of admiration, lingered on. However, as he affirmed on 25 February, 1827, one who carefully examined his thoughts would be astonished "to find how much he lives in the future."[3] Such a creature, he believed, "is probably immortal."[4] Despite the distance of the future, he sought to bring it into his present. However, his felt rift over deep-seated vocational ambivalence was accentuated as his thoughts turned to his Aunt Mary. Of all the members of his family, none pressed him into the family calling of the ministry with more ardor than his aunt. If he was, as he put it on 2 February, 1827, "designed to stand in sublime relations

---

[1]Ibid.

[2]Ibid., p. 187.

[3]Emerson, JMN, 3: 76.

[4]Ibid.

to God and to my fellow men," then he felt obliged to take up the matter with her, his most steadfast mentor.[1] In a letter written to his aunt from Alexandria, Virginia on 15 May, 1827 he referred to her as "Father Mum."[2] He mentioned that he was able to preach Sunday morning "without pain or inconvenience," but also that he was not sure he was "a jot better or worse" than when he left home in November.[3] However, the letter is important because of the way in which Emerson tied together mention of his illness with thoughts about his vocational prospects. For he appeared compelled to make a clear case about it to his aunt. Such an effort was somewhat unique, perhaps even over-labored. Though it was not possible to write to his father who lay silently in a grave, it was possible to communicate with his father's sister, "Father Mum," about these matters. She would remain silent about his struggle--"mum"--but also serve to restore the man's self-confidence as a good "mom" might.

He said to her that he was, despite his ability to preach on Sunday, "still saddled with the villain stricture" and that "perhaps he will ride me to death."[4] That his letter painted a gloomy picture of the soon-to-be minister, merely emphasized the intensity of his vocational ambivalence which, itself, undoubtedly was prompted by thoughts of his demanding aunt. Three months earlier when he had good cause to be much more urgent and vociferous about his lung complaints, he wrote to his brother and struck a note of optimism, one which betrayed the difference in regard he projected between his brother and his aunt: "I am therefore very decidedly relieved from my stricture" and "I flatter myself that I gain ground daily through God's blessing."[5] For some reason, then, Emerson's attempts to explain

---

[1]Ibid., p. 72. [2]Emerson, Letters, 1: 197-99.

[3]Ibid. [4]Ibid., p. 198. [5]Ibid., p. 189.

himself to his aunt were more labored than all his other communications at this time as well as at most other periods of his life.

The longest letters Emerson wrote during his journey were those to his aunt, letters which suggested the problem of a ministerial career rested uneasily on his mind. In this regard, it was no mere coincidence that after mentioning the continuance of his lung trouble to his aunt he also told her, "I have not lost my courage nor the possession of my tho'ts."[1] He confessed that in his "day-dreams" he hungered and thirsted "to be a painter."[2] Such reveries, he goes on to say "suggest a just idea of the world to come which has always been made repulsive to men's eyes from the inadequate representations of systems of religion which looked at it only in one aspect, and that (I am forced to use a word in a limited sense it ought not bear) a religious one."[3] He concluded by revealing his reliance upon a visual, Platonic frame of reference. In terms of that framework his sense of personal propitiousness sought fulfillment: "I grieve," he said, "to find myself clouding a gleam of truth with heaps of words:; and as he concluded his letter to Aunt Mary he requested, "Please disclose some of these lights to your poor blinded but very affectionate nephew."[4] Once again Emerson resorted to closing his eyes temporarily both to the Future and to the Past.

If Emerson sought to throw up something resembling a protective shield to ward-off his aunt's expectation that he fervently embrace the ministry, then he was not as ill in body as he may have represented himself to have been. In the first place he had gained substantial weight prior to his

---

[1]Ibid., p. 198. [2]Ibid.

[3]Ibid. [4]Ibid., p. 199.

letter of 15 May, 1827 to her. On 16 February, 1827 he reported his weight was 141-1/2 lbs., but by 25 March, 1827 his weight had jumped to 152 lbs.[1] This was some indication that his health had improved. Moreover, that his self-trust or self-reliance had been shored-up by the trip was evident as well. When he set sail from St. Augustine he was happy to report that even though he had "not written a sermon since I left home," he felt the relaxation strengthened him to begin preaching in the near future.[2] This he did in Washington, D.C. after getting "rid of a cold" during May.[3] However, Emerson was not alone, for he soon found a fit friend indeed.

Perhaps the biggest boon to his growing sense of new wholeness was derived with "equanimity and pleasure" from his shipmate, Achilles Murat.[4] A nephew of Napoleon (Napoleon would become one of the "Representative Men" about whom Emerson would write an essay in the 1840's), Murat was "a philosopher, a scholar, a man of the world very sceptical but very candid and an ardent lover of truth."[5] It was to the delight of Emerson, himself a nephew, that this "Atheist" applauded the young preacher's theological acumen: for a time, then Murat replaced Aunt Mary, and did so in terms which were much more congenial to Emerson's growing liberal bent.[6] Several months after the trip, during October of 1827, Emerson received a letter from Murat. In the letter Murat said the state of his mind had been altered since meeting Emerson: "Your system has acquired as much in probability as mine has lost in certainty, both seem to me now nearly probable."[7]

---

[1]Ibid., pp. 192, 194. [2]Ibid., p. 194.

[3]Ibid., p. 197. [4]Ibid., p. 193.

[5]Ibid., p. 194. [6]Emerson, JMN, 3: 77.

[7]See Ralph Waldo Emerson, Journals, E.W. Emerson and W.E. Forbes, eds.,

Because Emerson had never been in a position to think at all highly of a "consistent atheist," meeting and conversing "incessantly" with Murat until the Frenchman disembarked at Bordentown, New Jersey, was "a new event" added to "the quiet history of my life."[1] A quiet history perhaps, but hardly an uneventful one.

As he made his way up the Atlantic coast, Emerson shielded himself not only from his aunt, but also from other prospects. "No man can serve two masters," he wrote from Charleston on 17 April, 1827.[2] On the return trip he thought the choice ahead of him was between "greatness in the world" and "greatness of soul," and clearly he believed himself a party to the second alternative.[3] His lungs ached much less now and, indeed, he was beginning to lead "a new life": "I occupy new ground in the world of spirits untenanted before," he wrote, and "I commence a career of thought and action which is expanding before me into a distant and dazzling infinity."[4] His physical strength grew, disspelling the "bitter cold eye" that had shown down on him during January. "Strange thoughts start up like angels in my way and beckon me onward; I doubt not I tread on the highway that leads to the Divinity."[5] All this, therefore, would make it appear that the young pilgrim had decided firmly upon a ministerial career. However, he would come face-to-face with further trials.

Though Emerson was on a course toward "the Divinity," it was not clear at the time he wrote that statement that he meant he was committed to a church vocation. His ambiguity implied that he was, perhaps, committed

---

2 (Boston: Houghton, Mifflin, 1909): 188 (hereafter referred to as the "Forbes-Emerson Edition of the Journals"); also cited in Emerson, Letters, 1: 219.

[1] Emerson, Letters, 1: 194; Emerson, JMN, 3: 77.

[2] Emerson, JMN, 3: 78.   [3] Ibid.   [4] Ibid.   [5] Ibid.

to nurturing only a religious consciousness, only a sense of numinosity
that could give rise to feelings of basic trust. Moreover, we know that
once before, during 1820-22, he was on a path and, instead of meeting
Martin Gay face-to-face, he turned away "for no apparent reason." Perhaps
with a veil of humor Emerson wrote to his Uncle Samuel Ripley from Alexandria,
Virginia that--

> Here as every where else, where your illstarred servant has
> gone this winter, colder than was ever known since the Deluge.
> I believe; and I expect at every turn to be taken up and burnt
> alive as the genius of Winter traveling in disguise; for as soon
> as I come, so do the snow storms. You had better advise the
> farmers of Middlesex of these "signs that mark me extraordinary"
> as Glendower says as it may be worth their while to make up a
> purse to keep me at a safe distance from their cornfields.[1]

Undoubtedly he was not uninfluenced by what he had thought on 2 February,
1827, namely, that "I believe myself to be a moral agent of an indestructible
nature."[2] Though he believed himself to have weathered tuberculosis and,
perhaps, to have tasted "immortality," he reacted to the prospect of returning home to New England in a manner similar to his reaction to Martin Gay.
That is, he kept Gay at a distance, but felt merely seeing the lad's face
and blue eyes from such distance to be morally efficacious. Now Emerson
focuses on New England and Middlesex County in the same way. His playful
humor betrays its "glimmer in the horizon" but it bespeaks of his need to
effect a safe distance from New England as well. Even if he was primarily
concerned to nurture a religious consciousness for himself, it is clear
from the nature of his humor that he continued to hedge on committing himself
to the Church as a minister with daily responsibilities to others than
himself. An outlook is honed continually on the psychological crisis whose

---

[1]Emerson, Letters, 1: 196-97.

[2]Emerson, JMN, 3: 72.

widest and narrowest affective parameters are intimacy and isolation, all centered in geographical actualities.

The prospect of ordination lay before him when he arrived in Boston in June of 1827. At first sight it probably appeared somewhat enticing. For he had visited poverty-stricken William in New York City and tried during May, 1827, as he put it five months before, to get William "to go back like a good person" to Boston, "for 'happy is he who hath never seen the smoke of a stranger's fire.'"[1] However, Emerson's strengthened body thrusted the prospect of fulfilling a greater sense of destiny upon him, despite the fact he had received a preaching invitation while in New York City from First Church, Boston. Once again he took up residence in Divinity Hall at Harvard as a special student in theology, after visiting his mother in the Old Manse in Concord during June. He also began to increase his correspondence with his learned Aunt Mary at this time. Emerson's journey may have relieved his physical ailments but his entrance into a renewed dialogue with his theologically-attuned "Father Mum" implied not only the persistence of unfulfilled spiritual longings, but also the problem of bearing unresolved vocational ambivalence in the face of intensified social and economic expectations. "My eyes are not so strong as to let me be learned," he wrote to his aunt in August.[2] He indicated that the only way his aunt's orthodox God of Calvinism made sense to him was in terms of his unorthodox intuitive perception: "A mole's eye can discern when the beam is of pure light and when it is coloured. . . I see it with the force of intuition."[3] Significantly, only when the mole emerges from his shadowy Trophonius does it become possible to perceive any sort of light at all.

---

[1] Emerson, _Letters_, 1: 180.

[2] Ibid., p. 208.

[3] Ibid.

Moreover, despite his weak eyes, Emerson thought the "exalted person who
died on Calvary" was obscured, owing to "distance of time and in the confusion
of languages."[1] He had based his "Letter to Plato" on the same terms,
namely, a confusion of accrued "dialects." As he regarded Plato, so too
he thought of Jesus, namely, that "a portion of truth bright and sublime
lives in every moment to every mind."[2] Thus Emerson was gathering together
a mighty set of peers and, perhaps, he embraced them according to the model
of his family.

But the "indestructible" moral agent soon found himself preoccupied
by renewed concern for his health as he faced the hard work of supplying
pulpits in western Massachusetts during the summer and fall of 1827.
Emerson's preoccupation with his ills at this time had at least a curious
coincidental connection to the prospect of ordination as a Unitarian minister
in Second Church early during 1829. Returning from the South meant beginning hard work. However, our preparation for understanding the last episode of the cluster of 1825-33 can be begun at this point. It is possible
to suggest here that Emerson's engagement and marriage to Ellen Tucker
during 1829-31 served him as a reprieve, so to speak, from the meaning of
ordination or, as he put it, his imminent "execution day." In a subsequent
chapter about Emerson's last major journey of the period 1825-33, the
reprieve-like quality of his relationship to Ellen Tucker will be developed
as its opposite. That is, it will be suggested that on another level
Emerson's marriage to Ellen Tucker bore the taint of condemnation. In a
sense, his marriage made it possible for him to accept with resignation
what he thought to be an uninviting profession, and to labor as the "Reverend

---

[1]Ibid.

[2]Ibid.

Sisyphus" in a ministry at Second Church for three years. On the one hand, he accepted being "condemned" to the ministry as long as a relationship with Ellen granted him a temporary marital "reprieve." It was not merely coincidental, then, that his engagement to Ellen immediately preceded his ordination at Second Church.

In a subsequent chapter, this relationship between condemnation and reprieve will be depicted reversing itself. Then, Emerson will have mastered the former situation in which he felt under the thumb of those pressures in such a way that he will secure a vocational "reprieve" only insofar as he himself unconsciously "condemns" his wife to death. Following this, it was not merely coincidental that his resignation from his charge at the church was submitted shortly after her death. However, dealing with subsequent implications of the quality of "condemnation" is rightly postponed until the quality of "reprieve" which is at hand has been developed further. Moreover, it will be sometime later in our narrative until Emerson evidences that he has gotten "on top" of the entire situation in a masterful way. For the time being, he remains a pawn. What, then, can be made out of Emerson's renewed interest in his ills?

Hand-in-hand with his renewed preoccupation went hedging to commit himself to any one sort of pulpit for too long, that is, for any sort of "permanent engagement," as he would put it. Certainly one could say Emerson's hesitancy to take a permanent position resulted from his prudence, his desire to locate a good berth for himself in the Unitarian ark. But that his search was coupled with a preoccupation over renewed illnesses suggests a psychological connection he assumed to exist between sickness and vocation. Each time Emerson considered taking a position he found himself mysteriously set-upon by illness. The maladies supplied the excuse he needed for not taking a position permanently, at least until he became engaged to Ellen

Tucker. Then he secured the reprieve of being preoccupied with his fiancee

and wife more than with the subconscious link between sickness and voca-

tion. Therefore, Emerson's days as a pulpit supply ran from approximately

late June, 1827 when he returned from the South, to late January, 1829

when he accepted the offer from Second Church to be their junior minister,

along with the senior minister, Henry Ware, Jr. Emerson's ordination

would follow in March of 1829.

During that year-and-a-half long period of time Emerson had fairly

good health but put psychological distance between himself and vocational

commitments of any lasting sort. On the one hand, he attempted to settle

into the ministerial role which emphasized the preaching function, namely,

supply preaching. On the other hand, he succeeded in not becoming permanently

committed to any one single parish. In order to characterize the tenor

of this whole period of time best, we might very well jump ahead to a letter

to William which Emerson wrote on 3 April, 1828. Telling William he had

just returned from preaching at the church in Lexington (which, incidentally,

would be the last pulpit he would supply during the 1830's), he confided

he was "agreeably disappointed" having recently escaped "all engagements"

at a "New Church" in Boston.[1] He went on to say he was embarrassed "when-

ever any application" was made to him that "may lead to permanent engage-

ments": he continued to say, "For I fancy myself dependent for my degree

of health upon my lounging capricious unfettered mode of life and I keep

myself and I slowly multiply my sermons for a day I hope of firmer health

and solid power."[2] Yet, and somewhat ironically, he added the most telling

---

[1]Ibid., pp. 229-30.   [2]Ibid.

sentence: "Tis vacation at Divinity Hall, and so I am here."[1] Emerson

hedged committing himself when issues about his health crossed his mind, either

to a single congregation or, for that matter, to Divinity School when it was

in session. One will see later how a seemingly "permanent engagement" to

Ellen Tucker afforded him the "lounging capricious unfettered mode of life"

he wanted. Then the point will be that even though such a style of life

was desired, it was not necessarily needed to assure Emerson health. More

to the point, the question of career as an American lecturer hung in the

balance. The question of how (not "if") to abandon a ministerial post would

be in the offing. Then we will note that Emerson's personal style of acquiescence

will do the trick. At any rate, let us return to June, 1827 now that this

lead has been set.

In a letter to Aunt Mary dated June, 1827 Emerson allowed his shield

to drop somewhat and he hinted that the ministry, as a credal constraint,

was not his first vocational choice. Even to intimate such a thought to his

Aunt Mary was an act of courage in light of all she must have represented

to him, in particular, his father, and former generations of "Reverend Emersons."

Nonetheless, he wrote, "Although I strive to keep my soul in a polite equili-

brium, etc. I belong to the good sect of the Seekers, and conceive that the

dissolution of the body will have a wonderful effect on the opinion of all

creed-mongers."[2] The reality of physical woe, dare say death itself, was

the subject upon which Emerson's mind dwelled. To die, he felt, was of bed-

rock significance. Though he believed in his immortality because it rested

---

[1] Ibid.

[2] Ibid., pp. 202, 205; Forbes-Emerson Edition of the Journals, 2: 210-212. Emerson referred to himself as a "Seeker" several times. This note indicates other places where the same term is used in this way.

on Christian doctrines to that effect, the more pressing matter was hardly
so theological: "I mean the fear of death itself, the instinctive melancholy
which long trained philosophy does not strip off."[1] Characterizing his own
rush toward "execution day" more than he knew, he wondered why, "if it be
really true, and we plodders are to be so grand and infinite--mere beams
of glory--spirits,--one would think they should be so enamoured of the strong
suggestion that it would run before to meet its fate."[2] Would that the circumstances, which he took as portending his death, were that painless!

However, the future and the prospects of preaching as a minister for
the rest of his life, though edifying as thoughts may be, were vain wonderings
of mind. For Emerson's wonder arrived face-to-face with the soul which
does not rush toward death but which, instead, "is sedated . . . wallows
in the mire of life."[3] This attitude was consistent with that conveyed in
a letter written to William on 24 June, 1827 in which Emerson thought of
abandoning Divinity because of ill health: "I am all clay, no iron. Medi-
tate now and then total abdication of the profession on the score of ill
health."[4] But that raised the problem of finances, and with resignation in
his heart Emerson asked rhetorically, "Very sorry--for how to get my bread?
Shall I commence author? of prose or of verse. Alack of both the unwilling
muse!"[5] Failing that, he went on to report his personal mire: "yet am I
no worse in appearance I believe that when in N.Y. but the lungs in their
spiteful lobes sing sexton and sorrow whenever I only ask them to shout a
sermon for me."[6] Indeed, he would wallow in life's mire during the following

---

[1] Ibid., p. 202.
[2] Ibid.
[3] Ibid.
[4] Ibid., p. 201.
[5] Ibid.
[6] Ibid.

month as well. For he was yet unable to turn from the shadows of ill health
and hedged to make premature commitments to cultural vistas broader than
the Unitarian ministry.

By the end of July Emerson had turned down an appointment to serve
for three months as a missionary in western Massachusetts under the direction
of the Franklin Association.[1] Ironically, however, he decided shortly afterwards to journey to the same area early in September, 1827 in order to fill
a pulpit in Northampton. The pulpit had been vacated temporarily by one
Reverend Hall who, himself, had set out on a missionary tour of four weeks
which was similar to the one offered Emerson during July. Emerson believed
he would be able to preach all day in Northampton: "I suppose without
inconvenience."[2] About the same time, late in August, he reported his health
had "mended with the weather, heat being my best medicine," but that he was
not so well but that "the cold may make another Southern winter expedient."[3]
The point registered was not that another trip to the South might lay in
the future, but that if being a missionary led to the possibility of a
"permanent engagement," then he could use ill health as a way out of it.
By the middle of October the bucolic environs of Northampton, Emerson believed,
promised him "retirement, leisure for increasing my stock of sermons, and
such advantage to my health as this inland mountain air might bring me."[4]
However, "the frailty of human plans" were like "broken reeds."[5] The reason
for saying this was because after the stint at Northampton, he found himself
going from Lenox to Deerfield, to Northampton again, to Greenfield to New

---

[1]Ibid., p. 203.

[2]Ibid., pp. 210-11.

[3]Ibid.

[4]Ibid., pp. 212-13.

[5]Ibid.

Bedford, to Harvard, to Waltham, to Watertown, and to Boston before the start of December, preaching all the way! There is virtually no mention about how congregations received him in his letters during this time. What he was proud about was the fact that he helped pay the way of his mother and brothers by sermonizing. He described it to William at the end of October, 1827: "For as my sermons are worth several dollars apiece I am growing honest and beginning to pay my debts and advise you to take the early tide of my power and disposition."[1] Emerson's health held-up insofar as he felt financially independent, and, moreover, insofar as he could assume his family needed him at their financial helm.

Emerson was not only growing honest and free of debts, he was reading more as well. One of the two most important things that came under the survey of his keen eyes at this time was the letter from Achille Murat during October. It has already been mentioned in connection with his meeting and sailing from St. Augustine with the "consistent Atheist." However, coming when it did undoubtedly bolstered Emerson's sense of success as a minister of Unitarian doctrine, as one who would be listed to. A second piece of reading deserves even greater note. It suggests a subtle psychological connection Emerson made which would have even greater significance as the year of 1833 approached. "Please look in last Edin, Rev. XCI p. 185," he said to William in a letter of 31 October, 1827, "It is an account of Richter's wh. exactly describes Aunt Mary's style."[2] The pseudonymous reviewer, Heinrich

---

[1] Ibid., p. 217.

[2] Ibid., p. 218. The reviewer described Richter's work this way: "In the moral desert of vulgar literature, with its sandy wastes, and parched, bitter, and too often poisonous shrubs, the writings of this man will rise in their irregular luxuriance, like a cluster of date-trees, with its greens-ward and well of water, to refresh the pilgrim, in the sultry solitude, with

Doering, lauded Richter's life and work. He did, however, intimate Richter's heavy-handed and wordy literary style tended to obscure the sublime import of his message. What of this?

It was not his aunt's style which matters here. One should keep in mind that this pseudonymous review article Emerson singled-out he later discovered had been written by Thomas Carlyle. During July, 1832 Emerson would quote the pseudonymous author. By the end of October, 1832 he would know his new idol's name. It is possible to suggest that during October of 1827 Emerson first started to identify his Aunt Mary with that author and, more importantly, to plant seeds for an eventual switch or substitution for his deep-seated identification and devotion, from his aunt to Carlyle. At least, Emerson began raising his "literary" peer to a position higher in his peculiar mental world than his "theological" aunt. A similar process of identification was noted going on earlier between Levi Frisbie and Plato, and the instance at hand belies no less psychological plausibility. This subtle new interest in the likes of Carlyle was critical to Emerson's gradual shift of vocational identity, from the pulpit in 1829 to the lecturn in 1833 and thereafter.

Meanwhile, though Emerson grew stronger in body and professional resolve, his brother Edward found it necessary to consult Dr. Jackson, Charles' friend, because he suffered increasingly from a combination of nervous and tubercular symptoms. However, Edward soon held his own, so much so that Emerson accepted an invitation from one Colonel Kent, leader of the congregation in New Concord (Concord), New Hampshire, to preach for the rest of December as well as on Christmas Day, 1827 without worrying about letting down the

---

nourishment and shade." See Heinrich Doering (pseudo), "Jean Paul Frederich Richter's Life, with a Sketch of his Works," Edinburgh Review, 46, No. XCI (June 1827): 195.

family, especially his younger brother. Evidently inserted as an after-
thought into the preacher's journals and dated 15 December, 1827 was the
statement, "I ought to apprise the reader that I am a bachelor and to the
best of my belief have never been in love."[1] Whether or not he had in
mind his earlier relation to Martin Gay must remain a mute point.

Whatever the past significance that comment may have had, it obviously
also refers to the future. Emerson met his future wife, Ellen Tucker,
the step-daughter of Colonel Kent, sometime during that month in New Hampshire.
His relationship with her would bear striking resemblences to that with Gay
about ten years before. That is to say, the pattern of Emerson's relationship to her would be like the pattern of his relationship with Martin Gay:
As long as she lived and as long as they were married, Ellen would provide
Emerson with a suitable excuse to avoid deciding finally against a ministerial
career. While loving him in this manner, she would provide him also with
the kind of exclusive and unusual relationship he needed so as to believe
he lived a "lounging capricious unfettered" life, that is, a life without
any inescapable "permanent engagements." In like manner, Martin Gay was
viewed as a buffer between himself and a vocational commitment to school-
keeping. Emerson implied, as far as he saw it, that their relationship
was equally as exclusive and unusual as his first marriage turned out to
be. His relationship with Gay was hardly a "permanent engagement," even
thought its pattern was sustained. Emerson's marriage, too, would follow
the same pattern as well as be less than what could be called a "permanent
engagement" (he was well aware before he married that Ellen's tuberculosis
would, in all likelihood, bring about her death in the not too distant future).

---

[1] Emerson, JMN, 3: 99.

These psychological connections are put forth here by way of anticipating concluding aspects of the cluster of events of 1825-33.

January, 1828 began a year-long period of time during Emerson's life when he made some of his most decisive commitments during 1825-33, at least, he extended himself more in the direction of making what at the beginning of April, 1828 he feared, namely, "permanent engagements." In doing so he went beyond the plateau of achievement arrived at during 1825. Three "permanent engagements" stand out during 1828, all of which were intimately related to Emerson's psychological world of deepening associations in fantasy and in fact. They were his growing concern over Edward's failing health; his involvement with Second Church as a pulpit supply there; and, finally, his engagement to Ellen Tucker during December. One suggestion is that Emerson's commitments to Edward's health and to Second Church's pulpit, coming together as they did, served to externalize his own preoccupation with physical woes, insofar as they pertained to the "highway that leads to the Divinity." Emerson came down off his tightrope, so to speak, temporarily during 1828: By seeing to Edward's health, he affirmed his own strength, and by obliging Henry Ware, Jr.'s needs at Second Church, he affirmed his own inner freedom from a permanent ministerial charge. It might be said that during 1828 Emerson experimented at hard work quite differently from the "hard work" of field laboring in Newton and Chelmsford during 1825. He can be understood to have tried to employ another geographical pattern of travel in a psychological manner during 1828. That is, the "expansion" and "diminishment" of traveling of 1826-27 had been taken into his mental world and now was poised for use, readied for mitigating others' "illnesses" and others' "commitments." Because 1828 was the year when a process of externalizing his care was first evident in such a clear way, one can suppose that during that year the first clear indication was given that Emerson was beginning to enjoy a new, though temporary, freedom from ailments as well as freedom born of internal resistance to the Unitarian ministry.

Therefore, the first two engagements were, on the one hand, a mark of a fearless commitment to the ministry and, on the other hand, a courageous commitment to reshape the ministry in its broadest sense to fit his own needs and skills. Remember that by 1832 Emerson was convinced that in order to be a good minister in the broadest sense it was necessary to leave the ministry in the narrowest sense, in the sense of the "Unitarian" ministry. Though this may be a stark picture of what at the time were only nascent tendencies of the Emersonian disposition, they were, nonetheless, directions taken during 1828. Generally, during 1828 Emerson began to _care_ beyond the limited scope of his own frustrated quest after greatness. However, by caring about his brother and about Second Church Emerson was "expanding" beyond himself in a literal sense. Hence, the year of 1828 may very well be taken as the pivotal period during the whole of 1825-33. The hard work of being born to a wider world had begun.

Certainly Emerson was not as enthused about his two engagements as all that. But in light of his third commitment, they could be much more readily tolerated. The marital engagement to Ellen Tucker blunted the sharp responsibilities of caring for Edward and caring for Second Church. If Emerson had been attempting to externalize his struggle for three years to reconcile physical ill health and ministerial work in a parish (since his first vocational crisis at the Harvard Divinity School early in 1825), then his engagement to Ellen was a new, third variable which, happily, could take his mind off the other two engagements of 1828. But Ellen would die in 1831, and Emerson's reprieve would end with her death. This would bring on a _crisis_ of vocation par excellance, for then he would come, as it were, face-to-face with the ministry and its doctrinal demands which, as did Luther (a member of Emerson's pantheon of "Representative Men"), Emerson found intolerable. At that time he would, as usual, journey away for the benefit of health. Turning now to each of the three engagements, one's eye looks toward the completion of the second circle of Emerson's ritualized play, 11 March, 1829, ordination day.

Emerson began the new year of 1828 in Concord, New Hampshire explaining that he had read Charles' essay on "Friendship" in the Harvard Register, and was having difficulty finding a fit friend for himself.[1] By concerning himself with this particular interest at great length in a letter to Charles, he prepared to get involved with Edward's health, that is, to become more intimate with and actively concerned about his ailing brother. A theme of Emerson's correspondence during 1825-33 is isolation from his brothers in general. It was characterized by the metaphor of 1827, "brother barnacles," as well as signaled by the litany that they "Write. write.," which he requested of Charles in February of 1827, and of William during the following March.[2] Though he thought, "Brothers, even if I had decent ones, can never in any manner answer this purpose" of friendship, he turned to his brother's woes during February, 1828 nonetheless.[3]

Edward suffered from the capriciousness of paranoid delusions on top of a very frail constitution which, itself, was touched by the Brahmin legacy, tuberculosis. "Edward lasts so well," Emerson told William on

---

[1]Charles Emerson, "Friendship," in The Harvard Register (January 1828), pp. 333-36. The article is unsigned in the original manuscript.

[2]See Emerson, Letters, 1: 191, 201.

[3]Ibid.

18 February, 1828.[1] In spite of "these murderous diseases" about which

Edward talked, Emerson believed "his chance is good to last long," perhaps

quite as good as was his own chance, because salvation for all persons was

in "perfect living."[2] Edward's "rules," Emerson reported, "are the Medes.

Charles thinks Doctor Spittergen in Vivian means him."[3] The references to

"Medes" and to Disraeli's Vivian Grey (1826, 1827) are illuminating about

Edward's delusions. The first is an allusion to the story of the Biblical

Daniel and the Lion's Den, where Daniel is persecuted because he prays to

God, not to the king of the Medes (see Daniel 6: 1-29). Dr. Spittergen of

Vivian Grey was much given to telling about his views on diet and especially

on hygiene, matters relating to "purity" and to "contamination," both of

which are usually associated with the paranoid syndrome.

The first report on Edward to William appears curiously sandwiched

between two other passages. The first bears an affirmation of Emerson's own

strength and fearless commitment to a ministry. It also strikes to the core

of his attempt to reshape the ministerial vocation in broader terms, especially

in terms of expanding the vocation beyond doctrinal issues. In this sense,

Emerson's sermons actually became the substance of his redefinition. "Pray

Without Ceasing," for example, was something of an unorthodox point of view.

Henry Ware, Jr., as was mentioned already, looked upon Emerson's sermonizing

as being more liberal than he would have liked. In any case, Emerson wrote,

"I don't write because with all my leisure I have none. I am writing sermons.

I am living cautiously yea treading on eggs to strengthen my constitution.

It is a long battle this of mine betwixt life and death and tis wholly

---

[1]Ibid., p. 227.   [2]Ibid.

[3]Ibid.

uncertain," Emerson believed, "to whom the game belongs. So I never write when I can walk or especially when I can laugh."[1] The second passage portrays his gradual willingness to put his own troubles aside and to look after Edward" "I have not walked to the end of the rope of my rheumatism so have (a) little time for brotherly love. For tho it is strong as death yet wd. I not have death prove the stronger and so I must fight inches with him."[2] Such poised care for Edward was merely a beginning. Other circumstances intervened, making this particular "permanent engagement" more complex, more permanent and more engaging.

By this time Emerson had returned from New Hampshire to his Divinity Hall residence in Cambridge and was busy increasing his repertoire of sermons and supplying local pulpits. One can only guess his energy was activated partly by the presumed meeting of Ellen Tucker while he was in New Concord. For if Edward and Second church soon became the two major focal points of his care, then attending to his budding romance was a way of caring for himself. By the middle of April, 1828 he had written his letter to William stating that he sought a "lounging capricious unfettered mode of life," mentioned already. After preaching in Concord, Massachusetts during May he journeyed to New Concord, New Hampshire in order to preach during the month of June. Meeting Ellen there probably was hardly an obstacle to the leisurely life style he wished to live. Writing to William on 30 April, 1828, he stated, "especially do I court laughing persons," because after a "gossiping hour" where talk has been "mere soap bubbles" Emerson lost all sense of "the mouse" in his chest.[3] Because William worked so hard as a

---

[1] Ibid. [2] Ibid.

[3] Ibid., p. 233.

legal apprentice, Emerson proffered him a lesson: "Clear I am that he who would _act_ must _lounge_."[1] Therefore, if Ellen was to help Emerson "lounge," then Edward and Second Church called him to action. Certainly he was not aware of how little he would need William's advise about taking a church: "I have just refused an invitation to preach as a candidate at Brighton," he wrote on 30 April, 1828; . . . "It is the third No to which I have treated the Church Applicant or Vacant. Myself and some of mine advisers exhort me to wait a great while--2 or 3 years--for sound health and wind and limb and sermon barrelfull before I settle. I await the advice," he concluded, "of the Mogul--himself a divan (William)."[2] Emerson appeared hardly as desperate to receive word from Willaim as William himself had been to hear Goethe's advice three years before. Besides, Emerson lacked a sense of urgency about taking a church during the spring of 1828, urgency under which he would labor leaving Second Church four years later.

Only two letters are known to have been written during June, 1828, one on June 2nd, the other on June 30th. Most of the month was spent with Ellen in New Concord, New Hampshire. Neither letter was written while he was in the north. This suggests that when he was in New Concord Emerson was, indeed, more self-caring than he was caring for either Edward or Second Church, both focuses yet to loom significantly over the horizon of self-regard. In this sense, Ellen was his reprieve even before getting off the hook of duties at Second Church became a critical need. In any case, both letters of June paint a dire picture of Edward who, by 2 June, 1828, was "a great deal better" but who was, later that same month, "ill again--worse than before."[3] Toward the end of May, 1828 and during the early part of

---

[1]Ibid.   [2]Ibid., p. 234.

[3]Ibid., pp. 235-37.

June, 1828 Edward had "fainting fits, and delirium, and had been affected strangely in his mind."[1] Despite the fact that Emerson considered his brother restored to "his former habits of thinking" which, he injected, were "always perverse enough," Dr. Jackson was not convinced.[2] Emerson agreed with the physician that Edward would "never be cured" of his delusion of being "suddenly and totally recovered from his old disease."[3] By way of anticipating what is to happen to Ellen Tucker three years later, Emerson's reaction to Edward's physician should be singled-out for closer attention. What was Emerson's attitude toward men of medicine?

Charles' friend, Dr. Jackson, recommended that Edward "should not touch a book for a year."[4] Jackson would be the same physician who would attend Emerson's wife three years later, offer the recommendation that the couple leave Boston and go south for her health, and caution that if they went, then they would be prepared to stay there "for at least ten years."[5] Emerson wrote of Edward, however, that he (Emerson) was powerless to see to it that the doctor's advice was heeded by his brother: The "imperious patient" was up and dressed on that morning of 2 June, 1828, and Emerson felt that "the doctor's dominion" will shrink back into an "advisory council, and come in, I doubt not, for a due share of contempt."[6] Though he feared any future disorder may again affect his brother's nerves, he said help-lessly, "I confess I watch him with painful interest . . . for aught I know his health may be really recovering."[7] Therefore, Emerson's care for his

---

[1]Ibid., p. 235.

[3]Ibid.

[5]Rusk, The Life of Ralph Waldo Emerson, p. 147.

[6]Emerson, Letters, 1: 235-36.

[2]Ibid.

[4]Ibid.

[7]Ibid.

brother, was passive, evidencing a willingness to accede not to a physician's advice, but to the stronger will of a doctor's patient. This attitude is punctuated by the fact that Emerson's core in this instance was mostly visual, watching his brother and Jackson "with painful interest." This same passive posture of <u>vicarious suffering</u> will be used by Emerson in 1830-31, just as it had been expressed in 1820-22 in seeing but never effectively meeting and conversing with Martin Gay. During 1830-31 Emerson himself again will acquiesce over Dr. Jackson's suggestions. Then, Ellen's death will result. The trauma of losing her will mark the beginning of Emerson's vocational birth out of the Unitarian womb of his heritage.

After removing himself from the heat of this family calamity for several weeks in New Concord, Emerson returned to Cambridge where he wrote the letter of 30 June, 1828, the second known letter of this month. Evidently, Edward had suffered a complete nervous breakdown and Emerson wondered whether his brother required confinement in McLean Asylum in Charlestown as his other brother Bulkeley had needed from time to time. Edward was in "a state of violent derangement, so as to require great restraint."[1] Ruth Emerson spoke "of the Hospital, as perhaps a dismal necessity."[2] It was at this point that circumstances bore down on Emerson harder than ever before in his life. At this juncture, the choice of whether or not to externalize his preoccupations with personal illness and vocational commitments became critical.

Emerson's passive care (watching "with painful interest") was re-affirmed, but done in such a way as to make a telling connection. This is to say, he was concerned about Edward, and his concern had vocational implications which he soon realized. Besides the "state of feeling" produced by watching Edward

---

[1]Ibid., p. 236.   [2]Ibid.

"being unutterably wretched and ruinous to infirm health," he suggested his brother's illness was also sapping away some of his own health. That is, Edward's illness slowly pushed Emerson into a "permanent engagement." To take a job was necessary by way of supporting the family: ". . . it removes me from employment the profits of which are only more necessary to me on account of this calamity."[1] Nearing financial ruin and being true to his character, he took provisionary steps, steps which led him to his second major care:[2] "I have nothing else to say--no spirits to say anything else," he continued to say on 30 June, 1828.[3] But how mistaken he was! For he said also, "I have engaged to supply (Henry Ware's) pulpit," adding, "but shall probably relinquish it."[4] Circumstances forced Emerson to turn resignation to the ministry into a virtue of caring deeply for the health of his family at many levels.

Emerson believed that money might be needed in order to send Edward to the South for his health, and to take what would appear to be a "permanent engagement" as a pulpit supply was a giant step toward that end. Emerson knew that Henry Ware, Jr., Second Church's minister, was himself very sick. Though Ware's friends were not so sure of it, Emerson believed that as far as the senior minister's health was concerned, "no good ground of hope exists for a real restoration."[5] It was ironic, therefore, that at the very same moment when financial and vocational success seemed close at hand (Ware's pulpit soon would be vacant), Emerson exclaimed his "mowing tales of wo" to William saying, "Strange how all our prosperous days have been overcasted! As in case of both Edward's orations--and before--and

---

[1]Ibid. [2]Ibid. [3]Ibid.

[4]Ibid. [5]Ibid. [6]Ibid., p. 237.

since--and now again to be."[1] Edward was confined for the next month or
so in the Carlestown Asylum where, Emerson said, he had "been meeting with
Dr. W."[2] Emerson's resignation to responsiblity not withstanding, family
tension over the calamity of Edward's illness subsided somewhat during the
beginning of the summer, and this meant that Emerson could turn more of his
attention to supplying Second Church and to his prospects as minister there.
However, he remained ambivalent about the entire matter, hoping to "relinquish it" (his temporary position) soon. Though he may have wished to let
go of Second Church, immediate circumstances prompted him to hold on to the
direction which had been so tortuously secured.

During the beginning of July Charles delivered the valedictory address
to his graduating class at Harvard, and he probably struck jealousy in his
older brother's heart. After all, Emerson was elected poet for his own
class, not valedictorian, and he accepted that place on the program after
six other graduates had turned down the modest distinction.[3] Emerson felt
Charles' "performance deserves particular notice" because he was a "beautiful
orator" but, he thought, his brother was "never eloquent."[4] His main criticism
of Charles' rhetorical style was that it depended upon being a "spectacle
instead of being an engine," that is, "a fine show at which we look, instead
of an agent that moves us."[5] As he gave thought to his own eloquence as a
pulpit orator five days before, on 10 July, 1828, he felt a similar pride,
thinking himself beyond being a mere "spectacle" and "fine show." When
requested by congregations to fall into line with "popular ignorance and

---

[1]Ibid., p. 237.

[2]Ibid., p. 241; also, Emerson speaks of visiting Edward in a letter
dated 14 July, 1828 (p. 238).

[3]Rusk, The Life of Ralph Waldo Emerson, p. 84.

[4]Emerson, Letters, 1: 238.   [5]Ibid.

the duty of adapting our public harangues and writings to the minds of the people," he admitted uneasiness.[1] Emerson thought of himself as an "engine," and as such was not without a sense of strength and power. When he considered the "constitutional calamity" of the family, for example, which "in its falling on Edward" buried so many towering hopes, he said he had "little apprehension" of his own "liability to the same evil."[2] Even more affirmatively, "I have so much mixture of silliness in my intellectual frame that I think Providence has tempered me against this. . . .My practice conforms more to the Epicurean, than to the Stoic."[3] Emerson was ready to climb into the pulpit of Second Church, the failings and the inadequacies of his four "brother barnacles," whom he once saw from afar as something of a "spectacle," notwithstanding. Now they, not he, appeared high and dry, without health of spirit.

That William was having a rough time of it in New York City as a legal apprentice, that Edward was growing worse and more and more insane, that Charles was not an ideal orator as well as one subject to psychological depressions, and that Bulkeley was hopelessly retarded--all these deficiencies (and surely Emerson viewed them as such) were foils against which Emerson began discovering and cultivating his particular ego-strengths which would help solidify a personality effective later in cultural leadership. All of his brothers so far had shunned their ministerial heritage. Emerson himself was the only son faithful to the past, perhaps hoping it would bless him in the present. During July, 1828 he committed himself officially to supplying Ware's pulpit "thro' the whole of August" and "for an indefinite term" thereafter.[4] The distinction between circumstances and conscience seemed

---

[1] Emerson, JMN, 3: 136-37.

[2] Ibid.

[3] Ibid.

[4] Emerson, Letters, 1: 238.

muddled at best, but he was convinced by 30 July, 1828 that as a child is connected "to the womb of its mother by a cord from the navel," so too is man connected "to God by his conscience."[1] During 1832 when he would "sever the cord" that bound him to the congregation of Second Church, he would believe he was acting according to the dictates of conscience. However, then, too, other voices also would be heard. Thus for the moment, Emerson shouldered what amounted to full-time pulpit supply at Second Church early in August, 1828. He described his decision to take that burden upon himself late in July as one which, curiously enough, forced him to "enter into captivity."[2] One might add, the captive preacher awaited what he would call, again curiously, his "execution day" on 11 March, 1829. It would arrive exactly two months to the day after his being elected by the Society of Second Church as a colleague pastor.

At this juncture, Emerson's relationship with Ellen Tucker, somewhat suspended since June, 1828, began taking on major significance. It did so because Emerson soon made a habit out of being absent from his pulpit charge

---

[1]Emerson, JMN, 3: 139. That Emerson mixes feminine and masculine sources of infantile psychological identification suggests that throughout his vocational struggles whatever creativity he enjoyed was rooted in a basic acceptance of a sense of his own androgyny. Imagery of mixed expressions of sexuality not unlike that painted by Emerson here is the subject of the article, A.J.L. Busst, "The Image of the Androgyne in the Nineteenth Century," in Romantic Mythologies, ed. Ian Fletcher (New York: Barnes and Noble, 1967), pp. 1-96. That Emerson is drawing on androgynous identifications in his statement is evident because of the mixture of being attached to a mother and at the same time, being connected similarly to a father. One author has suggested that an anti-androgynous attitude, hardly that displayed by Emerson at this point, is distinguished by "its setting apart of all pairs of opposites--male and female, life and death, true and false, good and evil." See Joseph Campbell, The Masks of God: Occidental Mythology (New York: The Viking Press, Compass Edition, 1970), pp. 26-27. One is reminded of Emerson's earlier sense of ambivalence over Martin Gay, which presented similar mixing of sexual imagery, at least a blurring of what was a proper, nineteenth-century sense of masculinity.

[2]Emerson, Letters, 1: 242.

(the pulpit supply arranged for his own pulpit supplies!) ostensibly because
Edward was to be released from McLean Asylum during November (he had been
there since July) and it would be made easier for all involved if Emerson
took constant care of him. After all, Edward's mood swings were rapid,
and as late as August, 1828 he was still quite ill, believing as usual he
was "suffering punishment for great offenses."[1] Charles seemed too busy
as a schoolmaster in Boston to care for Edward, so the task fell upon Emerson.[2]
However, his irregular presence at Second Church was not unprompted by the
lure of New Concord, where Ellen Tucker awaited his visits. By the middle
of October, 1828 Emerson thought supplying Ware's pulpit during August would
lead to a more definite term of employment. He believed he probably would
"be expected" to supply Ware's place, "till December--an engagement which
suits my present convenience better than any other."[3] If the prospect of
replacing Ware left him cold, then circumstances soon worked to chill him
further. A more decisive turn would be taken by events during October and
push Emerson further into a full-blown commitment to the Unitarian ministry,
at least under a guise of permanency. Only after his ordination, then, could
he move his efforts toward a redefinition of the religious dimension of his
vocational role.

Though Edward was presenting the family with "the strongest hopes of
his entire recovery," Henry Ware was cause for increased worry.[4] Ware was
"ill again, and all good men are sorry," Emerson wrote on 17 October, 1828.[5]
He believed the rule of frailty, the Emerson family's chief bug-a-boo, pertained to Ware, namely, "to be a good minister and healthy is not given."[6]

---

[1]Ibid., pp. 244-45.   [2]See ibid., p. 244.   [3]Ibid., p. 248.
[4]Ibid., p. 251.   [5]Ibid., p. 249.   [6]Ibid.

Ware's illness, and its meaning within the context of Boston Brahmin culture;
implied for Emerson a greater ministerial commitment: "This event will probably
confine me where I am for the winter. It has some obvious advantages over
any other service but involves more labor."[1] True to form, Emerson hedges.
Coming right after a long paragraph about Edward in a letter to William,
the "obvious advantage" was clarified. The financial support to be received
from steady, assured employment would help pay the major part of the bills
for Edward's and Bulkeley's stays in the Asylum, as well as some for impoverished
William. A preoccupation over money was especially evident by the end of
the year, when Edward returned to the family fold and Emerson weaved a course
through the briar-patch of vocational expectations.[2] If he felt free to
relinquish his pulpit supply after the end of November, then the congregation of Second Church was at first oblivious to the depth (or lack of it)
of the preacher's commitment to them.

It seems as though the congregation wanted Emerson to continue on, after
the end of November, but that he himself wanted to do so was another question.
His tendency was to hedge somewhat, delaying because of very strange reasons.
That is, if Emerson wanted the money a "permanent engagement" would afford
him, then he acted in such a way that the church offered it to him that one
only can be led to see his ambivalence over the implications of their proposal.
He dealt with these "professional affairs" in a letter to the "Mogul"
(William) on 4 December, 1828. He betrayed his financial preoccupations.
In regard to money, he referred to family bills, or, as he called them,
"cards": He told William he had received and paid "the letters containing
the cards you sent" and offered his continued skill at money-handling; in

---

[1]Ibid.

[2]Ibid., pp. 252-53.

particular, "Had you not better send me half a dozen cards, without direction, to exercise my worldly wisdom in distribution? I am a great professor of that art, within these few months past, that I have meddled with Edward's matters."[1] In regard to his "professional affairs," Emerson verged on his first "permanent engagement" in a vocational niche, and this he communicated to his brother under the guise of secrecy and in carefully-worded confidences. The entire communication, one can suggest, was Emerson's attempt to act as if he were in control of a situation (i.e., to act "professionally"), most of the circumstances around which tended to convey the opposite, namely, his lack of control over his own destiny, and the pressure of circumstances mentioned already.

By stepping closer to the ministry at Second Church, Emerson stepped closer to what all his brothers had not chosen, namely, the family calling of liberal ministry. But along with his step he had to face the anxiety of the possibility of constitutional calamity, which might beset him at any time. Since he had survived blindness, tuberculosis, and had experienced the relieving of sporadic bouts of rheumatism by December of 1828, Emerson could feel more self-confident than ever before. Therefore, this sense would account for his sense of control over matters during 1828-29. But as a larger understanding of his "professional affairs" suggests, he was still worried about and motivated, at least in part by, a concern for bodily calamity all his own. In addition, he had in mind a reprieve from clerical "captivity" under the guise of a concern for Edward's health.

In that letter of 4 December, 1828 Emerson said at the outset that Edward was going with him "day after tomorrow to Concord, N.H. to spend three Sundays and then returns to Concord, Ms."[2] During the middle of

---

[1] Ibid., p. 252.

[2] Ibid.

November, 1828, when Second Church had not yet extended their offer of continuance to Emerson, he wrote to William that he proposed "getting an engagement to preach in ye country" and taking Edward with him, adding that he was "going to spend upon Edw.'s debts and can instead upon yours."[1] This sequence provides the kernel of insight needed to suggest concretely that going into "that dangerous neighborhood" of Concord, N.H. ("dangerous" because of his budding affection for Ellen Tucker who lived there!) was the major factor luring him away from Boston.[2] The communication of his "professional affairs" to his brother seems to have been conclusive. Explaining how he had preached a good while at Mr. Ware's, that he was on "no definite agreement as to time," and that "it was well understood Mr. Ware wd. shortly resign," he did not think it "very delicate" to hang on longer as the supply.[3] If the parish was to be regarded as "open for candidates," then he would be "monopolizing."[4] The point here is that Emerson was construing the situation much more differently than the Society at Second Church did. He was keeping the church at a distance.

The congregation of the church, it seems, had assumed all along that when Ware left, or at least just before he would leave, their new well-liked pulpit supply, the Rev. R.W. Emerson, would stay on as primary minister. The members of the congregation hardly would believe Emerson could ever "monopolize" their affections at all. In fact, they "made a fuss," he told William, and sent him word that "if they heard candidates there wd. be a division" among members.[5] There is little doubt that most members of the congregation liked Emerson best. He concluded, therefore, the "best people

---

[1]Ibid., pp. 251-52.

[2]Ibid., p. 256.

[3]Ibid., p. 253.

[4]Ibid.

[5]Ibid.

in the society" wanted him "by all means to stay."[1] Generally speaking,
the congregation was quite wholeheartedly in favor of their timid pulpit
supply. Despite renewed strength, Emerson thought little of himself in one
light of these proceedings, but held himself in higher esteem on the basis
of another light shining in their midst. On the one hand, he wanted other
candidates to be heard lest the congregation's choice of him would keep a
"better man from being heard."[2] On the other hand, "if I am settled," he
stated, "I choose it should be on my merits," not because the congregation
allowed a "better man" to pass by unheard.[3] Perhaps he hid his own religious
and vocational doubts behind a humble veil as William had not done when he
abandoned the ministry for a legal career during 1825. By confessing his
doubts to William now, and to do so while he allowed himself to be drawn
into a "permanent engagement" at Second Church, reflected juggling two
somewhat conflicting self-conceptions. On the one hand, he thought very
little of himself. This implied a diminished self-image. On the other hand,
he held out for the possibility of sensing greater self-worth. This meant
he hoped he would be granted an expanded self-image by the hand of Providence . . .
by the hand of what would turn out to be his own acquiescence.

When he finally accepted their official call on 30 January, 1829 Emerson
recognized clearly the overwhelming support he had from Second Church.
He said he was, "encouraged by the strong expression of confidence and goodwill" they showed him, their vote having been seventy-four out of seventy-
nine in favor of him.[4] However, prior to submitting to such positive regard,
Emerson would tell William in conclusion on 4 December, 1828, "I have left

---

[1]Ibid.

[3]Ibid.

[2]Ibid.

[4]Ibid., p. 261.

them."[1] He added a note about the promised benefits of this withdrawal at that time, that time just prior to the official offer from Second Church: "All this is in confidence, about the committee coming to me, and Mr. Ware's leaving. Why I should come away is plain as daylight. Now I have told you my whole story and my body is very well and I love you."[2] However, why he went away was not "plain as daylight." Another major factor was definitely at work beneath those tiresome "professional affairs." Specifically, a reprieve from Second Church which, in itself, would do more to tell the "whole story" as well as help his body be "very well."

Where Emerson arrived after confessing his professional tact to "come away" in December was not clearly depicted. However, psychologically speaking, one of the places with which he associated health at that time was Concord, N.H.: "Nothing but light and oxygen allowed in New Hampshire. . . ."[3] It was that place, and the young woman who lived there, which cleared the path along which he would "come away" further with Edward on 6 December, 1828. While in New Hampshire for the remainder of the month Emerson was obviously not dwelling too seriously on the imminent offer from Second Church or on his personal style of pulpit oratory. He wrote to Charles on 10 December, 1828 that he had "nothing very surpassing in the pulpit way," and that his younger brother's expectations for him, evidently communicated to Emerson a few days before, were "young falcons, sky high."[4] Other things were on his mind while Edward and he breathed oxygen and were dazzled by light in New Hampshire. For on 21 December, 1828 he recorded in his journal, "I have now been four days engaged to Ellen Louisa Tucker."[5] His continued reprieve from an

---

[1]Ibid., p. 253.   [2]Ibid.   [3]Ibid., p. 254.

[4]Ibid., p. 255.   [5]Emerson, JMN, 3: 148-49.

emotional commitment to Second Church, like his temporary vacation from Boston, seemed assured, at least for the near future. Three days after his entry in the journal he wrote to William and intimated a mild sense of trepidation over this particular "permanent engagement": "It is now just a year since I became acquainted with Ellen. . . but I thought I had got over my blushes and wishes when now I determined to go into that dangerous neighborhood again on Edward's account."[1] Not only had Edward served Emerson as an excuse to remove himself from supplying Second Church's pulpit and from the society's eagerness to give him a permanent position. He said also he was happily reprieved from appearing somewhat unusual: As a result of becoming engaged to marry he was "as happy as it is safe in life to be in the affection of a lady and the approbation of friends."[2] Nonetheless, he still seemed to be walking on eggs, that is, walking lightly lest he break the shell of convenient social accord and approvals.

There is no way of knowing whether or not this engagement had been on his mind for a long time. Had it been on his mind for a long time or not, we still do not know whether the thought of a marital engagement was spurred along by his needs to delay or, at least, to distance himself from his imminent ministerial charge. He knew that charge was, so to speak, "in his pocket," all "sown up." To plan to take a wife was a way pulpit supplying would be diminished, since his world would be appreciably expanded because of a new, added concern for Ellen. Coming when it did, Emerson's engagement to marry Ellen mitigated vocational certainties according to the visual pattern of expansion within diminishment. The meaning of the time and place of the marital engagement clarified Emerson's puzzle over "professional

---

[1]Emerson, Letters, 1: 256.

[2]Ibid.

affairs" of late November and early December, and afforded him a distinct advantage in controlling the issue of vocation. His first two growing commitments during 1828, to Edward's health and to Second Church, were planted in Boston's fertile soil. His commitment to Ellen, however, took him away from Boston and, in symbolic effect, carried him beyond concerns over Edward and Second Church. In a sense, both were aspects of his sense of ministry, that is, pastoral concern (Edward) and preaching (Second Church). Ellen meant neither. Thus, notable again, a geographical pattern was translated into one which was more psychological in nature. It was his pattern, or character structure which operated as a negotiated settlement between "illness" and "commitments."

After all, during his 1824 "self-assessment" Emerson acknowledged he considered the two functions of any ministerial charge to be pastoral care and preaching.[1] So, in a psychological sense, he was "role-playing" during 1828. Namely, what we have called "externalizing," seeing whether or not the ministry would fit his disposition and, moreover, seeing whether or not he might discover a way in which to redefine it around the core of his personal inclinations. Therefore, his engagement to Ellen, his third major commitment of 1828, marked a point when his role-playing came to an end, and when he poised on the verge of giving his play a seeming conventional cloak. Emerson's relationship with Ellen took his mind off just how uneasy he felt about wearing that cloak, the prized gown and band of the ministry. As long as he had Ellen with whom to muse, Emerson could tolerate a ministerial career at Second Church.

However, he still was not certain it was worth it. When he returned to Cambridge after Christmas he continued wondering about the "safety" of

---

[1]Emerson, JMN, 2: 237-42.

his engagement to Ellen. His concern for their future together was curiously ambiguous. When he turned to Aunt Mary on 6 January, 1829 he asked philosophically, "Can this hold? Will God make me a brilliant exception to the common order of his dealing, which equalizes destinies?"[1] His letter was written to his aunt for the purpose of informing her about his engagement to Ellen. However, the philosophical tenor of his questions, their probings into things ultimate, tended to betray something about his upcoming "permanent engagement" to Second Church. He asked his aunt if she believed his marital hopes would hold, but between the lines he implied he was asking her if the ministerial cloak which he was soon to don would hold too. For as he told her, "There's an apprehension of reverse always arising from success."[2] This was so, he believed, even though Ellen was regarded as God's "gift of his mercy."[3] As Emerson gained hold of Ellen, so too he held a faint anticipation of losing her, somehow.

It is now time to follow Emerson to the end of his second circle of play. It is necessary to recognize that Ellen provided the emotional support he needed in terms of an emotional reprieve in order to trek fearlessly toward ordination. One will note he began a subtle redefinition of the ministry in terms of his faith of 1824, the "telescope," much as he began actively externalizing in telescopic fashion during 1828. We will want to prepare to recognize Emerson's trek into Second Church's pulpit as a trek away from the need to depend upon Ellen for emotional support. In fact, an alert to this appears in the aphoristic statement he made to the effect that it was sometimes necessary to leave the ministry in order to be

---

[1] Quoted in Cabot, A Memoir of Ralph Waldo Emerson, 1: 147.

[2] Ibid.

[3] Emerson, JMN, 3: 149.

a good minister. Namely, as Emerson begins moving beyond the second circle
of play at ministry toward a third and final horizon of his formative years,
he first must solve the problem he had with marriage: Ellen was an obstacle
to his giving up the ministry in its narrow sense (Second Church), and to
his becoming a "good minister" in a broader sense (cultural leadership).
Emerson felt "condemned" to the Unitarian Pulpit due to the necessities of
marriage, of a marriage which emblemized his autonomy and strength apart
from his vocation-context of Boston. In terms of Ellen's physical condition,
which was poor indeed, marriage sustained Emerson in living "lounging capricious
unfettered" because such a style of life was required by his wife's condition. This also meant his eye turned toward prospects beyond the ministry,
usually idealizing a capacity for penning sermons and making a name for himself
as an eloquent preacher. Nonetheless, if Ellen placed smiles on his face
in Concord, N.H. in the past, then when he turned toward Boston it probably
seemed as if he were entering the cave of Trophonius, perhaps never again
being able to emerge from his fate happily.

By the strength of awareness of his own intuitive insight into orthodox
theology and into human nature Emerson was prepared to accept a position.
He did so as "junior pastor" of Second Church on 39 January, 1829, again
effectively as "Junio," even though the Society regarded their offer as the
office of "colleague Pastor" to Ware.[1] The decision was made for reasons
other than those related to the offer itself, reasons pertaining to its
feasibility in terms of the health of Ellen and Edward. These reasons
will be taken up in the next chapter. Let it suffice to say that Emerson
felt his fiancee and family were squarely behind him: "My history has had

---

[1]Emerson, Letters, 1: 260-61; ftnt. No. 4.

its important days within a brief period," he entered into his journal on 17 January, 1829.[1] Saying he was called to "an ancient and respectible church" to become its pastor, he recognized in the closeness of his engagement and new position not only the hand of his "heavenly Father," but also the accompaniment of "occasions of joy in the condition of my family," his mother in particular. The new dimensions of Emerson's expanded phenomenal world were rooted in a sense of androgynous unity, bringing together a man's vocational commitment with a fiancee and maternal jubilation.[2] On a similar joyous occasion, his engagement to Ellen, he wrote on 30 December, 1828, oddly, that he was "in a frame of mind" which invited him to repent sorrowfully "all my perversity," for he was stricken with a deep and contrite sense of the "enormity of sin" and the "evil of guilt."[3] In short, Emerson hardly made his decision to accept the call to Second Church in a vacuum.

Though his Aunt Mary may have had cause for a modicum of pride at the fruition of her efforts to see to it that one of her nephews entered her brother's profession, Emerson himself remained self-consciously in the position of an underling, in incubation at Second Church. Only with his resignation in 1832 would that nagging sense of inferiority be mitigated. Even though he became sole minister after Henry Ware, Jr. departed for Europe and secured the prospect of renewed health in July, 1829, Ware later joining the Harvard faculty, Emerson still withheld full commitment to the church. His ambivalence about taking the position to begin with was evident in his letter of acceptance: "If my own feelings could have been consulted, I should have desired to postpone, at least, for several months, my entrance into this

---

[1]Emerson, JMN, 3: 149-50.   [2]Ibid.

[3]Ibid., p. 149.

solemn office. I do not now approach it with any sanguine confidence in my abilities, or in my prospects."[1] The ministry, like schoolkeeping, could turn out to be a Gehenna. Nonetheless, he went against feelings of reticence because of the strong "expression of confidence and goodwill" of the congregation, and the bittersweet configuration, on the one hand, of family expectations and pressures and, on the other hand, the buffering reprieve of Ellen. "I well know," he wrote to the Society of the church, "what are the claims, on your part, to my best exertions, and I shall meet them, as far as in me lies, by a faithful performance of duty."[2] With the concluding remark, "I shall shun no labour. I shall do all I can," one realizes just how much his continuance in the ministry would require the inversion of the principle of "mind over matter."[3] Renewed physical complaints would soon be heard again.

For the time being, however, Emerson was content to take up a career, for time was "really nigh" when he was to leave forever the "delicious sloth of an unaccustomed life" and "go to work."[4] For now, he would refrain from taking in the life made possible by "delicious sloth," that is, a "lounging capricious unfettered" life. As he turned to labor he found he felt consumed by how busy it kept him. He felt fatigue "in every bone" of his body, he told his step-grandfather Ezra Ripley eleven days after ordination.[5] He seemed committed to his pastoral visits and to preaching, in spite of this minor complaint. However, he feared nothing, he confessed, "except the preparation of sermons. The prospect of one each week, for an indefinite time to come is almost terrifick."[6] Much of his fatigue was

---

[1] Emerson, Letters, 1: 261.   [2] Ibid.   [3] Ibid.
[4] Ibid., p. 265.   [5] Ibid., p. 267.

mental, since sermonizing meant taking sides theologically and, like Channing, Emerson was hard-pressed to do so willingly. Nonetheless, he did write sermons, and to this degree he began courageously to redefine the ministry for himself. One can recognize also how he was beginning a task to benefit his nation's cultural identity crisis, an ideological reorientation in germinal form. Later, his transcendentalism would be the summary expression of this bent.

His work began on 23 February, 1829, when he reaffirmed his faith in the telescopic principle. Work sped onward during July, 1829 when he transmuted his faith into the quasi-theological terms of his profession: "Some men see telescopically," he entered into his journal in February, and they are the ones who bring "the great and the infinite to our eyes."[1] This faith was carried over from 1824, through early 1829, and expressed in terms of the ministry. He believed the office of the Christian minister was to be the telescope for humanity: "What is the office of the Christian minister? . . . It is to see the creation with a new eye, to behold what he thought unorganized, crystallize into form, to see the stupendous temple uplift its awful form, towers on towers into infinite space, echoing all with rapturous hymns . . . aloof from the storm of passion."[2] Emerson fancied himself a beholder, not one beheld. He was an "engine," not a "spectacle." Therefore, even in his thought he was not outstanding. Instead, he stood out, believing himself to be hammering on the workbench of the American variety of human consciousness.

In drawing this chapter to an end a brief remark is in order about this whole period of serious play activity, that is, about the relationship

---

[1] Emerson, JMN, 3: 150.   [2] Ibid., p. 152.

of each of the three circles to the other two. This particular chapter
(second circle) admits less "expansion" than either the chapter describing
the first circle or, the next chapter describing the third circle of Emerson's
play. If the period of 1825-33 can be presumed to have been a single event
in the context of Emerson's first thirty-five years, then the beginning
would refer to the event of blindness and recovery in 1825, the middle would
be tagged to the event of preaching the first sermon and ordination. The
end would be associated with marriage, resignation from the ministry, and
Emerson's return from abroad in 1833. Therefore, from the point of view
Emerson achieved at the end of 1825, his capacity to see definitely had
been expanded beyond schoolteaching. Eyesight was restored from the point
of view of his achievement after returning from England in 1833, however,
his achievement of 1825 was "diminished seeing" by contrast with his new,
wider sight. That is, his budding career as a lecturer. The second circle
of 1826-29, then, was the point of Emerson's most diminished capacity to see
broader cultural vistas for vocational commitment when compared with each
of the other two circles that go to constitute the larger span of his entire
period of re-creative activity. Actually it was difficult for Emerson to
see beyond Newton and Chelmsford, so to speak. Even though restored vision
was involved, a less immediate more distant cultural horizon was not yet
recognized from within it. However, perhaps as a result of the involvement
of his eyesight, Emerson began seeing further, beyond Newton and Chelmsford,
as he entered into the second and third circles. In this sense, the physical
restoration of Emerson's eyesight served as a catalyst for the cultivation
of historical and charismatic parameters for his vision. Emerson may have
sensed himself a "captive" of forces and influences beyond his comprehension
during 1826-29, by his own avowal. But at the same time he began breaking

off fetters of personal capriciousness and to broaden his sense of vocational responsibility. One of his fetters and responsibilities would turn out to be the Unitarian ministry. First, however, he would have to break the chain of laughter and intimacy, for they bound him tightly in the grip of condemnation. In the following chapter, Emerson is depicted completing the action of turning his back on the darkness of the years of hedging to take a ministerial post and illness, having seen the light of future promise and solid self-confidence.

CHAPTER V

AMERICA, THE THIRD CIRCLE OF PLAY

Much like his journey South, Emerson's marriage to Ellen Tucker from 30 September, 1829 until her death on 8 February, 1831 was a pleasant and diverting alternative. This commitment to self contrasted to that of caring for Edward, as well as to that of being the responsible minister at Second Church. The marriage fed the fires of his need to turn aside from the Unitarian ministry, an institution virtually replaced, as he intimated, by the American Constitution (the next best thing, he believed, to the New Testament), and away from the sway of the heritage of both "Concords," the peace of narrowing one's sights to theological issues and a career in the service of the church. His journey to Europe and England not long after Ellen Tucker Emerson's death further expressed this expansive direction. Therefore, his resignation from Second Church, would be perfunctory at best. He had decided on the necessity of such a move by 2 June, 1832. The circumstances which surrounded his resignation were psychologically significant. They confirmed the presence of a line of continuity and sameness between his present struggle and his struggles of 1825, that is, whether or not he would muster the ability to trust his world as he trusted himself and, more than that, to feel intimately connected with it, with America (not just Boston and the northeast), but with his homeland. In this chapter, therefore, the salient episodes and themes of Emerson's life which led up to Christmas Day, 1832 will be depicted. On that day he departed for Europe and England after resigning from Second Church. Yet to come will be a study of the trip

itself and Emerson's meeting of Thomas Carlyle. The meeting with Carlyle
was the taking-off point of Emerson's return home, when he entered the
period of 1834-38, the time of his final and most expansive professional
formation.

If anticipation of marriage in 1829 was a major factor which pressed
Emerson into accepting the invitation from Second Church without "sanguine
confidence" in his ability to bear up to the job, then the termination
of his marriage may have occurred to him as one reason, at least, for
leaving the ministry, for going beyond that particular vocation. This
is not to suggest he deliberately planned to bring an end to his marriage
in order to leave the church. Some less than conscious sort of connection
between the death of Ellen (that is, loss of his "reprieve") and coming
to grips with his suppressed vocational crisis appeared to come into
play during the time at hand, 1829-31. For example, Emerson realized
when they were engaged she would not live much longer. Her bleeding
attacks were worse than his own tubercular symptoms. Moreover, years
earlier when he noticed his symptoms he thought he would die soon thereafter. Ellen's condition, thus, forced the couple into something of an
unconventional marital arrangement from the outset, to say the least.
Termination of this peculiar marriage might very well have entailed
termination of Emerson's conventional ministry. One cannot be sure
whether Emerson was aware of this possibility. However, one cannot rule
out the possibility, since the death of his wife seems to have pulled out
all the stops on his rush toward the lecture platform after 1833. Therefore, during the marriage itself the emotional quality of reprieve begat
its opposite emotional valence, condemnation. No doubt, because he
usually had succeeded doing so before, he searched his soul for a way

out of marriage now as well

As a general rule the psychologist is alerted to excessive depictions of love, for they often mask a grim taint of unconscious hostility, perhaps even hatred. Several Emerson scholars have pointed in this direction by suggesting that the Emerson-Tucker marriage was a most unusual and romantic one indeed, if only for the fact that each partner probably knew that the marital fruits of children and a lengthy future together were beyond their reach, let alone the whole matter of rigorous sexual intimacy.[1] Ellen's constantly failing health prevented all reasonable thought of bearing and raising children. Caring for her health in the face of tuberculosis filled not only her full attention, but also the attention of her husband. That their brief marriage was even consummated sexually is at least questionable. As a psychoanalyst might teach, such a relationship would be fraught with sexual repression and, as a result, would likely evidence unconscious hostility. Certainly this tenor resembled the texture of Victorian times, but that those times seemed particularly accentuated in the Emerson-Tucker relationship is unquestionable. Therefore, it is on this conflicted emotional back-drop that their marriage can be scrutinized.

A lot of the facts lend credence to the potent existence of such a

---

[1]See Henry Pommer, Emerson's First Marriage (Carbondale, Ill.: Southern Illinois University Press, 1967), pp. 19-20; Rusk, The Life of Ralph Waldo Emerson, pp. 134-35. Also, about a year after Ellen's death Emerson reported in his journal that he "visited Ellen's tomb and opened the coffin"; but it is unclear whether he actually did this or dreamed of having done so. In playing upon the theme of immortality, the reference indicates how "other-worldly" Emerson regarded the relationship. For the reference to opening the coffin and to a dream which paralleled the report about the same action, see Emerson, JMN, 4: 7; and Emerson, JMN, 3: 226.

back-drop. On the one hand, Ellen was a joy to Emerson since she took
his mind off his parish work. On the other hand, Ellen was an obstacle
and a bother in that she required not only financial support, but also
constant attention to her ever-worsening case of tuberculosis. Her illness, in effect, became the dominant preoccupation which they shared during
marriage. After two visits together during their engagement (during
January, 1829 and June, 1829), for example, Ellen was set upon by attacks
of worsened tubercular symptoms. Once, during July, 1829, she told Emerson
she thought herself not strong enough to see him again.[1] Her third and
last major attack came after she had been relaxing with her sister in
Philadelphia during June of 1830. Then Emerson had retrieved her, and
they went back to Boston, continuing housekeeping for about one month until
Ellen endured another attack in August. The closer Ellen and Emerson
became, geographically and emotionally, the greater the jeopardy in which
Ellen's life was placed. That Emerson persisted in desiring increased
intimacy with his wife was, of course, normal and natural for a husband to
do. However, the logical eventuality of intimacy of any continued sort
was the worsening of Ellen's condition and even her death. This fact
ushered in the emotional quality of isolation. Indeed, the irony of
Emerson's "one first love" for Ellen Tucker was that his desire to be
intimate with her veiled a deeper propensity to be isolated from her,
perhaps for the purpose of abandoning the pulpit she made palpable. The
structure of the marriage, therefore, required Ellen's physical demise.

---

[1]See Edith W. Gregg, ed., One First Love: The Letters of Ellen
Louisa Tucker to Ralph Waldo Emerson (Cambridge: The Belknap Press of
of the Harvard University Press, 1962), pp. 72, 76-77.

Only when she died was Emerson's deep emotional isolation poised and made ready for larger, cultural purposes. Emerson's isolation from Ellen was a prelude to his expression of national intimacy as a lecturer and seer to the American people.

By precipitating his resignation from the ministry and his subsequent journey abroad, Ellen's death opened the way for Emerson's active realization of charismatic authority fitting of a national leader. Yet these occurrences were not dissimilar to others from his earlier life. Being a husband resembled his trip and feelings in St. Augustine, Florida. There he was bored rolling an orange down the beach with a stick, wondering if ever he would find that special hour in one's destiny when he would find a proper "vent" for his "gift" of visionary eloquence. The structure of the period of 1826-29 in which that journey occurred kept him isolated from New England. He was in the South. Now, his marriage was poised and readied to carry that same structure to a new, broader plateau. If marital intimacy meant vocational isolation from the possibility of a career in a line of work other than the Unitarian ministry, then Emerson's marital isolation after his wife's death of 8 February 1821 turned the tables. Marital isolation was a pretext for vocational fulfillment. He extricated himself from his charge at Second Church, traveled abroad, and returned home to America. Thus, he began finding fulfillment in lecturing insofar as he felt intimately engaged in forging a distinctive American identity in terms of a national homeland. One recalls Emerson abided in assuming charge of his own family, his own home during 1828. Therefore, Emerson's wife was the "thumb in the dike" of his revolution of vocational identity. When that thumb was pulled out, flood waters of renewal washed away the past. At least, Emerson would report feeling re-born, symbolizing his resolution of unconscious conflict by embarking across ocean waters to Europe.

However, things were not as clearly portrayed as all this in the measured reflective life of the young minister during 1829-31, during the time of his year-and-a-half long marriage to Ellen. Nonetheless, it is possible to sort out most of the facts of those years and thereby lend credance to the plausibility of such a psychological interpretation. At least, insofar as it can point to distinct ways in which Emerson betrayed an emotional ambivalence about his marriage. Generally, this is done by way of understanding the third circle of play as the doorway to personal expansion, that is, from diminishment (i.e., the meaning of 1811-24), to play (i.e., the meaning of 1825-33), and to expansion (i.e., the meaning of 1834-38). One will conclude depicting the biographical cluster of events at hand by tracing three courses which Emerson's ambivalence appeared to take. Thus, the degree to which Emerson's joyful relationship with Ellen veiled his deeper ambivalence can be recognized first in his tactic of multiplying idealizations of their love; second, in the subtle way he identified with and responded to Ellen and his brother Edward; and, third, in the role played by Dr. Jackson in the life of the whole family during late 1830 and early 1831, and Emerson's regard of the physician's role. Generally, these three foci suggest Emerson's marital ambivalence was one of marital acquiescence, a failure to take decisive action when it was most called for by the physical condition of his wife.

Characteristic of Emerson's idealizing propensity was the public proclamation that "it was not the body but the spiritual properties that we loved."[1] The sermon in which this line was written on 21 December, 1828 continued, "The affections . . tended to expect perfection in the loved person, and from seeking perfection in the human friend were led to seek it in God."[2] Three days later he wrote telling William of his trip to the "dangerous neighborhood," where he was "as happy as it is safe in life to be," namely, New Concord, New Hampshire.[3] During the middle of January, 1829 Ellen became quite ill, according to Emerson's letter of 28 January, 1829 to William, "with that dangerous complaint which so often attacks the fairest in our stern climate."[4] Surprisingly, however, he quickly dismissed her illness as well as his worries over it and went on to talk about his "beautiful friend" who had "very elegant manners" and who knew the "difference between good poetry and bad."[5] We will note shortly how Ellen was thought of as a close approximation to Emerson's "ideal friend," whom he had sought during January of 1828 and would find after 1833 in the likes of "Representative Men" such as Luther, Plato, George Fox, and so forth--all of whom he idealized in his essays about each.

Emerson's lack of sustained worry over his fiancee's health is especially striking when it is remembered that it was his own very slight stricture in the chest which impelled the young preacher to seek comfort in the South just three years before. That Ellen's case of tuberculosis was much more serious than his stricture had been was obvious: unlike Emerson, Ellen continually "raised blood."[6] Though she would be unable

---

[1]Rusk, The Life of Ralph Waldo Emerson, pp. 133-34.

[2]Ibid.   [3]Emerson, Letters, 1: 256.

[4]Ibid., p. 259.   [5]Ibid.   [6]Ibid.

to muster the strength necessary to attend his ordination ceremony in March, he implied in his letter to William he fully expected that his "queen of Sheba" would be there.[1]

Therefore, from the beginning of his engagement, Emerson idealized his relationship with Ellen, and it smacked of a tenor similar to that of his relationship with Martin Gay. Ellen also was a similar an object of Emerson's vision. This form of idealizing was expressed best in about twelve love poems written during the time of their life together, during that time biographer Henry Pommer referred to as "this halcyon period."[2] Two examples should suffice to suggest the point about vision, that Emerson, as he had done in 1820-22, discovered emotional intimacy with Ellen insofar as he reacted visually to her. One of his love poems was called, for example, "Thine Eyes Still Shine":

> Thine eyes still shined for me, though far
> > I lonely roved the land or sea:
> As I behold yon evening star,
> > Which yet beholds not me.
>
> This morn I climbed the misty hill
> > And roamed the pastures through;
> How danced thy form before my path
> > Amidst the deep-eyed dew!
>
> When the redbird spread his sable wing,
> > And showed his side of flame;
> When the rosebud ripened to the rose,
> > In both I read thy name.[3]

Emerson not only saw Ellen in this accentuated manner, but also thought she bestowed efficacious radiances upon him. Perhaps with Charles' complaints in mind, namely, that Emerson was too wrapped-up in Ellen, the young poet

---

[1]Ibid.

[2]Pommer, Emerson's First Marriage, p. 33.

[3]Ralph Waldo Emerson, Works, 21 Vols., 9 (Boston: Centenary Edition 1903-1904): 99.

wrote, "Initial, Daemonic, and Celestial Love":

> The maid, abolishing the past,
> With lotus wine obliterates
> Dear memory's stone-incarved traits,
> And, by herself, supplants alone
> Friends year by year more inly known.
> When her calm eyes opened bright,
> All else grew foreign in their light.
> It was ever the self-same tale,
> The first experience will not fail;
> Only two in the garden walked,
> And with snake and seraph talked.[1]

Love poetry is one thing, friendship another. This, however, was also depicted in the "bright lights" which lit up Emerson's pantheon of great colleagues.

When he had written on 1 January, 1828 to Charles about his need of a fit friend, Emerson suggested he quarreled with his "race which will not give me what I want, either in the shape of man or woman."[2] In the next sentence to Charles he referred to a book from which he was drawing the allusion, "to ride my ray . . . in this quest" for a friend "with more diligence."[3] In parentheses he asked his brother, "you have read Tucker's vision," and referred to Abraham Tucker's The Light of Nature Pursued (1768), which had been recommended to him by President Kirkland of Harvard.[4] Emerson pursued Ellen, and in this new friend, also a Tucker, he saw light to which his poems would soon testify. The allusion of "Tucker's ray" would be used again on 20 May, 1829 in a letter to William in which Emerson would request a visit from this "New York Emerson."[5] Several months after her death he thought of Ellen in a way familiar to his deepest yearnings: "I sit alone from month to month filled with a

---

[1] Ibid., 9: 109-10.   [2] Emerson, Letters, 1: 225.

[3] Ibid.   [4] Ibid.   [5] Ibid., p. 271.

deep desire to exchange thoughts with a friend who does not appear--yet shall I find or _refind_ that friend?"[1] While in Rome early during his third journey during 1833 he lingered in bereavement, trying to retrieve his lost wife. He came to the conclusion that to realize his "ideal companion" was "never to dawn upon me like a sun-burst. . . . Yet," he assured himself, "I saw Ellen at once in all her beauty and she never disappointed me except in her death."[2] Eight years after she died, in 1839, Emerson, though married for a second time for four years, still idealized Ellen as a "great friend": He wrote that she "was never alone. I could not imagine her poor and solitary. She was like a tree in flower, so much soft, budding, and informing beauty was society for itself, and she taught the eyes that beheld her, why Beauty was ever painted with loves and graces attending her steps."[3] Emerson though, was alone.

Between January 30th and the middle of September of 1835, Emerson's journal entries paid three important tributes to Ellen. He wrote, first, that he had had visions of "Ellen's beauty and love and life"; and, second, "I love Ellen, and love her with an affection that would ask nothing but its indulgence to make me blessed"; and "I know no truer poetry in modern verse than Scott's line, 'And Sun himself in Ellen's eyes.'"[4] What makes these tributes all the more into nostalgic idealizations was the fact, first, that he wrote the second one just seven weeks after his engagement to Lidian Jackson in 1835 and, second, that he made no significant reference or allusion in his journals to Lidian, whom he

---

[1]Emerson, _JMN_, 3: 272.   [2]Emerson, _Letters_, 1: 376.

[3]Emerson, _JMN_, 7: 168.

[4]Ibid., 4: 263; Ibid., 5: 9, 85.

married on 14 September, 1835, the same year as that when he made new
entries about Ellen. Emerson no longer needed the old intimacy with
Ellen in 1834. Then he found lecturing on Milton, Fox, et al. to be an
acquaintance with the "friends" he long sought. However, Emerson evidently
had not worked-through the crisis he experienced as his relationship
with Ellen, perhaps the most acute one of the events of 1825-33. He
hearkened back to his memories of her for psychological reasons. Namely,
he remembered Ellen insofar as she suggested an emotional crisis of
intimacy versus isolation. This crisis was directly connected to the
geographical pattern of Emerson's lecture tours, of the lecturer's character,
"expansion within diminishment." In short, memories of Ellen heightened
Emerson's sense of the third circle of his play, the specifically American
parameter of his telescopic faith.

Besides idealizing his love for Ellen, Emerson's ambivalence was
contained as well in the subtle likeness and inherent differences he
expressed in regard to "sick Edward" and in regard to "sick Ellen," from
January of 1829 to February of 1831. Edward recovered to a reasonable
degree from his insanity in 1828, but he was plagued soon afterward by
tuberculosis. Ellen was stricken from the outset by the disease. The
way Emerson cared for each of these two sick family members was identical.
But one lived and the other died. Emerson's care would have killed both
had one not taken matters into his own hands. Edward was taken sick
with tuberculosis in New York City late in 1830. Ellen's health was
even worse at that time. Emerson, along with his mother, sought to have
both in Boston. In fact, at one point during November, 1830 he wanted
Edward to return home to Boston so he could be cared for and nursed to

health by their mother <u>and Ellen</u>![1] When this offer failed to attract
Edward home to Boston, Emerson was quick to say that travel to St. Croix
(where Edward said he might like to go instead of going to Boston) was
very expensive, perhaps prohibitively so.[2] That both Emerson and his
mother thought Ellen so healthy in contrast to Edward when, in fact,
the opposite was the case, since Ellen would be dead from her illness
in less than two months, was suspicious at least. Emerson had always
been his mother's favorite son since the death of her husband.[3] Now
she took steps to see to it that she and her son would join leagues to
bring Edward to <u>their</u> senses, if, as they assumed, not to his own.

When Ruth Emerson took the radical step of journeying to New York
City in order to retrieve Edward away from William, the "New York Emerson,"
and to return him to the household of the "Boston Emersons" late during
1830, she may have been seeking additional favorites. Nonetheless,
Emerson himself seemed to think the expectations placed on Ellen in regard
to Edward were appropriate, and saw nothing unusual in his mother's last-
ditch efforts to prevent Edward from sailing to St. Croix. While Edward
sought to flee from the suffocating grip of the tightly-knitted family
of Boston, Ellen could do little to do likewise. She was held tightly
and, it will be suggested in a while, she knew it. To be a family member
in the Boston household meant her imminent death. Edward would live for
three more years. But Ellen would die shortly after Edward's departure
southward to St. Croix. Somewhat symbolically, however, Emerson himself
would live after Ellen's death. Then he would realize he had paid whatever

---

[1]Emerson, <u>Letters</u>, 1: 310.   [2]Ibid., p. 311.

[3]Rusk, <u>The Life of Ralph Waldo Emerson</u>, p. 61.

debt he owed to the Emersons, especially to his mother, and was then free.

It is important to keep the full texture of Emerson's configuration of Edward and Ellen in mind as we proceed further. In addition, it is necessary to become aware of a third and most striking focus of Emerson's ambivalence toward Ellen and toward their marriage. This concerns the role played by the physician who watched-over Edward as the young man went gradually insane during 1828. Dr. Jackson was Charles' friend, the trainer of Lydian Jackson's brother later on, and the Emersons' family physician. Certainly the configuration of Edward and Ellen cast light on how Emerson regarded each of them. By focusing on the part played by Dr. Jackson in the decision to keep Ellen at home in Boston, and the part he played in the family's attempts to cajole Edward home, the plight and eventual solution of Emerson and his mother falls even more clearly before the eye of understanding. Dr. Jackson was no relation to Lydia Jackson, Emerson's second wife. However, he was no less significant than the two "Tuckers"--Ellen and the author of the book on light. Dr. Jackson's "vision" would lead to Emerson's availability to Lydia even as Dr. Jackson's "ray" led Emerson to Ellen. The context into which Jackson was called was one of an extended family in which two persons were very ill, though at some distance from each other. The family must have faced the question of what to do with each ailing member, and how best to do it. Thus, a decision-maker or authority figure was needed. This fact brought to the surface of family life the use of a most revealing precedent of care.

One has seen how Emerson gradually assumed a fairly dominant role in the Emerson family's household during 1828: He was earning enough money at the time to pay daily household bills as well as those of Bulkeley,

William, and Edward, and to support Charles partially as his youngest brother was just beginning to teach school in Boston. Also, Emerson probably was partly proud and partly angry over the fact that he alone was taking-up the family's inherited ministerial heritage. If he was, therefore and in effect, the head of the household, then Dr. Jackson was its unheeded medical expert. At least, he was heeded when Emerson foresaw no hitches of his own down the road of the doctor's advise, hitches which might thwart his growing sense of success in the Unitarian ministry.

Recall how Emerson acquiesced during June of 1828 when Edward was cared for by Dr. Jackson. Then Emerson was content to watch the "doctor's dominion" shrink back into an "advisory council," as Edward bordered on the breakdown that landed him in the Charlestown Asylum. Once in the Asylum, Edward was treated by other doctors who lived closer to McLean's than did Jackson, and Edward was discharged in reasonably good condition in November, 1828. The point is that Dr. Jackson, in effect, was regarded by Emerson as merely incidental to Edward's restoration. Only when a middle course was found, a course which promised Edward his health without going to extremes which might upset the household irreparably which Jackson suggested (Edward, he advised, should not touch a book "for a year") did Edward, in fact, recover. A short stay in the Asylum seemed a less stringent measure. Moreover, the antidote was not put forth originally by Jackson but by the Emerson family itself, Ruth Emerson in particular.[1] As the action proceeded, evidence indicates Emerson was most influenced not by the family's physician but by his mother. Though he thought of

---

[1] See Emerson, Letters, 1: 236.

himself as a success during 1829-31 and as the head of the household,
when the chips were down, he tended more to acquiesce, allowing his
mother's will to preside over such family concerns. Incidentally, he
had done the same sort of thing as a school-keeper during 1821-24 when
disciplining of his pupils was called for. Therefore, under the suasion
of his mother, Emerson would reject the welfare of his wife as the year
of 1830 gave birth to that of 1831.

These preliminary notes can be substantiated biographically. Though
the focus on the Edward-Ellen configuration and the focus on Dr. Jackson
come into clear view if one recognizes Emerson's tendency to idealize
his love for Ellen, the focus on such idealization is less important
here. However, as the record will show, the tenor of Emerson's own understanding of Ellen, Edward, and Jackson is itself an idealization. What
is really at stake not in the short run, but in the long run, was the
question of vocation. Would the Unitarian ministry hold, or, if not,
how would Emerson extricate himself from it and, finally, what would
follow from this episode? Emerson could not see very far down the line.
His inability to portend cast his portrayal of the episode of 1829-33 in
a form which was no less ideal than the form of his poeticizing about
Ellen. So now one returns to the record in order the follow these comments
out.

Ellen's first attack occurred just before 30 January, 1829, when
Emerson accepted the call to Second Church. He wrote to William two
days before that date and said he had "abstained in much hesitation and
perplexity" in giving Second Church an answer, "thinking that perhaps
the doctors might tell Ellen she ought to go away; and then . . ."[1]

---

[1]Ibid., p. 259.

The Kent family had moved to Boston for the winter and that made it easy for Emerson to regard their family as a part of his own or, at least, he could care for Ellen as if his family, not hers, was responsible for her health. Beza Tucker, Ellen's father, died in 1820. Not long afterwards his widow married Colonel Kent. The Colonel was Ellen's stepfather and leader of the New Concord Congregation. Evidently, Emerson's inclination held sway, for he did not consult "the doctors," but he "talked with Dr. Jackson" instead.[1] As a result he came to believe that on the following Sunday he would say "Yes" to the offer of a job.[2] William was eager to have Emerson in New York City for a spring visit, just as he would be enthused early in May, 1830. But his younger brother would place matters of profession and marriage first on both occasions. Late in January, 1829 Emerson was involved in juggling pulpit exchanges and anticipating ordination. These matters, he believed, would prevent him from going to New York City. Ellen was ailing but Edward appeared "more firmly established" than anyone could believe possible a year ago.[3] When he went to Second Church, then, caring for Ellen in Boston was paramount, and his care was intricately bound to getting his feet on the ground in the ministry.

The months from February through June were filled, on the one hand, by Ellen's mending after her first attack of raised blood and, on the other hand, by Emerson's professional first steps. March 11, 1829 was "execution day," but he quelled the thought by suggesting to William that Ellen was more important and that "Twould take more time than I can spare to tell how excellent a piece of work she is."[4] Later he referred

---

[1]Ibid.   [2]Ibid.   [3]Ibid.   [4]Ibid., p. 264.

to Ellen when he asked William, "Hast no curiosity to see the Beauty of the world the diamond idea that illuminates my retirements and rejoices my intercourse or if that is poor English makes my society."[1] Parish visitations were examples of social failure in the fiber of the new minister's resolve at best. They "cannot be numbered or ended."[2] Charles even referred to his bumbling brother as a "pelican in the wilderness."[3] Nonetheless, Emerson believed he was "labouring abundantly" in his new vocation but felt some drawbacks in that he had so little time "for study of books" and even less "for writing of letters."[4] It was due to winter's end and the fact of the return of the Kent family to New Hampshire during early May that he hardly expected to preach "at home" more than "half the time" for a "long while to come."[5] A "forlorn bachelor" soon journeyed to Concord, N.H. for the last part of May and early June in order to be with Ellen, hence, removed from Boston and getting a reprieve, as it were, from duties at Second Church.[6]

On 18 June, 1829, however, the strain on Ellen was great and she was "taken sick in the old way" with a second attack of bleeding.[7] Though the amount of blood raised this time was not as great as the amount raised during her first attack in January, 1829, the family in Concord, N.H. was hardly optimistic. Again Emerson took control of the situation before he returned to Boston at the end of June. Strangely put, he felt that Ellen's attack had "wonderfully changed" his visit--"I was perfectly happy now I am watching and fearing and pitied."[8] This remark

---

[1] Ibid., p. 265.   [2] Ibid., p. 269.   [3] Ibid.

[4] Ibid., p. 270.   [5] Ibid.   [6] Ibid.

[7] Ibid., p. 271.   [8] Ibid., p. 272.

would resonate with his remark on the day of Ellen's death. Then he would be "strangely happy."[1] Because there were no physicians in New Hampshire "in whom any kind of confidence can be reposed," he wrote on 19 June, 1829 he would "write today to Dr. Jackson . . . "[2] Despite his efforts, he seemed to invite one to think that he and his fiancee were well-aware that their imminent union would be short-lived: He wrote "Ellen has an angel's soul" and though she was "very skeptical about the length of her own life," she had a faith "as clear and strong as those do that have Gods kingdom within them."[3] One soon acquires a sense that Emerson thought God's kingdom was a place and a time in which to effect the "lounging capricious unfettered mode of life" he banked upon so heavily on 3 April, 1828. For, the moment "the queen of me gets relief," Emerson promised in mid-June, "her spirits return also and she is playful and social as ever" even though her conversation was "imprisoned in whispers."[4] He saw Ellen in this condition in New Hampshire intermittently from May through September, 1829, and he returned as well to Boston intermittently in order to attend to his duties at Second Church. He walked a tightrope between conflicting duties. By 1 July, 1829 he had become the senior minister at Second Church. Though he considered the neglect of his charge troublesome, he, nonetheless, considered giving all of his attention to his sick wife-to-be a "duty of impossible ommission."[5] He assured his family and friends of the congregation that he did not expect to be absent from Second Church in the fall, and when fall arrived neglect of his post lessened.[6]

But Emerson soon acceded to necessity. During August, 1829 Ellen

---

[1]Ibid., p. 318.   [2]Ibid., p. 272.   [3]Ibid.
[4]Ibid.   [5]Ibid., p. 279.   [6]Ibid., p. 278.

and Emerson set out on the first of four short trips for the benefit of her health. The significance of these trips to aid Ellen's health and spirits rested in the striking overlap they have with Emerson's own more widely spaced journeys. Emerson's trips were lending themselves as the structure in terms of which he was experiencing the growth of his wisdom during the 1825-33. But, as one shall see, the irony of the four small journeys was that they were too small. That is, while Ellen, Emerson, and the families were hardly optimistic about Ellen's prospects, all pitched-in to see to it that the short trips were pleasant affairs. If it was evident that the "major surgery" of a trip to a southern island was the key to Ellen's health, then the "bandaids" of small jaunts into the countryside added a torturous, almost victim-like under-current to her immiment demise. During August, 1829 Emerson, Ellen, and Mrs. Kent traveled "over 200 miles" in a chaise to a Shaker village called Meredith and to the environs of Conway, N.H.[1] Casting Ellen's renewal in visual terms, he described her to William during the trip as "the queen of me" who promised William "full leave to look at her--a sight I wd. go much farther to see." "Strange," he thought, "if you will not leap at the privelege."[2] Later in life, just as he divested himself of Martin Gay so too he would tend to play-down Ellen though with less success: "A highly endowed man with good intellect and good conscience is a Man-woman and does not so much need the complement of a woman to his being as another . . . Hermaphrodite is. . . the symbol of the finished soul."[3] The message conveyed appeared as a psychological statement of the resolution

---

[1]Ibid., p. 281.   [2]Ibid., p. 179.

[3]Forbes-Emerson Edition of the Journals, 4: 210, 378; Emerson, JMN, 3: 193.

of inner conflict. He would no longer need that particular female embodiment
of his alter-ego for his ego was mastering the situation all by itself.

But to work hard at separating himself from Ellen later in life was
a mark of just how very close to her he thought himself to be during
1829. During September, 1829 they journeyed out again, this time to
western Massachusetts and, perhaps, necessity was not acceded to as much
as a desire for fun. The couple kept a rhyming journal and wrote love
poems to each other. The results--"we read and scribble--but not sermons"
and "nursing a lame knee"--suggest Emerson was ready to settle down, at
least, to repair his sermonizing skill as well as his knee.[1] Marriage
seemed the natural course.

The wedding occurred on 30 September, 1829 in New Hampshire. Again,
that was at arm's length from commitments in Boston. Along with Ellen's
sisters, Margaret and Paulina, the couple returned to Boston and settled
into the Keating's boarding house on Chardon Street, where Ruth Emerson
was anxious to take them into her established household. The fact of
residence was perhaps portentious in light of the decision which would
soon carry Ellen to her grave. Meanwhile, however, a chronic inflammation
of his knee flared up at this particular point in time, causing Emerson
to wonder, "cannot a married man write and say that tis excellant to double
his being?"[2] Hermaphroditic he was not. But, then, he had to cope with
another person, a wife, not with "the symbol of the unfinished soul."
Lame, and unable to walk without a cane, Emerson reported, "Ellen has
been very well ever since she has been in town" but, as far as he was

---

[1] Emerson, Letters, 1: 284.

[2] Ibid., pp. 386, 385.

concerned, his major problem was his work, which was hardly made any easier by his unusual marriage and its dowry of ills.[1] "Sundays," he exclaimed, "I preach, _sitting_."[2] Literally, one may question even whether Emerson could "stand up" to the Unitarian pulpit, baring all implications brought about by the state of Ellen's health. "Woe is me my knee weak are."[3] One can say with some good psychological sense that when he thought of the Unitarian pulpit Emerson could not "stand" it.

An interesting thing happened during the first part of December, 1829, after about two months of marriage, which sheds some light on the psychological meaning Emerson used as a lens through which to view physicians in general. On 1 December, 1829 he reported his "old knee" was about the same; he was still "prisoner" of chairs and chaises.[4] However, he described he was expecting the visit that evening of "the quack doctor Hewitt," a forerunner of the modern chiropracter, having "quitted Drs. Warren and Ware."[5] Seven days later Emerson was happy to report he was now "walking about with great firmness," saying he was grateful to Dr. Hewitt, "who cured me in two hours."[6] The point here is merely a suggestive question: Does Emerson's estimate of Hewitt's quackery imply that Emerson viewed one who was not presumably a "quack," for example, Dr. Jackson, to be, perhaps, quite ineffective as a curer? Emerson seemed relieved and surprised as well by Hewitt. By implication he embraced Dr. Jackson with a different affection. Outside of some minor complaints about his foot afterwards-- due to "being put back to its old duties of carrying half the body"--

---

[1] Ibid., p. 285.   [2] Ibid.   [3] Ibid., p. 286.

[4] Ibid., p. 287.   [5] Ibid.   [6] Ibid., p. 288.

he "walked miles a day."[1] And, too, outside of some minor complaints,
he plodded along in the Unitarian ministry.

By the end of 1829 Edward felt well enough to join William in New
York City as his brother's legal assistant. Emerson was concerned above
all else about their financial and moral well-being: "As I hear nothing
of repentance much less of reformation from you N.Y. reprobates," he
wrote to them on 8 December, 1829, "I am to learn like mother to call
evil good . . . when the latest day of a windy purse comes send me word
and I will summon my forces."[2] Once of the most telling gestures made
by Emerson which betrayed how he felt about his two brothers was to
"enclose in this or some neighbor letter" Edward's key to the house on
Chardon Street.[3] At one level of analysis, Edward and William were away
from home geographically. At a deeper level, however, they were further
alienated from the "Boston Emersons" insofar as each, as well as Charles,
who was beginning a legal career of his own in Boston by now, had forsaken
the family's ministerial heritage. In relation to his society, that is,
to his brothers, Emerson withstood the longest under family pressure,
that is, pressure from his mother and aunt and now, in a subtle way, from
Ellen to pursue the Unitarian ministry. His brothers had wiggled out from
under such a pall. But because he actually held out the longest, Emerson's
propensity for suffering helped him reach the moral benefit of greater
national prominence later, after he left Second Church, than his brothers
were every to enjoy. Waiting was part of the sacrifice he would pay. In
this sense, then, Emerson was a "Boston Brahmin" par excellance. Though

---

[1]Ibid., p. 289.   [2]Ibid.

[3]Ibid., p. 288.

he may have assumed himself to have been a morally rich man because he suffered so in the ministry, he assumed he was rich by other standards as well: "But richer I surely am by Ellen," he concluded to William in December, "if she bro't no penny."[1] Indeed, Emerson would pay the price of being a rich man. Yet, that price would be his key to the homeland.

Emerson, Ellen, and her sisters took a third small journey to Philadelphia beginning in March, 1830. He returned to Boston alone during the middle of April, Ellen and her sisters following a month later when Emerson returned to Philadelphia in order to escort them home to Chardon Street. While he was away, Charles was put in charge of arranging to fill Emerson's pulpit with suitable preachers--quite a responsibility to foist upon the young lawyer![2] Ellen had grown weaker and all thought a southern trip, if only to Philadelphia, would speed the coming of her spring. Enroute to the city of brotherly love she made light of her condition and "she insisted," wrote Emerson, on pushing on despite being troubled persistently by her "red wheezers" and "considerable fulness in the head."[3] An interesting bind entangled Emerson while he was in Philadelphia seeing to Ellen's condition. It had three aspects: it concerned pulpit arrangements at Second Church which Emerson had mismanaged due to the greater attention he was giving to Ellen, Charles' helplessness to rectify the situation and, perhaps, some unconscious motivation on Emerson's part. In short, the Philadelphia episdoe was a blatant assertion of Emerson's dislike of the ministry with which, like his own bout with tuberculosis several years earlier, he was now "saddled."

Emerson had stayed, it seems, in Philadelphia two days longer than

---

[1]Ibid., p. 289.   [2]See ibid., p. 295.

[3]Ibid., pp. 295-96.

he had planned late in March, "in the expectation that Mr. Furness would decide to exchange" pulpits with him for two or three Sundays "as he had partly proposed."[1] Evidently Furness told Charles the exchange would not be possible. Though Furness had given thought to such a proposal, Emerson had understood that proposal to have implied set commitments. Furness was hardly committed to the exchange: Now "that hope is gone," Emerson concluded on 25 March, 1830, he realized the problem he had brought upon himself. He could not leave Philadelphia "soon enough to get home next Sunday" (the first Sunday he had believed Furness would supply his pulpit) and so he decided to stay "till the latest opportunities offer for returning," a week and a half away.[2] Had he decided to travel by land, he probably could have arrived home in time to have missed only a single Sunday's obligations. But because he waited "till the latest opportunities" for sea passage, Charles was kept busy taking up the slack for his brother, minister-in-absence. Another factor must be weighed into Emerson's acquiescence on this matter of vocational duty. His "faery queen" was pretty well but he preferred to see her "a grain more robust" before he left for home.[3] But one gets the impression that another reason mixed into this concern for Ellen's strength prevailed to detain him in Philadelphia. He wrote, there were "no females in the family" where they were boarding "except the hostess and she does not sit at the dinner table."[4] However, three gentlemen, "respectable people," did; and Emerson himself was a grain more robust and, perhaps, jealous, than usual because, as he put it, "Madame promises that when I go away she will sit at the table."[5]   If Ellen represented a

---

[1]Ibid., p. 297.   [2]Ibid.   [3]Ibid.   [4]Ibid.

[5]Ibid.

reprieve for Emerson, then his mismanaged scheduling of pulpit exchanges
as well as his tinge of marital jealousy combined to form a unified thrust.
In effect, it kept him at a distance from Boston, from home, and from the
entire matter of vocation. That is, away from the ministry in its narrow
sense but, beneath it, propelled him toward the ministry in its broadest
sense. Moreover, his fear of the possibility of having a flirtatious wife,
dare say an unfaithful one, may very well have testified to the existence
of some dissatisfaction with the marital relationship. In any case, he
behaved quite paternalistically toward Ellen.

That he would be so lax in securing Furness' promise to fill his pulpit in Boston, while at the same time be so concerned to secure the Madame's
promises over a situation of much less magnitude, in Philadelphia, supplies
grounds for suggesting that Emerson was, at least, avoiding vocational
responsibility whether he was actually aware of it at the time or not.
In this sense, he was closing his eyes to his Unitarian commitment, much as
he had done during 1825 when blindness prevented him from reading Unitarian
theology. However, now his reprieve was not nature's beauty in Newton and
Chelmsford, but Ellen's condition, her worsened condition, in Philadelphia.
Incidentally, Philadelphia was the place where the "Spirit of 1776" took
its first significant embodiment in the American Constitution. We know
Emerson thought the Constitution second only to the New Testament. Ellen's
"constitution" itself was faltering: As the psychological form prevailed,
Emerson acted as if Ellen's worsening health was the key to his own home,
to his own health, to his own constitution, to America. All this is suggested on the geographical backdrop of being separated from New England
and from Boston proper. But now Emerson can be observed turning his "isolation" from these foci into an "intimacy" with an even wider focus, namely,
America. Ellen's death would facilitate extricating Emerson from ever again

embracing the Unitarian ministry as he first thought he might from 1825 to 1831.

Four months earlier, during late October, 1829, he had written, "Say with Plato--Do not I think things unsound because I am unsound? as the blind man complained the streets were dark."[1] Emerson's horizon was expanding insofar as he realized his soundness. At the same time his weight rose to the healthy level of 157 lbs. during August, 1830, Ellen suffered her third and last major attack of "raised blood." The events which transpired afterwards suggest that, like the blind man, Emerson was closing his eyes to the magnitude of Ellen's rapidly deteriorating condition. Soon she would be better equipped to answer her question, "Whether the Spirits in heaven look onward to their immortality as we on earth, or are absorbed in the present moment?" than he. Moreover, if he was moved to sense Ellen's worsening health as an outgrowth or projection of his own unsoundness, then that explains the fact that, while Ellen slipped gradually into her heavenly abode, he turned to wonder over knowing and trusting himself. "Immense significance," he wrote on 30 July, 1830, "of the precept Know Thyself."[2] Alexander and Bonoparte were "ridiculous" to conquer men while they were yet themselves "unconquered, unexplored, unknown" to themselves.[3] Knowledge gave rise to trust: "I would have a man trust himself," he wrote on 27 September, 1830, because the "meanest human soul" contains a "model of action" which is "greater than is realized by the greatest men."[4] Thus, Emerson's eyes opened as gradually as Ellen's eyes closed forever. As Kenneth Burke puts it, the "machinery of transcendence" was activated and

---

[1]Emerson, JMN, 3: 167.

[2]Ibid., p. 192.

[3]Ibid.

[4]Ibid., pp. 198-99, 200.

Emerson moved through the expansive sequence of "I, Eye, Ay."[1] Ellen's demise was becoming an affirmation of Emerson's rise to a new cultural awareness.

By mid-summer Emerson and his wife had returned from Philadelphia to Boston and into his mother's household once again. Ellen's most fateful time of crisis was then only weeks away. Sufficient evidence exists to suggest Emerson was already alerted to the possibility of Ellen's early death even before they had spent much time together. On 22 January, 1829 a letter was written by Charles Emerson to William in which he said he believed Ralph Waldo sensed Ellen was "too lovely to live long," and he added another impression to the effect that even if Ellen died "tomorrow" their brother would consider it a blessing to have loved her.[2] The family thought he loved her "too much." Other evidence yields a similar ambivalence which Emerson assumed as he entered into marriage, a marriage which was quite fitting in terms of his own long-term needs, one of which was his need to be more than just an average husband and an average man. Writing to Aunt Mary on 6 January, 1829 Emerson scanned his own "particular felicity" (his marital engagement), and he wondered as was mentioned before, "Can this hold?"[3] His worry and fear over a quick end to his relationship with Ellen due to her faltering health was held in check by the "frank acknowledgement" of "unbounded dependence" on Providence.[4] This dependence he proposed

---

[1] Kenneth Burke, "I, Eye, Ay--Emerson's Early Essay 'Nature': Thoughts on the Machinery of Transcendence," in M. Simon and T.H. Parsons eds., Transcendentalism and Its Legacy (Ann Arbor: University of Michigan Press, 1966), pp. 3-24.

[2] Emerson, Letters. 1: 259, footnote No. 3.

[3] Quoted in Cabot, A Memoir of Ralph Waldo Emerson, 1: 147.

[4] Ibid., p. 148.

as a particular sort of "antidote," as a "sort of protest against ...
Ahriman," thus, hearkening back to the meaning of the recovery of his eyesight
toward the end of 1825.[1] Then and now were times of life, not death, as the
visual correlate of light implied. Though he appeared joyful in his new
love, he was daunted by the nagging sense that his reprieve was associated
with his personal destiny, with his vocational crisis and, more over, that
this particular association was not all what he might have hoped it to be.
Indeed, thanking Oromasdes for the boon of marriage was hardly enough when
it was in Ahriman, evil and darkness, that he found his most resilient adversary, unabated in haunting the young preacher.

In one sense, therefore, as his intimacy with Ellen grew his isolation
from the Unitarian ministry grew in like manner. Such was the reprieve of
Emerson's marital joy. But his abiding isolation from any sort of vocation
which might lead to "greatness" accentuated the fact that in this particular
way marriage stood in the path he walked most. Such was the condemnation
of his marital bond. For the family expected no more out of him than to
live up to his father's unretrievable reputation. In this sense, just as
Edward had fled from the clutches of home at the end of 1820, so too Emerson
sensed a need to escape from his own entrapping circumstances. For Edward,
escape meant health. But for Emerson, the Unitarian ministry meant sickness. It is possible to suggest that Emerson followed the pattern established
by Edward, and he did so with the aid of a vicarious "death." That is, he
embarked on a symbolic voyage into the ministry in the broadest sense only
after his alter-ego, Ellen, died. Therefore, if Emerson "died" in a symbolic
sense by a vicarious involvement in Ellen's death, then he was able to reap

---

[1]Ibid.

the moral benefit assumed by the Brahmin elite to result from any physical suffering. His particular benefit was that Ellen's death allowed him to see himself as "born" again because he himself survived the grave, so to speak. This new birth of a symbolic nature removed Emerson from the Unitarian ministry and placed him on the broader path "to the Divinity." Weighing his ambivalence over all Ellen meant to him, he wrote on 17 January, 1829, "Will God forgive me my sins and aid me to deserve this gift of his mercy."[1] Indeed, the full range of implications of Emerson's marriage would press in on him, making loving his wife more difficult than he knew.

The last part of 1830 was a critically important time in the life of all the Emersons. This was when the interplay between Emerson, his mother, Ellen, Edward, and Dr. Jackson reached its telltale crescendo. On 11 August, 1830 Ellen underwent another bleeding attack. From 23 August to 4 September, 1830 Edward visited her along with the family of the "Boston Emersons," and he returned to New York City, to his own problem of consumption. Ellen's attack presented Emerson with a choice which would turn the tide of his vocational struggle over the ministry and, in a more long-range way, determine the "dark or bright dye" his later years would assume forever.

By the beginning of September Ellen had mended sufficiently enough to permit her and her husband to take a short trip--their fourth--to Lexington, Massachusetts. Then she proceeded alone to New Concord, New Hampshire. It was a venture filled with false promises if ever there was one. Emerson joined her two weeks later, preached in New Concord for the last time, and then returned with Ellen to Boston late in September carrying high hopes. The history of Emerson's many marital anxieties and changed plans might

---

[1]Emerson, JMN, 3: 149.

seem to be the record of well-oiled decision-making. However, appearances can be deceptive. On 6 September, 1830 Ellen had sent word to Emerson that she had arrived in New Concord two days before. Evidently her 11 August, 1830 attack had raised the possibility that a southern trip, one which went further than Philadelphia, might be best for her health. On the one hand, Emerson believed "she mends fast" in her hometown but, on the other hand, "we ponder many plans."[1] Ponder they did, but no more than that. Deliberate action that might best serve Ellen's health was not forthcoming.

Ellen weathered the excursion remarkably well, Emerson thought, and her spirits seemed lifted: "she inclines after all to stay at home this winter."[2] Moreover, Dr. Jackson, Emerson said, "leans to that opinion."[3] The doctor, who was in Boston at the time, had no way of knowing about Ellen's condition when she was in New Concord, except by means of her letter to her husband about her arrival there and her fast mending. One can take it from this that Emerson, at least, reported Ellen's optimism about her health to the doctor. Perhaps he was blinded by the facts related to her failing health. At any rate, the question can be raised about what happened within the Emerson family by early October, 1830 in regard to another southern trip. For on 4 October, 1830 Emerson painted a different picture, reporting that Ellen was "pretty well" and that they hoped "in a fortnight" to begin "housekeeping," and were currently busy buying "carpets and the like" for their home.[4] What led to this seemingly hasty decision (or lack of one) to shelve all realistic thoughts about another southern trip?

Ellen's excursion to New Concord and back undoubtedly played upon

---

[1]Emerson, Letters, 1: 307.   [2]Ibid.

[3]Ibid.   [4]Ibid., p. 310.

Emerson's thoughts about whether or not he and his wife should hazard another winter in New England. With cold, damp air fastly pouring over the coastal regions of New England, Boston in particular, and with the prospect of Ellen's consumption becoming worse, the entire Emerson family stepped onto centerstage and began to weigh the pro's and the con's of sending the young couple south, perhaps to Cuba, for possible benefit to Ellen's health. Prior to her trip Dr. Jackson had discouraged a voyage (the risks of winter sea travel being well known). But the point the family seemed to overlook for reasons that may begin to emerge soon, was that the physician said nothing to discourage southern travel by land.[1] In regard to this, the doctor's "dominion" shrank back "into any advisory council" and, perhaps, engendered a due share of tacit contempt within family ranks (emotional vestiges from Edward's mental collapse). Ellen's short and successful trip in Massachusetts and New Hampshire itself confirmed she could possibly endure such travel if the North Atlantic and its cold, damp atmosphere were avoided. However, Dr. Jackson confessed traveling itself was not the remedy Emerson and the rest of the family had thought it might be in Ellen's case. In her present condition, he believed, Ellen should not "migrate to Cuba or elsewhere unless she was prepared to stay for ten years."[2] Thus, the doctor's initial advise to the family was to the effect that only if the couple re-located themselves on a more-or-less permanent basis (a "permanent engagement") in some warmer, dryer climate, might the chances of Ellen's survival be reasonably increased, dare say, assured. The implication was that without going to that particular extreme the entire family would place Ellen's life in jeopardy if they

---

[1]Quoted by Pommer, Emerson's First Marriage, p. 43-- from an unpublished, private manuscript.

[2]Rusk, The Life of Ralph Waldo Emerson, p. 147.

insisted on a less certain hope, for example, if they decided another New England winter could be conquered. Clearly, Ellen was prepared to migrate to Cuba and to live there permanently. Emerson and the rest of his family balked emotionally.

Henry Pommer, a biographer of Emerson's first marriage, has put forth several hypotheses about why Dr. Jackson's advice discouraging a voyage in particular and travel in general was offered.[1] First, Jackson may have felt, Ellen really could survive a Boston winter; second, she was too weak to travel far; third, she was doomed in any case and might die happier if close to familiar places and persons. Pommer also believes, "because of Doctor Jackson's reputation," Ellen and Waldo "probably accepted the advice."[2] This, Pommer believes was emphasized because of the known hazards of sea travel, Waldo's professional responsibilities, and the pleasure of looking forward to their own home for the very first time.[3] As a biographical interpretation, this might suffice. However, when psychological suggestions are added to such a biographical interpretation the facts of the matter can be read in a different light.

It is difficult to dispute all Pommer puts forth about Dr. Jackson's advice if it can be presumed Emerson was wont to be decisive in following a doctor's advice in the first place. This was noted already in terms of Emerson's "care" of Edward during 1828 to be simply not the case. But, even so, if his own active decision was not to be forthcoming, that is, that Emerson would not choose even the hope of the "middle road," namely, relocating by land to a Southern state (if not Cuba) in order to benefit Ellen's health, then further scrutiny of his acquiescence is needed. As the record will

---

[1]Pommer, Emerson's First Marriage, pp. 43-44.

[2]Ibid., p. 44.   [3]Ibid.

show, reasons related to Emerson's profession, not reasons related to Ellen's condition and health, seem to have held sway. Pommer's conclusion as to why the Emersons remained in Boston is based upon what he believes a doctor might use as a criterion for deciding in such cases, namely, an assessment of the balance between Ellen's "strength" and her "weakness." And he would do this in light of the alternatives for curing her. However, one might be inclined to wonder, first, why the "middle road" alternative was not seized upon, that is, why it met with family silence and Emerson's acquiescence. Also, second, whether such distantiating, as a psychological strategy, could be confirmed by similar precedents. Already an affirmative answer to the second query has been suggested by noting Emerson's manner of relating to physicians in general. Answers to the first query emerge from noting some of the interrelationships within the whole Emerson family at this time, especially noting how those social relationships were oriented and directed by the subtle sway of maternal authority. It has been noted already that these relationships were presided over by-and-large by Ruth Emerson. If Emerson thought of his Aunty Mary as "Father Mum," then the logic of his personal style of life and general outlook implied Ruth Emerson was "Mother Mum." That is, if Aunt Mary was a father mum because she was an erratic letter-writer and an often silent mentor, then Ruth Emerson was a mother mum because she was a very predictable mother and mother-in-law. By contrast with Edward, Ellen would receive only "second-best" care from her mother-in-law.

Therefore, the doctor's initial advice fell on deaf ears or, at least, the Emerson family failed to catch the implication of the discouraged ocean voyage to Cuba. Emerson's own ambivalence about whether or not to travel southward, especially over the idea of re-locating himself permanently, career and all, reflected the general tenor of his brother's equally ambivalent concern over how to respond to an invalid in their midst, especially the wife of the promising young minister of Second Church. Thus, Charles, who was the only other Emerson son living under his mother's roof at the time, displayed this general tenor of ambivalence best by acting in what might be called an "antiphonical" manner in relation to Waldo, stating his doubt while his brother asserted hope. Quoting Charles' letter to William of 11 August, 1830, the editor of Emerson's letters reports Charles indicated Ellen's bleeding cast the family into "trouble and anxiety" mainly over "her husbands prospects" in the Unitarian ministry, that is, he thought his brother would carry through professional suicide, since "they will probably go off this Fall to Southern Latitudes."[1] The sound this sort of statement might have made had Emerson heard it would have been a counter to his intention, namely, to see to his wife's mending. Charles, like his mother, could not fail to see the vocational implications for Emerson in Ellen's deteriorating health and the necessity of a southern trip. Emerson, if given the benefit of the doubt, could not bring them into view as readily. Three days later Charles wrote that his brother seemed set on traveling south but, he added perfunctorily, even if Waldo thought so, he himself doubted whether any climate could save Ellen.[2]

Charles may have been stating what Emerson himself had within him but could not easily bring to the forefront of articulated considerations. Charles may have been stating what Emerson probably thought, what, in effect, they both knew their mother had on her mind. Namely, separation from the household meant disaster, virtual bodily and professional death. It has

---

[1] Emerson, Letters, 1: 307, footnote No. 71.

[2] Ibid.

already been shown how, when at her lowest financial ebb, Ruth Emerson under-
took and succeeded in sending William and Ralph Waldo to Harvard.[1] She
was not about to allow her son's professional life go down the drain. One
suspects Mrs. Emerson, believing Ellen could not be saved, could not ever
support Ralph's short-term absence, or the time it would take Ellen to die
in the South. Perhaps she felt he had already shirked his professional duty
enough for Ellen. In any case, bodily and professional "death," then, was
the unspoken sense of her son's travel in the past. It would lace together
the meaning of her own desperate trip to New York City during the up-coming
December.

The family was in general accord several years earlier when Emerson
decided to flee southward in order to relieve his own "stricture about
the chest." By comparison, his illness then was far less serious than
Ellen's was late in 1830. But during 1826-27 all realized he would eventually return home to Boston after his southern excursion. It was to be
merely a journey, not a permanent re-location. Also, during his bout with
those strictures about the chest he consulted not one, but several physicians,
but they could not diagnose his plight adequately. The point being that
he did not rely simply on the advice of one doctor alone but several when
he was sick. Then the family contented itself following his reports of
recovery in terms of his increased capacity to preach as he journeyed up
the Atlantic seaboard, that is, in terms not of his health alone but in
terms of his budding professional skill, preaching, for which reasonable
health was needed. All in all, the family saw Emerson's "professional
prospects" grow brighter and brighter insofar as he made his way to Boston,

[1]Rusk, The Life of Ralph Waldo Emerson, pp. 55, 63.

New England, that is, to home where he could learn to fill his father's shoes as a minister. Familial regards in terms of the equation between professional success and proximity to the Emerson household (over which "Mother Mum" presided) would be carried over and relied upon when Ruth Emerson would try to fetch home Edward when his health took a turn for the worse during December, 1830.

In any event, late in September, 1830 Dr. Jackson believed it would be better for Ellen and spouse to spend the winter "quietly keeping house like good and sensible people."[1] One can only assume that at that point in the course of her illness he felt the task to be done consisted in salvaging what little life remained in her frail body, especially since no serious discussion about re-locating in the South had taken place among family members, let alone between Emerson and his wife, both of whom continued wide-eyed with what would turn out to be false hopes.

Therefore, Emerson's specific ambivalence over saving his wife or making a career for himself tended to be regarded by the family as mutually exclusive alternatives. Moreover, family tension increased as a result of this struggle. This is indicated by the way in which Ellen soon was regarded once the choice of remaining in New England for the winter had grown less critical, if still existent at all, by October. No longer holding the option of re-locating in a warmer, dryer climate, the family seemed to respond to Ellen with either of two extremes, one response was quite premature and the other response was too late to do much good. On the one hand, the family regarded her to be healthy and whole and capable of being the active wife of their latest contribution to Boston's Brahmin elite. When the pace of

---

[1] Emerson, _Letters_, 1: 307, footnote No. 71.

such regard increased, so did the activity of the Rev. and Mrs. Ralph Waldo Emerson: They purchased a home of their own in Boston as well as a complete line of the latest in home furnishings, all this by the middle of October, 1830. Even more astonishing was the fact that Ellen started to make extensive preparations for entertaining the entire family, the Kents and the Emersons, on Thanksgiving Day. Generally, Ellen was taxed beyond her capacities by domestic life but she seems to have found some happiness in a somewhat normalized marital role: "Here I sit in my own little domicile," she wrote during that fall "and realize that I am Mrs. Emerson to the full for Betsy and Nancy and Martin (servants) must have their daily and nightly tasks allotted--and Mr. Such a one with his wife are in town and they must come to tea tomorrow--no cake--bless me how many eggs? how much sugar? . . ."1 When Edward reached his crisis in December, it was Ellen whom her husband volunteered to nurse him to health, if only he were to return home to Boston. In short, Ellen was not well but the family behaved toward her as if she were quite sound indeed.

The other extreme of familial regard and treatment, on the other hand, was expressed after the thirteenth day of January of 1831, after Ellen suffered another bleeding attack and after she was forced ever after to be bed-ridden until 8 February, 1831, the day she died. A hush of surprise fell over the household when in the short time of less than an hour the eager domestic administrator and Boston socialite became a stricken invalid once again. Emerson was forced to cancel several services at Second Church. Dr. Jackson came daily, nurses rubbed Ellen's hands to quicken her circulation, and Emerson, Charles, and their mother kept watch around the

---

1Gregg, ed., One First Love, p. 134.

clock, issuing frequent bulletins to the rest of the family, especially to William and to Aunt Mary. In short, the family's regard and behavior shifted in reverse from their behavior toward Ellen when she was merely ailing. But now it was too late. Now she required nursing day in and day out. Therefore, it is possible to assume that it was unusual indeed that only when Ellen underwent her last and most severe bleeding attack, did the family and her husband give her the kind of nursing care which might have benefited her more had she received it long before January. In one sense, had the couple nursed their relationship and made their way to the South in rapid order before autumn greeted winter things might have worked out differently. However, by the second month of the new year their feeble efforts would prove to be fruitless.

This treatment of Ellen would appear to have been somewhat insidious to boot. The reasons for saying so are, first, Ruth Emerson's failure to trust Edward with his own dire condition. And, second, the regret which hung over the family because of not sending Ellen to the South. At least, regret was submerged beneath concerns for Emerson's "professional affairs." On one level Ellen probably thought being at home with the Emersons at her bedside was her needed balm. But evidence suggests, on another level, she actually knew she was doomed when the decision to remain in New England for another winter was made.

Edward was taken ill in New York City with symptoms like Ellen's during early November, and it is clear that his sister-in-law identified intensely with his trouble. Moreover, it so happened that Edward was the brother with whom Ellen felt closest. Edward was with Emerson when the marital engagement took place, and Edward visited Ellen after she had her major attack of August, 1830 (William remained in New York). Debate went on about whether Edward should remain in New York, go to Boston, or go to the West Indies for the benefit of health. He reached his own decision in December, 1830 to sail for St. Croix. Evidently, Ruth Emerson became panicky: "Mother had arrived in New York" in order to fetch Edward back home to Boston or, at least, to prevent him from sailing away to the West Indies, Emerson told his grandfather Ripley on 15 December, 1830; but she had been "detained two days in Newport by weather so that Edward sailed out of New York about half an hour before she arrived, on Sunday morning."[1] Ten days before, Emerson, Charles, and their mother had "talked over the matter" and were "all pretty strongly of one mine" that Edward "ought to come here" (Boston) rather than "go alone to sea."[2] The importance of the "Boston Emerson's" sense of loyalty to home was conveyed by that single word, "alone." Why, one could ask, was it necessary for Edward to be with some- one else? Had not he decided on sailing southward? Nonetheless, it seemed better to the Emersons to "roll him up in hot blankets" in Boston, and in the spring send him temporarily to Carolina "if need be."[3] When Ruth Emerson returned to Boston on 16 December, 1830 "disappointed," she was comforted by seeing a visitor who had not brightened her door in about four years, her eldest son, William.[4] However, Ruth Emerson's comfort in having most of her family together and around her was Ellen Emerson's regret.

Emerson's first letter to departed Edward was written on 24 December, 1830, on Christmas Eve, exactly two years before the eve of his own depar- ture abroad. Attached to the letter was a note from Ellen which betrayed her regret. With the kind of irony that grows out of naivete, Emerson

---

[1] Emerson, Letters, 1: 313.

[3] Ibid.

[2] Ibid., p. 312.

[4] Ibid., p. 314.

asked Edward to follow "Ellen's advice about inquisitiveness" in asking about the nature of life on St. Croix.[1] Obviously, Ellen was very interested in some sort of vicarious attempt to gain health through thoughts about Edward's brighter skies. He asked Edward to "make written minutes of places and prices and persons and climate" that may be of use to "any of us hereafter."[2] With telling flourish, Emerson concluded his part of the letter by betraying his own character. He said he trusted in the Heavens to care for his brother and he believed they all would yet pass pleasant days of health together: "But let us rejoice in the New Testament," he added soberly, "which makes sickness and distance safe to us."[3] One month later Emerson's demeanor became less rigid, less conventional: Ellen was "more sick" on 24 January, 1831 and her husband wished "we were both of us with you," writing to Edward.[4] He still believed, "as soon as the snows melt" and "as soon as she recovers her diminished strength" they would set out "for Philadelphia or Baltimore."[5] That Emerson blinded himself from seeing the writing on the wall was hardly in the interests of his wife's welfare which, itself, had worsened beyond all hoping. He reiterated again with the same blinded eyes a similar hope on 31 January, 1831 but, as he wrote a week earlier, by that time he and the rest of the family, Ellen included, had "come to prefixing of if to all our plans."[6] In short, under family pressures which were laced together by professional hopes and aspirations, Edward's plight received more attention than it actually required. When proper care arrived at Ellen's bedside, it arrived too late to be of use. Emerson

[1]Ibid., p. 315.

[2]Ibid.

[3]Ibid.

[4]Ibid., p. 316.

[5]Ibid.

[6]Ibid., pp. 317, 316.

acquiesced, allowing his mother's presiding presence a position on center stage.

Both Emerson himself and Ellen herself intimated that if Ruth Emerson's presence had been less commanding, then they might very well have taken the possibility of a southern relocation more seriously than they did. When he was about to enter Harvard Divinity School late in 1824 Emerson made it a habit to visit the Reverend William Ellery Channing in order to impress upon the famous preacher that, as Emerson put it, "I am studying Divinity."[1] Certainly Channing was a role-model of a sort for Emerson, of a minister, of course, but also of a man with a highly developed moral character. In many ways Emerson adorned this "idol" as he wished. During September, 1830 when family discussions about Ellen's health were at an anxious pitch he wrote that Channing's situation was like his own: "Dr. Channing, I learn goes to Cuba this winter for his wifes health!!"[2] The fact was that Channing spent the winter of 1830-31 in St. Croix instead, and for his own health.[3] The point is that not even sickness tarnished the lustre of Emerson's idol. Even if Emerson was unaware of Channing's actual condition, the young man implied that men of moral character see to it that their sick wives get well, whatever the price. However, Emerson was not to live up to the high standards he associated with his Channing.

In vain hope, Ellen sailed vicariously with Edward. On 24 December, 1830 attached to her husband's letter to his brother Ellen wrote "hug yourself for your timely retreat," herself unable to embrace the "beautiful

---

[1]Rusk, The Life of Ralph Waldo Emerson, p. 103.

[2]Emerson, Letters. 1: 308.

[3]Ibid., p. 308, footnote No. 74.

[4]Gregg, ed., One First Love, p. 135.

balm" of the South.[1] She continued, "Pray speak kindly to the Santa Cruzians

of all your kith and kin and pick out a pretty spot for Waldo and wife to

live--for such golden dreams in spite of 2d church and blk gown Bostonians?

Concordians do I indulge. . . . Cold winds and changes here (,) scorpions

and debilities there--The latter I urge are not so soul annoying as the

former--One is slow, uncertain death or an ill-spent life (,) the other a

quick and sure remedy or a certain an [sic] not agreeable but more preferable

death--You perhaps are so new to and transient in the invalid table that

you will never understand me when I speak so strongly."[2] Even Ellen her-

self felt tormented by circumstances in Boston more than she did when away

from that particular city. Cold, damp winds, one has been suggesting, were

not the only uncontrollable forces to which she was subjected there. How-

ever, dream as she did, her fate was all too clear. On 5 February, 1821 her

mother-in-law went to some unusual lengths to depict Ellen telling the

family of her gratitude to God and of "her benevolent interest in all her

friends, saying they all had been very kind to her."[3] Perhaps Ruth Emerson

wanted it noted that Ellen felt all had helped, including her mother-in-law.

One can rightly remain somewhat skeptical about the real meaning of Ruth

Emerson's emphases, however, Even if the emphases were those of Emerson's

mother alone, for whatever psychological reasons, and not an accurate depiction

of Ellen's true feelings, Ellen's next breath betrayed her own more pressing

and imminent disappointment and regret. She said she hoped she would live

---

[1]Gregg, ed., One First Love, p. 135.   [2]Ibid.

[3]The quotation is taken from a letter written by Ruth Haskins Emerson
to Edward. It is quoted in Pommer, Emerson's First Marriage, p. 48.

"to hear of Edward's safe arrival" in St. Croix.[1] Such knowledge would do
her little good but it might lend her some vicarious comfort as she poised,
winged for flight to Heaven, not to the South with migrating flocks. Thus,
Ellen knew she was doomed when Emerson acceded to professional necessity
in terms of the meaning of family interrelationships, especially as the family
sought to deal with the whole matter of illness, tuberculosis, during September,
October, and December of 1830. When it was too late to do anything about
it, Emerson and his wife wished they, as well as Edward, had been on their
way to St. Croix and, for Ellen, instead of being on her way to the grave.

Emerson's acquiescence smacked of passivity, especially insofar as
passivity worked as a pretext of acknowledging some sort of "higher authority,"
sacred power, or, simply, just a broader cosmic vision of his place within
the expanding American world. That is, what Erik Erikson has suggested is
the emotional sense first experienced in the universal experience between
a mother and her infant. Then, the mother's eyes are the infant's first
stars, her smile the moon, and her voice the infant's first breezes. In
order that infants derive maximum advantage from these first relationships,
it is important for the relationship to be an exclusive one, one not subject
to interruption or inadequacy. In this sense, then, Ellen diverted Emerson's
eyes from his mother. However, the authority of his mother's presence in
the household sustained him through his short marriage and, thus, was in
the end a more abiding presence than the presence of his wife, though some
associational over-lapping undoubtedly occurred (e.g., Emerson's love poem
for Ellen, "Thine Eyes Still Shine"). In any case, locked into such a
relationship required the budding cultural leader to preserve the integrity

---

[1]Emerson, Letters, 1: 321.

of his special relationship with the stars he saw.

In this regard, on 7 January, 1831 he confided in his journals that he placed great moral value on the power "to withhold," which was more difficult to exert, he believed, than the power to give.[1] To withhold is to imply self-control. Such self-control is rooted in the fundamental modality of "taking in" or, in other words, of trusting oneself to hold on to what already has been secured in life. To try to choose this higher and more difficult form of virtue as a Christian often meant one was "much mis-understood" and, thus, "thought stingy."[2] Emerson was persuaded "many men are miserly because of their dislike of miserliness."[3] Then he went on to explain how a "husband" exercises the "greater good" by withholding his capital worth from others, so that the husband does not "peril his liberty and power to fulfill his promises" by any wanton giving.[4] In this sense, Ellen required wanton giving. Relocating might very well have done the trick. It could be said that by "withholding" the real hope of a life in the South from his wife, Emerson found his new sense of personal freedom from the Unitarian ministry confirmed, and imminent institutionally. This was an ongoing pattern in his life. For example, he withheld the possibility of a "more familiar intercourse" from Martin Gay as well as a "permanent" engagement from the Unitarians. After all, who was he to seek the arrest of the force of Providence. It was Providence which averted over-spending oneself!

As Providence would have it, Ellen died on 8 February, 1821. Emerson's

---

[1]Emerson, JMN, 3: 221-22.   [2]Ibid.

[3]Ibid.   [4]Ibid.

reaction to her death coalesced in three directions: (1) letters written
to his Aunt Mary and to Edward (2) the administration of the sacrament
of the Lord's Supper at Second Church (3) and his journey abroad and return
to America during 1833. These points display the course of his genesis
of an expanded vision within the immediate confines of a world now diminished
by the loss of his wife.

His first reaction to Ellen's death was to write a letter just several
hours after she died to his vocational sparring partner, Aunt Mary, about
the passing of his "angel." He most readily associated his aunt with his
vocational crises as we have already seen.[1] He said, "I am alone in the
world and strangely happy . . . Ellen is present with me now beaming joy-
fully upon me . . . I see plainly that things and duties will look coarse
and vulgar enough to me when I find the romance of her presence (and romance
is a beggardly word) withdrawn from them all."[2] One can only suggest in
passing that Emerson was projecting his "withholding" upon the screen of
Providence. It was Providence, he thought, which now withheld Ellen's
presence from him. Days spent with Ellen, he said, were "the most eventful
of my life" but now they were a "dim confusion," though they "shine brilliantly
in my spiritual world."[3] At this point in time, just after Ellen's death,
he took the first of two short trips which would help him get beyond personal turmoil and grief. His first journey would help him resolve his
grief over Ellen. The second, about a year later, in 1832, would help him
decide what to do about his commitment (or lack of it) to Second Church.
His larger journey during 1833 would go beyond both of these smaller ones.

---

[1]Emerson, Letters, 1: 318.   [2]Ibid.   [3]Ibid.

It would precipitate his vocational revolution as a cultural leader.

Reacting to that first small trip (a several day long walk in the mountains of western Massachusetts during June of 1831), he reported traveling was a "sad recreation" to one who "finds Ellen nowhere yet everywhere."[1] However, a pattern had been set already and a connection between "seeing" and "trusting," evident in a letter to Edward, began to emerge clearly as a lesson Emerson gradually recognized as his own. In the letter to Edward he betrayed his own source of faith, namely, the activation of the pattern of expansion within diminishment. Moreover, he hearkened back to his "particular felicity" of his 1829 engagement to Ellen, to which the recuperating Edward was party, and anticipated the form and content of his dream of 1840: "Keep your tranquil temper as the apple of your eye and if it comes, as I hope, from a spirit of boundless trust, come life, come death, come eternity, this shall be armour and preparation."[2] If Ellen had been the "apple" of Emerson's eye, then he had learned how to trust her as she lived and, more significantly, as she died. When Charles' health failed during September and October of 1831 Emerson referred to him then as a "wilted apple."[3] In any case, guilt may have invited Emerson to think "the grave" was "pleasanter . . . than the house" during March of 1831.[4] As a world without Ellen lay before him his horizons widened. Though his trust in Ellen was bound to her short existence, he found it possible to expand this kind of affection to "boundless" proportions.

Marks in the record of this time suggest, furthermore, that Emerson carried a burden of guilt, perhaps due to Ellen's condition of the last

---

[1]Ibid., p. 324.   [2]Ibid., pp. 324-25.

[3]Ibid., p. 332.   [4]Ibid., p. 319.

months of 1830 and his response to it. During August, 1831 Ellen's sister,
Margaret, had an attack of tuberculosis. The same symptoms beset Charles
in October. Emerson's reaction was one of unusual concern, perhaps even
more than he showed when Ellen was so stricken with even worse symptoms.
And he did so, quite revealingly, in terms of trying to arrange for each
of them to journey to St. Croix in order to join Edward! The implication
of this is that now, late in 1831 and after Ellen's death, he believed
Edward had made the right decision for himself during December, 1830, namely,
to "escape" from Ruth Emerson and flee southward.[1] Apparently, he could
now question his mother's wisdom. It is possible to suggest he viewed
Ellen's death as his having paid a debt owed to his mother. She had won
the struggle for him against Ellen, but now he could detach himself from
both of them. That a sense of guilt usually arises from the smoldering
fires of so-called "repressed hostility," or failure to assert confidently
one's initiative, is a standard psychological rule of thumb. Emerson
seems to be no exception to it.

Clearly he was not unused to feeling some sense of inner hostility
which, because of how he expressed it during November, 1831, seemed to
invite one to believe he wished it aimed at his mother. At least, because
she lived with him for the rest of her life he realized he could not "escape"
from her, nor, in a sense, did he really want to. Years earlier he was
bothered by how she relieved him of the task of disciplining refractory
pupils at the School for Young Ladies when "the will of the pupils was
greater than the will of the teacher." During November, 1831, however,
the tables were turned somewhat. The teachers at Boston's Mayhew School

[1]Ibid., pp. 330, 334.

had been accused of using harsh disciplining methods on their students by the parents of the pupils. When the parents threatened the teachers with violence, Emerson took it upon himself to intervene, and he secured protection from the office of the mayor of Boston. Furthermore, he joined the teachers in helping campaign against a proposal to end corporal punishment, a proposal which, in fact, was defeated. The point is Emerson contained his hostility in this instance as he was unable to do during 1821-24 when he himself taught school. That Charles, Edward, and William remained away from Boston for the rest of their lives also testifies to the suggestion that their mother was, at least, somewhat overbearing, if polite. Emerson, try as he might to have acted otherwise, was constrained like the narrator in his short story about "The Magician" (circa 1820), to be faithful to his "lonely mamma."[1] One can suggest that Ellen's death carried away the previously ineffective character of expressions of hostility over his maternal "captivity," a captivity in the Unitarian ministry just because it was the "family" heritage, and pressed him into more appropriate channels by which to direct hostility's course. One of these more appropriate streams flowed into Second Church. It pertained specifically to an act of violence central to the Christian faith—the crucifixion.

Debate of the sacrament of the Lord's Supper was a psychologically significant means by which Emerson managed his vocational problem of whether to remain in the ministry or not. It raised quite a clamor at Second Church. Having "taken in" the Unitarian Church (perhaps being "taken in" by it, as well by his family), he would now "eliminate" it. No longer did he have to support a marriage and, besides, he received a small legacy from

---

[1] Ibid., p. 341.

the Kent family (the estate of Beza Tucker) by which to support himself,
though not lavishly by any means. In June of 1832, almost a year-and-a-
half after his wife's death, he wrote to the Society of Second Church
requesting they excuse him from administering the rite, since he believed
it was not Christ's intention to have the supper repeated for centuries in
his memory. This is a suggestion that the past deserves being left in the
past, not repeated as a current experience. That is, Ellen (the sacrificial
lamb) is dead; and Emerson did not want to be reminded continually of man's
guilty past by repeating the rite. Emerson preached a sermon with a similar
message in September, probably forged by his resolve of 2 June, 1832 that
"in order to be a good minister it was necessary to leave the ministry"
since he believed the profession was "antiquated."[1] By July he had taken
his second short trip with Charles, this time to the White Mountains and
in order to work out his reasons for resigning from his charge. "The
good of going to the mountains is that life is reconsidered," he thought
on 14 July, 1832, for at "such a distance" from Boston one could assume
"a just view" and make no mistake as he would were he to follow the "round
of customs" which he observed in Boston, in Second Church.[2] His conclusion
then was that "Jesus did not mean to institute a perpetual celebration"
and, therefore, he himself could not go habitually "to an institution"
which the parishioners would continue to "esteem holiest."[3] He would have
to resign from his pulpit. In this way the more "appropriate" channel of
an ideological conflict, which betrayed his own religious doubts and now
was unearthed for the parishioners to see, was the tool by which extrication

---

[1] Emerson, JMN, 4: 27.   [2] Ibid., pp. 27-29.

[3] Ibid., pp. 29-30.

from the ministry in the narrow sense became possible. His final sermon at Second Church was preached on 22 December, 1832. Meanwhile, and prior to actually resigning, his preoccupation with the Lord's Supper early in 1832 eventuated in his request on 11 September, 1832 of a "dismission" from his pastoral charge, an acknowledgement of his resignation. It was granted on 28 October, 1832 but not until after sixty-two ballots! However, the Society dismissed him with "affectionate regret," and agreed to continue his salary to the end of the year.[1]

Through August of 1832 Emerson continued to suffer from that 1828 sprained knee which flared up sporadically (and conveniently) to prevent him from standing while preaching. He suffered as well from persistent diarrhea which he mistakenly associated with the death-inducing epidemic in Boston that year, cholera.[2] Again, these ailments, particularly the diarrhea, were regarded as "the design of Providence," a "divine plan."[3] His refusal to administer the sacrament of the Lord's Supper, a rite during which one "takes in" food, was a symbolic means of refusing to "take in" (or be "taken in" by) the Unitarian tradition. Thus, Emerson, in a very straight-forward psychological sense, did not "incorporate" the church into himself. He refused to accept the church by making himself unacceptable to it. It was clear he felt he could not "trust" the church with his future, with providing the proper vent for his "gift" enroute toward his rightful destiny, that pathway to "the Divinity." Diarrhea was a symbolic means of removing or "eliminating" the church, as it was represented in consummate

---

[1] Emerson, Letters, 1: 356, footnote No. 45.

[2] Emerson, JMN, 4: 37; Rusk, The Life of Ralph Waldo Emerson, p. 162.

[3] Emerson, Letters, 1: 354.

form in the sacrament of taking in the body and the blood of the crucified Christ. Emerson refused to participate in that sort of "violence." Emerson rinsed clean the Unitarian heritage while all the time digesting parts of it which were of fundamental significance to him, for example, preaching, which later became lecturing. His current identity then was a negative one as a result. He was <u>not</u> a Unitarian minister. One month prior to his writing of the letter of resignation he reported, "under the diarrhea I suffered now one fortnight and weak am as a reed."[1] However, he pointed to a new course of allegiance before him, though only "ideal," by means of asserting that "still the truth is not injured, not touched though thousands of them that love it fall by the way. Serene, adorable, eternal it lives . . . "[2] Though he divested himself of the ministerial office, he retained a ministerial devotion to the cause of divine truth."[3] At this point he departed from Boston and New England on Christmas Day of 1832 for Europe and England, again for the benefit of health. Nine months later he would return, reborn an American with a vision.

Both his letters and his preoccupation with the Lord's Supper as foci in his relation to his wife's death suggest that Emerson re-activated the pattern of play evident during earlier years, namely, to set out on a journey shortly after the appearance of signs of personal crisis. His journey abroad (his longest and most distant to date) transposed the geographical pattern of "going out" (expanding) and "going back" home (diminishing) to the more psychological pattern of expansion within diminishment. That pattern itself has cultural, historical, mythical, and charismatic affinities.

---

[1]Emerson, <u>JMN</u>, 4: 33. [2]Ibid.

[3]Emerson, <u>Letters</u>, 1: 357.

It has been suggested all along that this particular psychological pattern
is primarily a pattern of visual response, a seer's response. This has
been noted already, for example, in the two love poems which Emerson wrote
about Ellen. There the visual way in which Emerson construed his relationship with his wife touched-base, so to speak, with the similarly patterned
visual relationship with Martin Gay, a relationship in which, curiously,
no conversation was ever exchanged. Though Thomas Carlyle would be the
next recipient of a similar regard, before Emerson departed for points east,
omens were in the air. If Ellen's death darkened his world, then darkness
became the ground upon which he began finding new things to behold, new
light to fill his world. His journey would help him "take it in."

Approximately a full-term of nine months transpired from the time
he left for his trip abroad to the time he arrived home on 7 October,
1833, "reborn" as a lecturer on natural history. His authority to shift
from pulpit to lecture platform derived mainly from his resignation from
the ministry in the narrow sense. This he intimated seriously, but not
without the "excitement" which he had craved during October, 1820, in a
letter to William written in November, 1832, just prior to his departure:
"The severing of our strained cord that bound me to the church is a mutual
relief. . . thought it will occasion me perhaps some (possibly much) temporary
embarrassment yet I walk firmly toward a peace and freedom which I plainly
see before me albeit afar."[1] He went on saying, "shall I pester you with
half the projects that sprout and bloom in my head, of action, literature,
philosophy? Am I not to have a magazine--my ownty and downty-scorning
co-operation and taking success by storm."[2] If it was Ellen's death that

---

[1]Ibid., pp. 357-58.   [2]Ibid.

brought about the severing of the umbilical cord between Emerson and Second Church, then it was he himself who, though "bound" by that cord to the tradition represented by the church, employed diarrhea as a means of working out a state of "mutual relief" to himself and to the congregation. After all, if man was connected to God, not to any church, by the umbilical cord of "conscience" as he thought during July, 1828, then the same should hold late during 1832.[1] When he severed that "strained cord" he "flattered" himself that he was "getting better at last," that is, he was emerging from a prison "sentence," he said, which had had "Egyptian darkness."[2] When Margaret Tucker succumbed to death during November, 1832 he cast her life in terms of a prison sentence as well: "Go rejoice with Ellen" in freedom from "painful corporeal imprisonment."[3] Later the seer would unshackle their necks so they, too, could see his light. Emerson would call Americans to the "higher calling" of being "Americans" first, Unitarians or whatever second. However, though in his enthusiasm he "saw" his future fairly clearly, his twenty-four hour visit with Thomas and Jane Carlyle on 25 August, 1833 in England made the most decisive impression on the emerging seer to date. The concluding chapters of this study can be prefigured somewhat by sketching-out the parameters of this meeting, especially in terms of its pre-1833 antecedents.

On 31 October, 1827, All Saints' Day, Emerson first noted, we have mentioned already, the man he would later know as Carlyle. Then Carlyle was just an "anonymous (sic) author."[4] During his trip of July, 1832 to

---

[1] Emerson, JMN, 3: 139.   [2] Emerson, Letters, 1: 357.

[3] Emerson, JMN, 4: 60.   [4] Emerson, Letters, 1: 218.

the White Mountains with Charles, Emerson noted Carlyle for a second time still as an "anonymous author," by inserting a quotation from The Corn Law Rhymes: ". . . Imitation is a leaning on something foreign; incompleteness of individual development, defect of free utterance. Ed. Rev. No CX."[1] Emerson's last reference to the "anonymous author" occurred on 1 October, 1832: he said he was "cheered and instructed" by the paper on Corn Law Rhymes in the Edinburgh Review by "my Germanick new-light writer whoever he be."[2] The author, Emerson thought, "gives us confidence in our principles. . . he assures the truth lover everywhere of sympathy."[3] Blessed art that makes books and so joins me to that stranger by this perfect railroad."[4] Not an umbilical cord, but a track reached across the Atlantic. Evidently, Emerson felt incomplete. For his railroad would stretch to England and would assure him the strength and self-confidence he needed. He would, as he put it, be "leaning on something foreign," Thomas Carlyle, whose name Emerson discovered only several weeks before setting sail on Christmas Day, 1832. His journey, he believed in light of his new finding, would have to be consummated in England.

Carlyle was Emerson's best and new-found "friend" in the most magni-minious sense of that word, from 1833 on. The nature of Emerson's relationship with Carlyle implied a mode of vision, of not pretending "to have solved the great problems" but being "an observer of their solution as it goes forward in the world."[5] Emerson wrote about Carlyle, "I

---

[1] Emerson, JMN, 4: 28. [2] Ibid., p. 45.

[3] Ibid. [4] Ibid.

[5] Emerson, Letters, 1: 394.

loved him at once."[1] He felt he had met men of far less power who did
not have as great an insight into "religious truth" as did Carlyle.[2]
He reported that Carlyle's isolation on the Scottish moors facilitated
an intimacy with the inner-most recesses of his self: Carlyle was not
"filed down" by "city society."[3] The relationship between these two
kindred spirits enabled the American to take great delight in possessing
his own identity afterward in terms of contemplating his personal "saints"
or "spiritual heroes," such as George Fox, Michaelangelo, and, of course,
Plato. From the likes of all of these representative men Emerson would
work to differentiate himself. One-third of his lectures of 1834-35
are devoted to biographies of these sorts of great figures.[4] Carlyle was
a similar "fit friend." Indeed, the English hero-worshipper raised
Emerson's sights to figures of the past who were far greater than any of
those persons had been upon whom he had depended all his life. On 5 September,
1833, however, when Emerson "saw the last lump of England" receding over
the eastern horizon, he did so "without the least regret," but insofar
as his future was concerned, his mild apprehension on the occasion of
returning home was justified, if only momentarily as in the life of a
man growing wise.[5] For Emerson had his "umbilical cord" cut, and his
future was bright with promise. Moreover, lecturing would prove increasingly,

---

[1]Ibid., p. 395.

[2]Ibid., p. 394.

[3]Ibid., p. 395.

[4]See Stephen E. Whicher and Robert E. Spiller, eds., The Early
Lectures of Ralph Waldo Emerson (Cambridge: Harvard University Press,
1959), pp. 93-201.

[5]Rusk, The Life of Ralph Waldo Emerson, p. 197.

as he would assure his mother in 1838, to be "good bread."[1] In short,
Ralph Waldo Emerson's dire play moved quickly to closure. Therefore,
he commenced gathering together ("taking in with his vision") persons
soon to be recognized the world over as "Americans."

Emerson's lack of regret for having left English soil behind when
he embarked for New York City in September, 1833 marked the spirit of
his incipient vocational revolution as a lecturer. Also, it supplied
the pattern his lecture tours would take later. His journey abroad,
though it may have been a "fool's paradise" as he looked back upon it
many years later, soon ignited his concern to view traveling as a means
for calling a populace to nationhood.[2] By not feeling regret as he watched
England slip over the visible horizon he could turn confidently to the
horizon that stretched-out almost limitlessly to the west, to America.
Like the action of turning from shadows to light in the platonic cave,
Emerson's geographical and psychological expansion, his visionary faith,
mitigated his apprehension with an invigorated spirit of national pride.
Therefore, as the sight of England diminished in the east, his eye greeted
an expanded horizon in the west. Indeed, during the nineteenth century
westward expansion reached unprecedented heights in the United States.

By returning home, specifically to America and not merely to Boston
or to New England, but to "America" as symbolic entity in itself geographically
and psychologically, Emerson affirmed the validity of a unique national
consciousness. Though the Revolutionary War severed the Colonies from
England, most Americans retained much of the cultural and literary styles

---

[1]Emerson, Letters, 2: 120.

[2]The phrase, "fool's paradise" can be found in Emerson's essay,
"Self-Reliance": see Works.

of colonial times. Thus, a situation of cultural ambiguity prevailed: a United States with an exclusive edge on the cultural life of England. Because Emerson had cut the "umbilical cord" to one vestige of colonial times, the Unitarian ministry, he was, in effect, quite prepared to effect a severing of the apron strings, so to speak, which by-and-large bound his country men to Mother England. Not child's play, but cultural ritualization was being called for. However, his irony was that he never could sever completely the ties which bound him to his own mother. In any case, he facilitated a resolution of cultural ambiguity in terms of his personal resolution of vocational ambivalence. This he did by his ritualized and growing capacity to envision an "American" literature and a general but personal artistry according to the pattern of expansion within diminishment.

Taking up the lecture platform and traveling westward, then eastward, became the tool he used to finalize what had been begun in 1776 with the Declaration of Independence. As the nation grew in size and spirit in independence, Emerson followed westward "expansion" while at the same time affirmed national "consolidation" in the east, in the Government in Washington, D.C. If his own lesson of playfulness was to hold sway for others, that is, if "Self-Reliance" was to become infectious nation-wide, then independence would have to follow the pattern of expansion within some sort of commonality. Emerson believed the formation of a national literature would set some standards for this sense of commonality. However, the mold by which his hopes were shaped in this regard had been forged already during the period from 1825 to 1833, during his play at vocation-making, ego-mastery. Thus, the pattern of expansion within diminishment, which was engendered during this incubation, would serve his culture as a meshing of his "personal odyssey" with its "national formation," on the east coast as well as on the frontier, during the mid-nineteenth century. Finally, the charisma he would soon come to bear was that of a leader who, as he said in his manifesto of 1836, <u>Nature</u>, like a "transparent eyeball," is able to "take in" the universe.[1] Emerson was becoming a cultural laborer because he was becoming skilled at showing Americans how, as he had learned, to trust themselves. He attempted to secure for his countrymen a firmament that stretched from coast to coast, from sea to shining sea.

Let one turn now to the man born amidst these sorts of waters. For the period of 1834-38 is one of clear expansion. It sets the standard for the man and his work for the rest of his life.

---

[1]Emerson, <u>Nature</u>, p. 6.

CHAPTER VI

SHRILLS FROM THE MARKET PLACE:
THE LECTURER AND HIS PROPS

If one were to pause to reflect on the cluster of events of Emerson's

life occuring between 1825-33, then two biographical coincidences stand

out. Each carries through the entire period of time. The first coinci-

dence concerns Emerson's physical ailments, each of which appears as a

thwart not only to his personal state of health but also to professional

commitments. The second outstanding factor is Emerson's commitments to

the Unitarian ministry. Physical ailments and Emerson hedging to commit

himself fully to the Unitarian ministry are two major concerns that appear

to go hand-in-hand during the period from 1825-33. Writing on 16 April,

1833 when he had abandoned all serious commitment to a Unitarian ministry

of his own, Emerson mentioned to Charles, "I am in better health than ever

since I was a boy."[1] Clearly, an onslaught of physical ailments gave Emerson

a practical excuse for carrying out his desire to hedge on becoming a minister

for life. As we pause to reflect on the time during 1825-33, let us turn

to examine this coincidence further. By doing so, we will better understand

the significance of Emerson's personal and vocational accomplishments during

the period from 1833 through 1838.

The cluster of events of 1825-33 might be segregated as a single unit

if only because Emerson was persistently without good health during that time.

No other time in his life had he been so plagued day after day, week after

week, month after month, and year after year with bothersome but hardly dire

---

[1]Emerson, Letters, I:373.

complaints about an assortment of illnesses--blindness, rheumatism, lameness, tuberculosis, and diarrhea. Before 1825 and after 1833 Emerson was remarkably healthy according to his own report. This is striking when Emerson's health is measured by the standards set by his ailing and frailer brothers and sisters. The testimony of his lecture tours later during his life was even more striking. The extensive travel they required, especially during winter months, suggests that he was fit enough to do it. In short, Emerson was at his lowest ebb during the events of 1825-33, and his condition was marked oddly by the appearance of a plethora of physical illnesses.

One can speculate on the irony of this curious fact of illness during this time. One might, for example, point to 1806, Emerson's third year, and suggest a traumatic connection between the boy's attendance "again" at Mrs. Whitewell's reading school, and intestinal disturbances which appeared shortly afterwards and which, for lack of a clear cause, were blamed on worms. It is likely that the boy's attempts to assert himself as a reader like his father were repressed, those unconscious checks being shored-up by illnesses visible to himself and to others. In any case, these episodes of 1806, about which very little source material exists, must remain a shadow. However, it seems no accident that during Emerson's lowest ebb, when physical illness racked his body, he also fought for his life in the high tides of vocation indecision, as well as with the mental torment which resulted from the battles.

A pause for reflection on the meaning of 1825-33 also must dwell on Emerson's commitments (or lack of them) to the ministry. During 1825 Emerson entered Harvard Divinity School. During 1832-33 he resigned from his ministerial charge at Boston's Second Church and traveled abroad. If one were to ask the question, were his physical ailments connected somehow to the commitments he made to the Unitarians during 1825-33, then the answer would be in the affirmative.

Not only were these two facts biographically coincidental. They also allowed
Emerson the strength of a neat psychological maneuver. His physical ailments
appear and persist insofar as Emerson himself appears and persists to be committed to the church and to a career in Divinity, as he might say. As the
record will show, when he becomes ill it is also at the same time when he
wishes to avoid or delay some sort of ecclesiastical commitment. For examples,
studying Unitarian doctrine in 1825, taking up the missionary field of western
Massachusetts in 1826-27, ordination in 1829, administering the Lord's Supper
in 1832, and so on. However, Emerson enjoyed preaching very much and he
experienced little consternation over that particular ministerial duty. Becoming
approbated to preach in 1826 suggests this, even though Henry Ware, Jr., senior
minister at Second Church, had some reservations in regard to the liberality
of the young man's sermons.[1] At any rate, the curious confluence of _illnesses_
and _commitments_ was mediated and neutralized somewhat by a simple technique
Emerson employed almost automatically, a pattern of response to the coincidence
of these two facts at critical moments in his life which reflects his pattern
of play. This time Emerson's play is clearly play. He enjoys the leisure of
travel.

Emerson mediated and eased the torment of physical ill-health and vocational indecision by traveling. To recognize Emerson's traveling is to open up
the possibility also of seeing reflected within it the pattern of expansion
within diminishment. By recognizing the presence of Emerson's style of playful, ritualized vision within his travels during 1825-33 (and thereafter), we
confirm the drift of the overall meaning of the cluster of events of 1811-24.
Emerson appeared to be trapped waiting for some highwater-mark to appear to

[1] Rusk, _The Life of Ralph Waldo Emerson_, pp. 135-36.

end his torment over health and vocation. To wait meant to be locked in
a diminished state of affairs. However, to travel meant to begin projecting
new horizons of expansion beyond his present. Emerson was anticipating
future "expansion," but for the time being felt as if he were waiting,
wrapped in a period of incubation which only that form of play, which is
travel, could animate. However, broader social patterns pressed in on
his immediate needs and kept Emerson from seeing clearly his situation
during 1825-33. At least, he seemed preoccupied by the shadows of vocational
incubation and its hand-maiden, travel.

It was suggested in preceding chapters that the Brahmin rule of frailty
was shrewdly and, perhaps, unconsciously used by Emerson, to talk himself
into a commitment to the Unitarian pulpit. The popular logic of his social
environment suggested that in order to be a good minister it was necessary
to act like a Boston, Brahmin minister and appear continually ill. One
would hardly pretend to be ill all the time, just that there was a popular
association between being a minister and being ill and this idea was
available to Emerson as unconscious intentions sought expression. Illness
seemed dictated for a minister by the larger social pattern of Boston
Unitarianism, because most ministers, so it went, were of faltering health.
If he did, in a sense, welcome illness, Emerson was able to hedge in his
commitments to the ministry and, at the same time, appear headed in the
direction of an apparently genuine ministerial commitment. Hardly hindered
by social regard, Emersons' immediate more personal needs placed the rule
of frailty in the background. Out of that background emerged Emerson's
deep-seated preoccupation with ritualized vision. In this narrower area
of immediate personal pressures traveling came to have its most dynamic
effect on the course of his life by helping him see beyond the frailty

of his own commitments to the Unitarians.

During 1825-33 Emerson resorted to traveling not only for seeking
poetic inspiration, but also to seek restoration of good health. The
total effect of linking together illnesses, commitments, and travel is
Emerson's realization that, indeed, "faith is a telescope," as he believed
during 1824. By removing himself from the torment of 1825-33 on three
successive occasions and then returning home afterwards, Emerson touched
upon a potent modus operendi by which he would later make his contribution
to American life: By traveling ("expanding") he was able to relieve self-
suffering and to see the course of his life in clearer perspective, with
greater resolve for future promise. By 1829 he was convinced about the
efficacy of his faith: "Some men see microscopically: some see telescopically.
One magnifies and one microfies. One exaggerates the familiar and homely
into notice and honour"; he says, "and one bring the great and the infinite
to our eyes."[1] During the summers of 1831 and 1832, during short trips with
Charles to the Green and White Mountains, a similar visual sense prevailed:
"Here among the mountains . . . one should see the errors of men from
calmer height. . . ."[2] This self-report of an immediate biographical
circumstance dealt with being in the mountains at that point in his life.
It lends concrete embodiment to a less immediate formulation of similar
curative techniques, namely that a "telescopic faith" helps one reach
"calmer heights" even without being atop a mountain. In short, the cluster
of events of 1825-33 states better the overall drift of his pattern of
play, which first was discerned in the record of 1811-24. This is so

---

[1] Emerson, JMN, 3: 150.

[2] Ibid., 4: 27, 27-29; 3: 257-58.

because of the close correspondence between the journeys of that period as carriers of the meaning of travel. That meaning is clearly associated with the pattern of expansion within diminishment. This is a mark of the use of Emerson's ritualized vision.

Therefore, by way of drawing to a close these summary reflections on the period of 1825-33, the following review of Emerson's ritualization of that time would proceed as follows. The first event of the cluster of events of 1825-33 began in 1825 when Emerson experienced partial blindness shortly after embarking on theological studies at the Harvard Divinity School under the tutelage of Andrews Norton. It continued into late 1825 with his first journey to the country, and concluded with the restoration of his eyesight during September and October, precisely with his report saying so early in January, 1826. The second event began with the preaching of his first sermon in 1826 and continued with his voyage to Florida during the winter of 1826-27, with which Emerson intended to alleviate symptoms of tuberculosis. It ended on his ordination day, 11 March, 1829, three months after his engagement and six months prior to his marriage to Ellen Tucker of Concord, New Hampshire (New Concord). The third event began with his marriage and the subsequent death of his wife in 1831, leading to resignation from his ministerial charge at Second Church in 1832, which was related symbolically to persistent diarrhea. It continued with his trip to Europe and to England and his fortuitous meeting with Thomas Carlyle, and concluded in 1833 with Emerson's fateful decision to take up the lecture platform or, at least, to move quickly in that direction, after his return from abroad.

*   *   *   *   *

One of the more attractive aspects of the Unitarian ministry to Emerson during 1825-33 was the steady income it brought him. However, the ideological sacrifices incumbent upon the young minister were great ones, and the tear in his disposition which they elicited helped him resign from his charge at Second Church. During 1834-38 the tables were turned. In fact, Emerson soon became sole party to virtual financial independence because of the part of the Tucker estate to which he fell heir after Ellen's death. But, because of legal complications involving intricate probate hearings, the estate would not be settled finally until 1837. Therefore, though he received an advance on the estate during 1834, Emerson was forced to find other means of support in the meantime. However, support came to him not only in terms of finances. He was heartened and guided as well by other almost as equally important props as financial rewards. On the one hand, he was pulled into the growing lyceum movement in New England. And, in a sense, found his style in the pulpit but a stone's throw away from the demands of the lecture platform. The lyceum network supplied the equivalent of pulpit supplying as far as he could tell. However, in the lyceum he did not have to worry about carrying on his back or in his voice the burden of vocational ambivalence over the Unitarian ministry. On the other hand, and perhaps a more psychological sort of support, was Emerson's identification with his first literary friend of consequence. During 1833, August, Emerson visited Thomas Carlyle and his wife (who, by the way, Emerson though "a most agreeable accomplished woman"). The Carlyles lived, thought Emerson, "in perfect solitude."[1] Visiting with them was, to use Emerson's own visual image, a "white day" in his years, when he found "the youth" he sought in "Scotland,"

---

[1] Emerson, Letters, 1: 394.

and believed "good and wise and pleasant" Thomas Carlyle seemed to be.[1]
Incidentally, it is possible that the visit to Carlyle was part of a biographical formula with which Emerson could have been familiar and which
itself was similar in usage to some kinds of ancient biographical traditions.[2]
Both Emerson and his brother travel to Europe and use their experiences
there as the bases for "secular" careers afterwards. The seemingly stereo-
typical nature of seeking inspiration may very well reflect some larger
cultural pattern which guided these Brahmin sons. At any rate, Emerson's
new vocation took shape largely because of his identification with an outstanding literary figure, and because of the established lyceum movement
which facilitated securing speaking engagements. Each of these props will
be probed in greater detail. It will be suggested how inheriting Ellen's
share of the Tucker estate precipitated both securing the stability of
"person and place," one's sense of being in the world, and renouncing the
ministry forever.

Emerson's personal "railroad," one noted him saying, led directly
to Carlyle, and it is clear the young American leaned heavily upon the
foreigner at first. "Drawn by strong regard to one of my teachers,"
Emerson wrote Carlyle on 14 May, 1834, "I went to see his person. . . at
Craigenputtock."[3] Certainly Carlyle had been regarded as at least one,
if not the only, of those ideal "instructors" whom Emerson believed were

[1]Emerson, JMN, 4 : 219-20.

[2]Ernst Kris, "The Image of the Artist," Psychoanalytic Explorations
in Art (New York: International Universities Press, 1952), pp. 64-84.

[3]Joseph Slater, ed., The Correspondence of Emerson and Carlyle (New
York: Columbia University Press, 1964), p. 97.

necessary to "instruct the instructors" during 1826.[1] To the degree he filled this eminent position in the eyes of the young American, Carlyle joined the ranks of Emerson's personal, mental pantheon of "great men" (already noted) especially insofar as Plato was its oldest leading figure. Since an attitude of adulation poured from Emerson, that pantheon, which included Carlyle, could readily be transported home to the United States. When Emerson bid adieu to England he felt no regret "in the presence of the best of its sons" that he was not born there; in fact, he said he was "thankful" to be an American as he was "thankful" he was a man, and that the "best merit" of England to his eye was that it was the "most resembling country to America which the world contains."[2] He could readily feel that Carlyle, off in Scotland at that time, was not unlike himself, off in America. Both were at a distance from the heart of Mother England proper. However, separation from this common cultural well-spring made them allies in the ideal world of friendship: "Strange," Emerson wrote during 1837, "that any body who ever met another person's eyes, should doubt that all men have one soul."[3]

Martin Gay also was a young man "at a distance," separated from Emerson himself. But distance and separation made Emerson's heart grow fonder or, at least, honed the edge of his fascination ever more acutely in regard to Gay and Carlyle. Carlyle, in Craigenputtock, resembled a hermit who chose to isolate himself from "city life," as Emerson had put it before. It is interesting to note that during his entire nine-month long journey abroad much of Emerson's self-understanding was built upon a similar image of the hermit, not just one isolated from "city life,"

---

[1]See Emerson, Letters, 1: 167.   [2]Emerson, JMN, 4: 81.

[3]Ibid., 5: 364.

but one seeking a friend of outstanding proportions. He virtually staked his career on whether or not he could sense "fitness for friendship" in Wordsworth, Landor, Coleridge, and Carlyle. These hardly were ordinary men of standard intellectual and artistic proportions. Writing to William on 26 February, 1833 he told how the "courts of the old world impress the poor hermit," though every place he entered, he said, was "a new lottery; chance may make you acquainted with an honest and kind man therein then will that place disclose its best things and you may know nobody then will go out of it ignorant and with disagreeable impressions."[1] Again he referred to himself as a "hermit" during communication to Williams' fiancee, Susan Havens, on 22 March, 1833. He reiterated that "every town is a lottery" insofar as one would have to take his chances on finding fit friends of outstanding proportions in them.[2] Therefore, for this single reason, Emerson could say readily to William on 23 March, 1833 how, "I hate travel- ling. Happy they that sit still! How glad I shall be to get home again."[3] However, the magnetic pull on the hermit from home was partly counteracted by Emerson's new sense of an international, transhistorical "home," an idealized place of intellect filled with a corps of "fit friends," lifting high banners of "virtue."

Though Emerson thought traveling was a "poor profession," it evidently was "good medicine" and, like seasickness, it could help to "break up a morbid habit."[4] That habit, of course, was Emerson's propensity to become ill (or, at least, to rely on illness as a convenient excuse) when faced with committing himself to the Unitarians. In fact, why 1825-33 ended at

---

[1]Emerson, Letters, 1: 364.

[2]Ibid., pp. 368-69

[3]Ibid., p. 370.

[4]Ibid., p. 371.

the very moment when he departed from England to return home to America
was because he himself reported early in 1833 that he was "in better health
than ever" since he was "a boy."[1] When he wrote to Aunt Mary on 18 April,
1833 he explained to her he had set sail "away from home a wasted peevish
invalid" and he had been "mending ever since," and as a result he was "in
better health than I remembered to have enjoyed since I was in college."[2]
Hardly could he have framed the cluster of events of 1825-33 better than
that, since he said his health had been at a peak of fitness sometime
during 1811-24. He harkened back to pre-vocational ambivalence days,
implying his crisis of vocational identity had been resolved by 1833.

However, though the hermitage of traveling removed him from the
Unitarian church, it did not fill the void in his life. "I am a poor
asteroid in the great system subject to disturbances in my orbit," he
added to his Aunt on 18 April, 1833, "not only from all the planets but
from all their moons."[3] He went on to say, the "wise man--the true friend--
the finished character we seek everywhere and find only in fragments."[4]
He was not able to persuade himself that all the "beautiful souls" were
fled out of the solar system or that he would be "excluded from good company
and yoked with green dull pitiful persons . . . with various little people."[5]
He believed his concern for meeting a noble model for his own dawning sense
of vocation was far more intense and critical than the cares of his seasick
traveling companions. They wanted only for the seas to calm. He enjoyed
the crests, which thrusted his eyes to more distant horizons.

Emerson's seas did not churn enough. It hardly was coincidental that

---

[1]Ibid., p. 373.

[2]Ibid., p. 375.

[3]Ibid.

[4]Ibid.

[5]Ibid.

when he wrote to his aunt four long months after his departure (the first
letter written to her during his journey) he bemoaned his inability to find
adequate inspiration. Aunt Mary, proud during 1825 when her nephew set
sail into theological studies and perplexed by his three journeys during
1825-33, undoubtedly felt betrayed. In his letter Emerson was more arti-
culate than anywhere else during this period of time about his inability
to meet the ideal of "friendship" which Charles had set-out for him early
during 1828, or about his own sense of the hermaphroditic quality of the
"finished character."[1] The way he put it, he had met many upstanding people,
but no outstanding teachers: "I want instructors. God's greatest gift
is a Teacher and when will he send me one, full of truth and of boundless
benevolence and heroic sentiments. I can describe the man, and have already
in prose and verse. I know the idea well, but where is its real blood
warm counterpart."[2] Aunt Mary was Emerson's teacher of old, perhaps
exemplary of a "Teacher" imprinted earlier in his life. By suggesting he
had not yet met his great Teacher, he was implying that his aunt's guiding
hand had loosened its grip on him, and that he was well on his way toward
wriggling free from ancestral theological and vocational confines. Indeed,
Jesus, "that excellent Teacher," was not as important as "my brothers
my mother my companions" as a friend of the most ideal sort.[3] However, on
21 October, 1833 he believed that "Jesus Christ will be better loved by
being less adored."[4] In effect, he thinks he can love his Aunt Mary better
by adoring her less. That is, by being more self-reliant. Christianity

---

[1]See ibid., p. 225; Emerson, JMN, 4: 210, 378.

[2]Emerson, Letters, 1: 376.

[3]Ibid.; a similar reference to Charles is ibid., 2: 24.

[4]Emerson, JMN, 4: 92

rested in the "broad basis of man's moral nature," not the reverse.[1]
Aunt Mary was to become further estranged from her nephew during 1835 after
his second marriage. But, having worked through his feelings about his
aunt, whom he had considered a teacher par excellance, Emerson still faced
a gnawing sense of loneliness.

In a letter written from Rome on 20 April, 1833 to his best friend,
George Sampson, Emerson linked together loneliness and the solace of home.
However, these two concerns would take on a meaningful twist. What can
be extracted from this connection is that the American "hermit" was being
readied by circumstances to meet the "hermit" of Craigenputtock. "I
tell you," he said to Sampson, "I love real men and therefore I meet continual rebuffs and disappointments in seeing so many and yet none."[2]
Emerson had looked for and had found Ellen "nowhere yet everywhere" after
her death during June, 1831.[3] Now, however, she, like Aunt Mary, somehow
could not suffice in fulfilling his yearnings. So obstinate was his own
conviction that "in minds of the first class this hunger for truth from
others must exist" that he preferred to deny he had met "any wise man" than
to admit anyone could be "indifferent to the topics" which interested him.[4]
Evidently Sampson sensed the hermit's plight, for Emerson reiterated Sampson's
query, namely, "Do you say I ought not to have wandered from my place: I
found sincere people at home--why did I not stay there?"[5] Emerson agreed
with his friend that perhaps traveling, especially with finding a fit
friend in mind, was folly. But the void of this hermit's loneliness was

---

[1] Ibid.

[2] Emerson, Letters, 1: 378.

[3] See ibid., p. 324.

[4] Ibid., p. 378.

[5] Ibid.

not. And it had not yet been turned toward the likes of one Thomas Carlyle. Emerson hoped "better things of Carlyle" on 16 May, 1833 while slowly enroute to London from Rome.[1] He hoped the "lottery" of England would turn the tides of fortune his way, and help him forge a product marketable from the lecture platform at home. The chances he took were good ones.

If he had run amuck finding others who had glanced into eyes and realized all men were of one soul, then Emerson's "white day" with the Carlyles confirmed his conviction. Almost instantaneously he had lifted the meeting into heights similar to those reached during his "astronomical reveries" of times past, embellishing them with ideal meaning: If Aunt Mary had sufficed as his Teacher and, as his earlier openings of his letters to her phrased it, his Friend, then she had been replaced by Thomas Carlyle. In effect, from within the diminished relationship and meaning he now associated with his aunt, Emerson expanded beyond that more-or-less theological nexus of intellectual vitality, and moved toward a literary identification. Carlyle was Emerson's God-sent "gift," a "Teacher."[2] Because there will be reason to recall it later, Emerson's most poignant characterization of Carlyle can be quoted now. The reason for including this thumbnail characterization here is, on the one hand, because it states clearly Emerson's fulfilled "love" of "real men," one of whom he considered to be Carlyle. And, on the other hand, because it soon will be suggested that Carlyle's "person and place" (i.e., his wife and location) were worthy of imitation as far as Emerson was concerned. Suffice it to say here that Emerson's stability of "person and place" paralleled Carlyle's situation almost point-for-point, from emotional rapport (such as it was) with his

---

[1] Ibid., p. 383.

[2] Slater, ed., The Correspondence of Emerson and Carlyle, p. 106.

wife to the solitary life they shared on the isolated moors. Thus, of Carlyle Emerson wrote on 30 August, 1833 in Liverpool that, "He talks finely, seems to love the broad Scotch, and I loved him very much, at once. I am afraid he finds his entire solitude tedious, but I could not help congratulating him upon his treasure in his wife and I hope they will not leave the moors, tis so much better for a man of letters to muse himself in seclusion than to be filed down by the common level of compliances and imitations of city society. . . . "[1] Early in 1835 he would say Carlyle was "one of the best" of all time, even though he would add, "my friends think I exaggerate his merit."[2] Therefore, Emerson's love for Carlyle was a love of adulation which was not unlike the love of a prodigal son for his father.

If Carlyle was the Teacher who was to be loved, then he prompted Emerson beyond the small society of his mother, brothers and daily companions who, themselves, were no less morally efficacious than Jesus, as he told his aunt. When Edward died in Puerto Rico on 1 October, 1834, Emerson sent word about it to his literary master shortly afterward. In this letter of 20 November, 1834 Emerson acknowledged receiving the first letter from his new Teacher, Carlyle, one week before, early during November. Emerson had written his first letter to Carlyle on 14 May, 1834; and the letter from Carlyle was dated 12 August, 1834. The received letter, Emerson said in his second letter, made "a bright light in a solitary and saddened place. . . . As (Edward) passes out of sight, come to me visible as well as spiritual tokens of a fraternal friendliness which by its own law, transcends the tedious barriers of Custom and nation, and opens it way to

---

[1]Emerson, Letters, 1: 395.   [2]Ibid., p. 432.

the heart."[1] Edward had been away in Puerto Rico for over three years.
Although Emerson stood somewhat alone as his brother passed "out of sight,"
the fact of the matter was that Edward's death marked the beginning of
Emerson's sense of ritualized expansion. This was directly connected
to the larger society represented by Emerson's new literary friend.

Edward was the brother who fled southward for his tuberculosis during
December of 1830. Possibly Emerson felt relieved by hearing Edward had
died, that is, news of the death may have relieved him of his guilt.
Perhaps Emerson realized that going south permanently only prolonged Edward's
life. It did not cure him. This was partial consolation that the best
he could have done for Ellen was to prolong her life. If this was all,
then perhaps he could feel it was, after all, more merciful to let her
die earlier than later. In any case, receiving the "bright light" of
"fraternal friendliness" from Carlyle at the time of Edward's death eased
Emerson's mind, and freed him to chart other vocational seas than that of
the Unitarian ministry. That is, as the familial circle Emerson had known
contracted when, as had Ellen, Edward passed "out of sight," that circle
gave rise to a wider, and more expansive civil sense with its own incipient
mandate. Emerson's railroad to Carlyle seemed to be making a return trip
by means of the letter dated 12 August, 1834. Touching a Platonic notion
that gave animation to the soul shared by himself and Carlyle, Emerson
thanked his "jealous Daimon" for the "true consolation" which came as a
"godsend so significantly timed."[2] Carlyle's letter, for the moment,
realized the "hope" to which he had "clung with both hands, through each

---

[1]Slater, ed., The Correspondence of Emerson and Carlyle, p. 106.

[2]Ibid.

disappointment," that he might talk or converse with a man "whose ear of
faith was not stopped," and whose argument he "could not predict."[1] He
asked rhetorically, "May I use the work, 'I thank my God whenever I call
you to remembrance.'"[2] As his literary ally, Emerson used his relationship and subsequent identification with Carlyle as a means of extricating
himself from the constraints of family pressures. The relationship was
used as well as a means of poising himself so as to be ready to meet the
destiny of a higher calling in the context of American cultural transformation he believed he faced--a patently civil undertaking, worthy of mature
regard.

Carlyle was like Emerson's ancient Teacher, Plato, and insofar as
he was, Carlyle became aggrandized as a member of Emerson's mental pantheon
of "Representative Men." Carlyle was included not only because he represented
virtue, but also because he was a consummate literary scholar, as far as
Emerson was concerned. The association between Carlyle and Plato was integral
to Emerson's appropriation of Carlyle's style of historical writing, that
is, history as a record of great biographies. Emerson relied on biography
(as well as upon natural history) as the subject matter of some of his very
first attempts to succeed on the lecture platform late in 1833 and through
1835. This particular interest remained with him throughout his life.
Generally, then, of all his literary friends later in life, Carlyle was
the one who most readily was associated with the Athenian philosopher so
dear to Emerson's sensibilities.

When he glanced into Carlyle's eyes, so to speak, and saw his own
soul, Emerson was penetrating into his own most abiding framework for

---

[1]Ibid.

[2]Ibid.

relating to his phenomenal world. Spoken of here is the <u>exclusivity or</u> <u>solitariness</u> of the mother-infant relationship, in which vision is paramount and in which all external demands upon that relationship are taken as being "less real" than the relational interplay itself between mother and infant. On 25 February, 1834, just as he was getting his feet on the ground of the lecture platform, Emerson said he knew of a sure way of achieving "solitude"--"go to the window and look at the stars."[1] He said, "if they do not startle you and call you off from the vulgar matters I know not what will."[2] Recalling the Eriksonian discussion, what Emerson described as his means of achieving solitude during 1834 is an analogue to the mother-infant relationship which is characteristic of the game, "peek-a-boo." That is, the "stars," like a mother's eyes, lift one's own eyes to less "vulgar" heights. Here is a clear example of the ritualized visual pattern of expansion within diminishment. The room confined his vision, but the window opened upon greater, dare say, maternal, sights, a "cosmos" into which, at least for fleeting moments, Emerson felt granted peeks. Another example of Emerson's tendency to cast Carlyle into a role which was more than that of being only a fit friend also can be cited.

When he was in Sicily on 13 January, 1833 Emerson depicted clearly his telescopic faith: "A man looks upon himself as a mere circumstance and not as a solid, adamant, mundane ground plan of a universal man."[3] It was suggested that if a man would "turn the telescope" on his "internals," and if he compared them "with durable things," then he would discover that those "internals" would always "outshine the sun and will grind to powder the iron and the stone of outward permanence," just as the "power" and

---

[1]Emerson, JMN, 4: 267. [2]Ibid.

[3]Ibid., p. 119.

"peace" of "memory" reach further into antiquity than to touch the "side
of the pyramids."[1] These examples of Emerson's more mature use of the
infantile relationship have a larger purpose than merely to serve as examples
of the pattern of expansion within diminishment. They implicate Emerson
in a not so immediate process of taking for granted more similarities than
differences between Plato and Carlyle. Generally, it would seem as if,
when faced with a would-be adversary, Emerson engaged in a psychological
process by which that would-be adversary was converted into a "mother,"
at least into a mother-like father or older brother. One may recall that
before he entered into theological studies Emerson first felt called upon
to justify himself to Plato. Then the "Letter to Plato" was the result,
a letter with a thematic structure identical to the structure of expansion
within diminishment. And that particular pattern, we have said all along,
was rooted in the mother-infant relationship, or that sense of mutuality
with others which gives rise first to payful reciprocity and then later
may spawn ritualized forms of regard and behavior. If Plato resembled an
adversary or, at least, the challenge of a figure to be reckoned with, then
Emerson placed the Athenian in his maternal pantheon. Carlyle, too, was
a would-be adversary whom Emerson recognized as Plato's peer.

Carlyle taught Emerson to affirm the exclusivity of the primal infantile relation, or a relation which in the examples above existed between
Emerson as an observer or beholder and a celestial vault or some ideal,
cosmic realm of ideas which served symbolically to replace trusting and
trustworthy gazes shining down on the life of the nascent lecturer. "All
the mistakes I make," he reported during April, 1834, "arise from forsaking
my own station and trying to see the object from another person's point of

view."[1] On the one hand, Emerson reported an end to personal identifications.
However, he went on to say that when he read "so resolute a self-thinker
as Carlyle," he was "convinced" of the "riches of wisdom" that ever belong
to the man who utters "his own thought with a divine confidence that it must
be true if he heard it there."[2] In spite of a more-or-less permanent identification with Carlyle, his Teacher, Emerson was able to realize what he had
to do in order to create for himself the ground of self-trust and personal
independence, and do so within the context of his identification. Here was
an analogue of the Platonic Cave, where Emerson's identification with Carlyle
was the cave while the bright light of day coming from the mouth of the cave
was the wisdom of self-trust and the goal of personal independence. Moreover, it was in terms of the same kind of solitariness that the hero, Socrates,
evidenced his highest virtue. He turned away from all knowledge other than
self-knowledge. Thus, Carlyle's message fit in with Emersonian preoccupations.
Therefore, Carlyle and Plato were of the same divine cut in Emerson's eyes.
But the association also was even more overt than this.

One needs not hunt for expressions of visual expansion within diminishment alone, since Emerson made clear references to the affinity he perceived
between Carlyle and Plato. If the meaning of Plato for Emerson was carried
best by the ritualized pattern of play represented, for example, by the imagery
associated with Plato's allegory of the cave in book VII of his Republic,
and if Plato was associated with Carlyle as another great Teacher, then
Carlyle too was regarded as an embodiment of the structure, expansion
within diminishment. This has been seen insofar as Carlyle was believed to
have been a step beyond Aunt Mary. So, references which confirm this pattern
of mental association, this particular relationship in Emerson's pantheon

---

[1]Ibid., p. 274.   [2]Ibid.

of Teachers, can be cited.

Critical of Carlyle's somewhat unorthodox literary style (humor), Emerson wrote to him early in 1834 advising that, "Bacon and Plato have something too solid to say than that they can afford to be humorists. You are dispensing that which is rarest, namely, the simplest truths--truths which lie next to Consciousness and which only the Platos and Goethes perceive."[1] In a sense, Emerson was pleading with Carlyle to be to him what Goethe had been to his brother, namely, a moral hero. Literary style might dull the truth, but Emerson was certain his hero did not tarnish it very much. Emerson acknowledged that the "true argument, what we call the unfolding of an idea," had been demonstrated best specifically in two works, namely, in "Plato's Dialogues, in Carlyle's Characteristics."[2] Sampson Reed, theologian by training and druggist by trade, whose book, Observations on the Growth of the Mind (1826), Emerson believed would "give him Frisbies chair" at Harvard during 1826, became one of the most influential American Swedenborgians during the 1820's and 1830's.[3] Emerson sent Carlyle a copy of Reed's book along with the first letter of 14 May, 1834. Carlyle praised Reed's work, saying the "Swedenborgian Druggist" was a "faithful thinker, with really deep Ideas."[4] Then Carlyle quoted a line from his own book, Sartor Resartus, indicating further praise for Swedenborgianism in general: "Thro' the smallest window, look well and you can look out into the Infinite."[5]

So much for the Plato-Carlyle connection. Now it is time to consider

---

[1]Slater, ed., The Correspondence of Emerson and Carlyle, p. 99.

[2]Emerson, JMN, 4: 289.   [3]See Emerson, Letters, 1: 176.

[4]Slater, ed., The Correspondence of Emerson and Carlyle, pp. 101-102.

[5]Ibid.

some of the more psychological implications this connection spelled-out

for Emerson, since the association became integral to the American's bio-

graphical propensities late in 1833 and ever afterwards. Emerson arrived

in New York City from abroad early in October, 1833, and was in Boston

by the ninth day of that month. Emerson would constantly beseech his

great Teacher everafter to see the United States soon (as he had been in

the habit of beseeching his Aunt Mary to visit the family years earlier),

but the Englishman would keep postponing a visit (Carlyle never did manage

to visit the United States, although Emerson's two visits to him later

in their lives might be said to have given Carlyle little reason to do so).

In any case, throughout the years, as Joseph Slater, editor of the Emerson-

Carlyle correspondence, has put it, the men maintained a "sort of visual

communication by means of photographs; in the lean years after the (civil)

war photographs sometimes crossed the ocean when letters did not."[1] In

effect, Emerson could have before his eyes images of the man with whom he

shared a Platonic rapport. Carlyle stabilized the "pictorial air" of the

world. Therefore, Emerson relied on the individual Teacher as an emblem of

the expansion he sought from within the confines of his distance from all

Teachers, distance in time and, as was the case with Carlyle, distance in

space.

"The secret of the teacher's force," Emerson wrote on 20 April, 1834,

"lies in the conviction that men are convertible. And they are. They want

awakening."[2] Just as Carlyle continued to open Emerson's eyes in pictorial

form as the latter arrived across the ocean, so too any teacher should

---

[1] Ibid., p. 50. Some of the photographs are included between pages
52 and 53 of this volume.

[2] Emerson, JMN, 4: 278.

open the horizon of one's vision to "God's universe, to a perception of its beauty."[1] But late in 1833 Emerson still wondered about how to assess the churches from whose "habitual sleep" he had awakened a year or so before. He called both Calvinism and Unitarianism, as well as broad Christian or pagan faiths, an "imperfect version of the moral law" in the hands of "incapable teachers."[2] The "true Teacher," he believed, penetrates to the "depth of the Original" and exhibits it to men . . . because of "this One bottom . . . men of each church, Socrates, A Kempis, Fenelon, Butler, Penn, Swedenborg, Channing think and say the same thing."[3] In summary, then, the teacher of the coming age must occupy himself in the "study and explanation of the moral constitution of man," at least more than in the "elucidation of difficult texts," especially the Bible.[4] This was remarkably consistent with evangelical Protestantism which was spreading throughout the land, especially to the west of New England, insofar as its point of view was neither wholly Calvinistic nor Arminian.[5] Whereas the evangelicals employed revivalistic machinery in order to engender a facsimilie of this point of view, the Bostonians relied on the lyceum. In both cases, life itself could readily become a perpetual scripture. The individual life cycle afforded all persons the "lottery" of trying to go beyond themselves by striving to perfect their moral integrity.

In order that Emerson's psychological preparedness to link together Carlyle and Plato in terms of the pattern of expansion within diminishment

---

[1]Ibid.

[2]Ibid., p. 83.

[3]Ibid.

[4]Ibid., pp. 93-04.

[5]See William McLoughlin, ed., The American Evangelicals, 1800-1900 (New York: Harper and Row, 1968), p. 26.

be poised, ready for actual expression in the American Lyceum, another propensity must be recognized. This tendency is noted to be one step removed from the less immediate reality of a mind-set filled with associations of "great men" and, with the same step, a move closer to the lecture platform after October, 1833. Quite simply, Emerson followed Carlyle's lead and found biographical study a worthy pursuit. By means of biographical study he was able to fix his eyes on the "One bottom" of all men: "Does it not seem as if a perfect parallelism existed between every great and fully developed man and every other?" he asked during December, 1834.[1] For example, one might take men of a strong nature like Luther, Socrates, or Sam Johnson--men upon whom events have acted powerfully. Chances are that one would find no trait, no fear, no love, no talent, no dream in one that "did not translate a similar love, fear, talent, dream, in the other."[2] This belief, thus, was the ground for developing the "Portraiture of Man," the ideal.[3] Moreover, as a professional speaker, Emerson was giving birth to a "strong nature" all its own, one which was approximating in fact this ideal portrait.

The fascinating fact of biography was that it cast one into a market place where the relative and absolute merits of many persons, as well as oneself, could be adjudicated and either rejected or made one's own so that one could reap moral benefit: "Is there not always a silent comparison between the intellectual and moral endowments portrayed and those of which we are conscious?"[4] Luther, Newton, and Buonaparte were subjects of panegyric because, in the opinion of the lecturer, in "some one respect" this particular man "represented the idea of Man."[5] As far as one accords with the lecturer's

---

[1]Emerson, JMN, 4: 336-37. [2]Ibid. [3]Ibid.

[4]Ibid., p. 256. [5]Ibid.

judgment, the picture can be taken "for a standard of Man"; and "so let every line accuse or approve our own ways of thinking."[1] Thus, by means of comparative biography we learn how truly to live, not just "get ready to live."[2]

Hardly at a loss for a metaphor to describe the effect of not venturing into the "biographical market place," Emerson believed most men were chained to great men, that they "buy" but never are satiated: Who says, he wrote, "we are not chained? He lies . . . See how greedily you accept the verse of Homer or Shakespeare; the outline of M. Angelo; the strain of Handel; the word of Webster; how thoroughly you understand and make them your own. . . I say you are chained."[3] What Emerson implied here was what he himself was unable to do, even if he sensed it was called for. One may shop for suitable identifications or "role models," but one is chained to them unless those identifications serve only as pretexts for growing beyond them. Though he may have been able to grow beyond Luther, Michaelangelo, et al., Emerson himself was by-and-large chained to Carlyle. Yet the identification seemed not to thwart Emerson's sense of vocation. After all, Carlyle was a man of letters and Emerson had not yet achieved a similar recognition in his own country. Emerson was disappointed in himself, believing he labored under an "optical deception of the mind."[4] On 23 December, 1834 he defined what he meant by this "optical deception" in terms of an identification. An ingenious man, he thought, is disappointed "hearing opinions and truths congenial to his own announced with effect in conversation. . . . they are so near his own thought or expression that he thinks he ought to have spoken

---

[1]Ibid.   [2]Ibid., pp. 276-77.   [3]Ibid., p. 365

[4]Ibid., pp. 370-71.

first."[1] If disappointment was the overall tone of the cluster of events

of 1811-24, now that same disappointment had risen to scrutiny. Moreover,

once scrutinized, it was readily dispensed with as a "deception." When,

just four days later, on 7 December 1834, he said there were two kinds of

blindness--"one of an incapacity to see; the other, of preoccupied atten-

tion"--he implied that biographical identifications could be all shadows

or all light.[2] In either case, one could not "see"--he would be blinded

or be myopic. One needed identifications, but one did not need to worship

heroes. Because Emerson relied above on the metaphor of chain, and because

of the notion of "optical deception," it was not difficult or unusual for

him to have had a feeling that all identifications were like caves and to

act accordingly. Only from within the cave could one see beyond shadows

to light. Thus, even in terms of his identification with Carlyle and his

biographical preoccupation his particular ritualized vision held sway as

it did for the seer in the Platonic allegory of the cave.

During November, 1835 and after less than two months of marriage to

his second wife, Emerson would suggest that his biographical yearnings were

like a marriage in that both marriage and biographical study needed close

attention in the present, in spite of the realities that so much of biography

and marriage was of the past: "People think that husbands and wives have

no present time, that they have long already established their mutual con-

nexion, have nothing to learn from one another, and know beforehand each

what the other will do."[3] However, popular belief was illusory, and the

"wise man will discern the fact; viz., that they are chance-joined, little

---

[1]Ibid.   [2]Ibid., p. 377.

[3]Ibid., 4: 108-109.

acquainted, and do observe each the other's carriage to the stranger as curiously as he doth."[1] Implied was that, like marriage, much of biography is carried on in the future by scholars eager to identify with "great men." Having lost his first wife whom, he told Aunt Mary on 18 April, 1833, he had envisioned "in all her beauty," Ellen, nevertheless, "never disappointed" him "except in her death."[2] If this statement is seen to be consistent with his thoughts on "optical deceptions," then one can only infer he was implying that his first marriage was, indeed, disappointing. If it was not, then he would have little need to make it into a platform beyond which he thought he had to go. For a fleeting moment from 1829-31 Ellen held in check Emerson's need for Teachers. She herself was "God's gift of mercy," a Teacher, and "sunburst" in a way quite inimical to his lessened rapture over his second marriage.[3] Also, exactly at the same time that he became acquainted with Ellen Tucker, during the winter of 1827-38, he was unusually preoccupied with finding a "useful person," one who, perhaps, would help him and not degrade him.[4] That is, he sought a "clear soul" who, in passing by, divided "our good and bad angel" so that one might "best amputate" those persons with dull, degrading souls.[5] Psychologically speaking, Emerson was defining his autonomy at the same time he was seeking to merge with his Teachers, and with the soul of the universal glance at some idealized time of consumation in the future. Such was the lingering remnant of his psychological crisis of intimacy versus isolation which had begun during 1824-33 but now was being resolved during 1834-38.

---

[1] Ibid.

[2] Emerson, Letters, 1: 376.

[3] See Emerson, JMN, 3: 149; Emerson, Letters, 1: 376.

[4] See ibid, pp. 222, 225.

[5] Emerson, JMN, 5: 298.

Now is the time to shift gears. That Emerson had been inspired by Carlyle is beyond doubt. Inspiration had been "taken in" through Emerson's initiative to form an identification of literary mutuality with Carlyle. The upshot was that Emerson was prepared, at least at first, to model his nascent career as a lecturer and author on Carlyle's success. Thus, the Englishman was Emerson's first major prop during 1834-38. His second major prop was the already-established network of educational societies, known together as the American Lyceum movement. Just as Emerson found entering the Unitarian framework convenient during 1826-32, so too the Lyceum was a convenient place to begin anew. Besides, a resolution of his vocational crisis was on the offing.

The first lyceum was founded in 1826 in Millbury, Massachusetts by Josiah Holbrook, a teacher and lecturer.[1] It was named after the place where Aristotle, among others, lectured to the young men of ancient Greece. As one of the first forms of concerted adult education in the United States (Charles Grandison Finney made his debut in New York the year before. He also was concerned about adult education, insofar as methods later were codified by theological thinkers such as Horace Bushnell and Henry Ward Beecher), lyceums were voluntary associations that gave people the chance to hear lectures and debates on topics of current interest. The lyceums multiplied rapidly after 1826, chiefly in New England, New York, and in the Middle West, and by 1834 over 3000 local groups were, by and large, organized into the network called the American Lyceum. At first, lyceums were local affairs, with speakers being chosen from the community. Later, by 1840, they became more of an institution, and professional speakers traveled the lyceum circuit for fees, in a manner akin to "speakers bureaus"

---

[1]See Carl Bode, The American Lyceum: Town Meeting of the Mind (New York: Oxford University Press, 1956).

of the twentieth century Rotary Club. Emerson, of course, owed his reputation to the American Lyceum, since his major essays were the product of the demands of his audiences. Generally, the lyceum movement can be understood as the earliest educative component of the broader national movement toward social and humanitarian reform during the nineteenth century. It worked to help form the ideological dimension of the new American self-understanding or identity.

However, Emerson would have had this conception reversed, namely, that the zealotry of social and humanitarian reform was merely a component of the broader consciousness of virtue which, he declared on 1 October, 1837, was the axial spine of the world: "The young man relying on his instincts who has only a good intention is apt to feel ashamed of his inaction and the slightness of his virtue when in the presence of the active and zealous leaders of the philanthropic enterprises of Universal Temperance, Peace, and Abolition of Slavery . . . Trust it nevertheless."[1] Seeming not unlike what he wrote early during 1831 on the virtue of "witholding," he made an analogy between "zealous versus inactive" commitments and a man's financial worth: "A man's income is not sufficient for all things. . . . It is a grandeur of character which must have unity, and reviews and pries ever into its domestic truth and justice, loving quiet honor better than proclaiming zeal."[2] He continued to say in a way which by now had become characteristic of his thinking, that he thought "the zealot goes abroad from ignorance of the riches of his home. . . . But this good intention" of the young man toward inaction and virtue, which "seems so cheap beside the brave zeal," is the "backbone of the world."[3] That the "Representative Man" was to be

---

[1] Emerson, _JMN_, 5: 380-81.   [2] Ibid.   [3] Ibid.

at the helm of the redeemer nation also eventuated in a somewhat more concrete difference and likeness between the two religious ideals of "quiet honor" and proclaimed "zeal."

Implied by the appearance of the lyceum movement were two things at least. On the one hand, the lyceum grew out of local communities, and insofar as it did it tended to shift concern for education away from what usually had been under the auspices of ecclesiastical guidance during the past, namely, education as the achieving of personal and doctrinal congruity. In this sense, the lyceum replaced much of what the church had done in local liberal communities. On the other hand, however, a broader perspective suggests that lyceums and churches were less rivalrous than it would seem, that they were meeting needs together in concerted fashion. If evangelical energies were channeled increasingly into social and humanitarian reform during the first half of the nineteenth century, then one of the major reforms that also took place at the time had to do with the initiatives to found American public schools. These initiatives were a direct contribution of the American Lyceum movement insofar as the issue of public education for each citizen was a dominant topic discussed on the lecture platform.

Therefore, public education might be understood as a counterpart of what the evangelical preachers referred to as "conversion." One needs not to go into evangelical Christianity here. But it can be pointed out that by concentrating on the practical aspects of soul saving, the evangelicals, as did Emerson and the transcendentalists, avoided intricate debate over creeds, doctrines, and dogmas. Both public education and religious conversion were merely expressions of the national propensity to stabilize a unified cultural consciousness, a "national identity." It is interesting to note in this regard that a parallel movement occurred after the Civil War, one which did not appear side-by-side with the more liberal churches of New England earlier in the century. Growing directly out of a more evangelical corps, the Rev. John H. Vincent and Lewis Miller met at Fair Point on Lake Chautauqua, New York in 1874 and organized an assembly for the training of Sunday School teachers and church workers.[1] When the assemblies became annual affairs they were referred to as "Chautauquas," and, though at first they were strictly religious in nature, they gradually assimilated such activities as lectures on secular subjects and dramatic entertainment. William Rainey Harper, later the president of the University of Chicago, got his start as the educational director of the Chautauquas in 1883. The institutional similarities of the American Lyceum movement and the Chautauquas suggest that the ideal of the "Representative Man" and the ideal of the "Redeemer Nation" intermingled in peoples' minds during the nineteenth century.

However, Emerson believed leadership could not be crammed down the throat of his country (his phrasing). The psychosocial oral mode of "incorporation," he sensed, was inappropriate. Rather, seeing himself as a leader, he thought his eyes themselves were beacons of national direction: "It is enough for him that he has eyes to see that he is infinite spectator without hurrying uncalled to be infinite doer. . . . If you sit down to write with weak eyes and awaken your imagination to the topic you will find your eyes strong."[2] The point to be made was that his national service was laid upon men indirectly or, as he put it,

---

[1] See Joseph Gould, The Chautauqua Movement (New York: New York State University of New York, 1961).

[2] Emerson, JMN, 5: 26.

1

"obliquely"--a modest, inoffensive influence.

On 28 November, 1828 the Exchange Coffee House in Boston was again the site of patriotic zeal. A meeting was organized, presided over by Daniel Webster, to discuss the founding of a local lyceum. Out of that meeting was created the Boston Society for the Diffusion of Useful Knowledge. The committee appointed to oversee the activities of the Society was made up of two persons, George B. Emerson (Ralph Waldo's second cousin) and William Russell, editor of the American Journal of Education. When Emerson returned from abroad in 1833 a place for him seemed at hand, if only because of being well-connected. With assurance of a growing network of local committees of arrangements and subscription, as well as membership audiences eager to hear new things, Emerson jumped into the fray.

To his favor was the reality that one need not be an expert in the field of one's topic. It was well-known that virtually anything said from the platform usually was soaked up into some kind of popular understanding, usually referred to as "appreciation." Often lectures were built around a single topic, many lecturers addressing themselves to it. At other times a lone lecturer would deliver an entire series on a topic by himself. Evidently Charles and George B. Emerson made the initial arrangements for Emerson's debut as a lecturer. On 11 October, 1833, two days after arriving home in Boston, Emerson wrote to William, "I have engaged to deliver the introductory Lecture to the National History Society in November."[2] Sufficiently motivated by Carlyle, Emerson now was familiar with the game plan.

Characteristic of Emerson's professional life during 1834-38 was

---

[1] Ibid.

[2] Emerson, Letters, 1: 397.

his single-minded devotion to the lecture platform, which was not unprompted by envy of Charles' growing success as a Court Street attorney. Emerson had gone to great lengths during 1829-31 to free himself from pulpit responsibilities at Second Church. Now as he plunged headlong into these new professional commitments he also accomplished placing his emotional life out of the decisive sway of family life. This was demonstrated in a short letter written on 18 November, 1833 to William who was anticipating marriage on 3 December, 1833. Emerson told his brother he was happy William's "lonely days" would soon be ended by the advent of the "real happiness of a home."[1] However, he went on to say that he was too busy and too committed to a lecture series and, as a result, he would be unable to attend the wedding ceremony, which was to take place not far away in Portsmouth, New Hampshire: "I should have been glad to accept your invitation and accompanied you to Portsmouth but could not easily avoid or shorten this engagement of mine in this town (New Bedford, Massachusetts) . . . besides I am not hero at festivals."[2] Even more to the point was that William had asked Emerson to be the best man, the "groomsman," and now the commission fell necessarily upon Charles by default, or so Emerson assumed.

In addition to sending his regrets, he informed William that their mother also would not be attending the wedding. This was because the "ride could give her no pleasure at this season and the seeing the form, amidst an assembly of total strangers," seemed "scarcely worth the journey for her."[3] It was not that he was being rude to William by begging-out, just that weddings had become low priorities for him. Speaking for their mother was not customary for the Emerson sons and the fact he did do

---

[1]Ibid., p. 398.   [2]Ibid.   [3]Ibid.

so at this times implies that Emerson, not his mother, was in control of things. The point is not that a church ceremony and a chilly trip in a chaise prevented Emerson and his mother from attending William's wedding. Instead, the point is that Emerson refrained from conceiving of the event totally as a "family event," with the implication that he had done all he could to try to be in attendance. At least, other factors worked to place this event lower on Emerson's list of personal priorities than it would have been if, perhaps, his brother had married during the previous decade. Emerson's regard at this point was psychologically interesting because it contrasted with his regard of his family and his first wife during 1829-31. We shall see how this new regard was regard of distance or "isolation" and, moreover, how it became the mold into which the tenor of his second marriage would be poured.

A cursory survey of his early lectures, more by way of a listing, should suffice to suggest that, indeed, he was too busy for much else, let alone family life of the sort he knew while engaged and married to Ellen Tucker. After his first lecture on 5 November, 1833 at the Masonic Temple in Boston (again made possible through the connection of George B. Emerson) the lyceum welcomed the delivery of "The Relation of Man to the Globe" for the Franklin Lectures, a series arranged for people of modest means; "Water," for the Boston Mechanics Institution; and "A Correct Taste in English Literature," for the American Institute of Instruction, through 1834. He read lectures on Italy before the Unitarian congregation at New Bedford during 1833-34, and presented lectures and sermons in Waltham and Plymouth during 1834-35. After 1835 he lectured as well as preached occasionally in Waltham, Lowell, Roxbury, Framingham, Charlestown, Watertown, Portsmouth, East Lexington, and Concord--so that his fame spread slowly to the degree to which his circuit widened. Before 1843 he was also invited to lecture in Providence, Rhode Island; Worcester, Massachusetts; Philadelphia, Pennsylvania; Baltimore, Maryland; and New York, New York. In addition to these tours, he also gave occasional lectures (one of which will soon be noted to serve as a point of culmination for the period of 1834-38): one for the Concord sesquintennial celebration (12 September, 1835); one at the Green Street School in Providence (10 June, 1837); one at the annual meeting of the Phi Beta Kappa Society at Harvard College (31 August, 1837); a lecture to students at the Harvard Divinity School (15 July, 1838); and lectures at Dartmouth College (28 July, 1838), Waterville College, Maine (11 August, 1841) and Middlebury College, Vermont (22 July, 1845). Emerson was a busy man.

His "Divinity School Address (15 July, 1838), and the psychological components of his life which attend to it at the time of its appearance, will culminate the elaboration of the cluster of events at hand. For it is clear that by 1838, when the address was delivered, Emerson had set himself firmly in the vocational identity that he would carry for the rest of his life. Therefore, 1834-38 might appear as an "anti-climax," his resignation from Second Church during 1832 having been the appropriate "climax." However, though he had been, as it were, born anew after 1832-33, he continued to preach occasional sermons as well as to lecture. But only when the quantity of lecturing increased, did Emerson actually "work through" his act of 1832 emotionally. Only then had the psychological crisis of intimacy versus isolation been negotiated to a point of sufficient resolution that his life could expand into other vistas. The appearance of the "Divinity School Address" in itself--a lecture in form, delivered to men trained preach sermons--and Emerson's last sermon following it, marked the time in his life when psychological closure on the past (i.e., the ministry in the narrow, denominational sense) gave rise to a re-centering on the future (i.e., the ministry in the broad, civil sense). Not incidental to the vitalizing of the props of Carlyle and the American Lyceum movement was the reality that, in one sense, Ellen Tucker Emerson continued granting Emerson a "reprieve" even after her death.

Ellen Tucker literally "bought time" during which Emerson could slowly turn his sights away from the "pale negations" or shadows of Unitarianism and work through the act of 1832. On 24 May, 1831 he wrote to William that "Ellen is to continue to benefit her husband whenever hereafter the estate shall be settled. . . . I please myself that Ellen's work of mercy is not done on earth, but she shall continue to help Edward & B. & Charles."[1] Part of her father's estate, long probated, would soon be his. Beza Tucker, who had been a Boston merchant, had died on 16 May, 1820.[2] However, because of legal complications Emerson's claim to Ellen's part of her father's estate was uncertain and, he added, "I am going fast in arrears."[3] Ellen had not reached twenty-one years of age, the legal age, when she died. In question was whether or not, after what would have been her twenty-first year (1833), her share of the Tucker estate would automatically go to her husband. It was not that Ellen's family tried to keep Emerson from getting the money, though this might be read easily into their acquiescence over pressing the legal issue one way or the other. Rather, their financial situation was not as critical as his was. They could over-look slow-moving legal machinery, but he could not.

---

[1] Ibid., p. 323.

[2] See ibid., 6: 169.

[3] Ibid., 1: 323.

During June of 1831, Ellen's inheritance remained "wholly unsettled" and Emerson did not wish to appear too aggressive pressing his case, since to do so might offend Ellen's mother, Mrs. Kent, and Ellen's sisters, Paulina and Margaret (who would die late during 1832): "I may have legal rights which I shall not choose to enforce."[1] But his career was at stake, and when he learned during January, 1832 from Mr. Cutler, the executor of Beza Tucker's estate, that the day of final settlement was "far off," perhaps not for "as long as I live," Emerson filed a suit against the estate.[2] When he was in Naples on 12 March, 1833, however, he felt betwixt-and-between about his future. Then he was wont to think of himself as the "plain old Adam, the simple genuine Self against the whole world."[3] Nonetheless, he was convinced that in such a state one's need was to "assert yourself," so that he would not find himself "overborne by the most paltry things."[4] John Hooker Ashmun, law professor at Harvard, acted on Emerson's behalf and took out letters of administration for him and filed a petition with the Supreme Judicial Court in Chancery. This action subpoenaed Mr. Cutler, Mrs. Kent, "and other surviving heirs, to appear before the court 'to abide such order and decree as to your Honours shall seem agreeable to equity and good conscience."[5] Despite his amiable relations with the Tuckers and Mrs. Kent, Emerson was out to enforce his legal rights at a time, no less, when he was only weeks away from the "climax" of his vocational conflict at Second Church. However, about two years would elapse before the first steps toward a final settlement would be reached.

---

[1] Ibid., p. 327.

[2] Ibid., p. 345.

[3] Emerson, JMN, 4: 141.

[4] Ibid.

[5] See Emerson, Letters, 1: 345; Rusk, The Life of Ralph Waldo Emerson, p. 157.

Margaret's share was willed to Paulina and to a Boston Hospital and school when she died late in 1832, about a month before Emerson sailed for Italy. Charles was left in charge of the whole matter of securing his brother's money, just as he had been left in charge of Emerson's responsibilities at Second Church during 1830. Emerson was certain he would be richer "for Ellen's estate" when he was again in America during December, 1833, believing whenever that day came he would buy "a hearth somewhere to which we pious Aeneases may return with our household goods from all quarters of our dispersion."[1] When he hoped for this, he simultaneously was basking in success from his lecture at the Masonic Temple and was preparing the lecture, "Water," for the Mechanics Institute, which he delivered in January, 1834. The legal initiative of 1832 evidently offended Joshua Nash, husband of Paulina and Emerson's brother-in-law, who thought the action was one of greed.[2] But Emerson, if he actually felt some pangs of guilt as a result of stepping on Nash's toes (the heat of the Nash-Emerson relationship seems to have cooled by April, 1837),[3] found them mitigated by his new-found profession. In addition, he soon realized his initiative would not be without its rewards.

During May, 1834 Emerson received a substantial portfolio of stocks (67 shares, City Bank; 19 shares, Atlantick Bank; 31 shares, Boston and Roxbury Mill Dam) and an advance on what case was being decided as his share of what was left of Beza Tucker's cash resources. This advance amounted to between $3000-4000. Though the other half of Ellen's share

---

[1]Emerson, Letters, 1: 402.   [2]See ibid., pp. 345, 349.

[3]See ibid., 2: 66.

was still in Mr. Cutler's hands (a value of about $11,647.99), Emerson esti-
mated that the half which now was his (a value of about $11,600) would start
producing the full $1200 he expected to be earning annually because of
Ellen's "work of mercy."[1] In terms of his distinction between "Understanding,"
or the lesser faculty of the soul, and "Reason," or the higher faculty of
the soul--"it simply perceives; it is vision . . .," he suggested to Edward
that with his new annual income "the Reason of Mother and you and I might
defy the Understanding upon his own ground, for the rest of the few years
in which we shall be subject to his insults."[2] Little did Emerson realize
during 1832 that by severing the cord that bound him to the church he not
only would find new autonomy, but also his achievement brought about new
forays and initiatives into the real world, the world of the "market place."
He seemed confident that he could generate sufficient business, so to speak,
by lecturing. Especially since he would receive the full settlement during
July of 1837. Twelve hundred dollars per year was about equal to two-thirds
of his salary at Second Church during 1832. He thought it a good start.

There is no conclusive evidence to suggest either that Emerson married
Ellen for her money, or that he allowed her to die knowing that her estate
would fall into his hands. Money was not a big issue during 1829-31, the
time of their relationship, because he was earning more than he ever had
earned before as the minister of Second Church, his first real job. Nonetheless, it is difficult to banish the thought of less than honorable motivations
on his part surrounding her death and the question of Beza Tucker's estate.
It is possible that the "pay off" of marriage was not only the assertion of

---

[1]See ibid., 1: 412-13; Ibid., 2: 86-87, 91-92.

[2]Ibid., 1: 413-14.

personal autonomy and strength, but also the basis for financial rewards in the future. Even prior to the onset of his full-blown ambivalence in 1825, long before meeting Ellen, Emerson was aware of the wealthy Tucker family. He had passed their house on his way from Roxbury to Boston on the Dedham Road during 1823-25 and, moreover, Beza Tucker was a pew-holder in his father's church, First Church. Emerson was especially aware the family had a reputation in the neighborhood of succumbing easily to tuberculosis.[1] Generally, one suspects a multitude of factors involved. But one also has the feeling that a young man, who had been deprived of many of the niceties of life, including a satisfying vocation for most of his life, was hardly inclined not to think of the financial side of romance. However, this seems to be only the drift of the evidence, not conclusive in itself.

By the time he was half-way through 1834, the lecturer's props supported his single-minded rush to the lecture platform. He had carried home from England an identification with his only live literary mentor; he had found ready connections and successes in lyceums in and around Boston; and he had received half of his wife's share of Beza Tucker's estate, with reasonable assurance of receiving more several years later. Being propped-up by these supports, and now knowing what he expected of himself as a professional person, Emerson was ready to turn his attention elsewhere. With his professional life set firmly afoot, he moved to adorn it with the stability of "person" (a wife) and "place" (a home of his own). His shrills from the lyceum marketplace required harmonizing. Only as he cultivated a personal life with a compatible wife and in comfortable surroundings

---

[1] Rusk, The Life of Ralph Waldo Emerson, p. 134.

did he feel free finally to let go of the pulpit completely. Somehow, he felt it necessary to certify that he had severed his own "umbilical cord" to the church. Taking his own wife, and purchasing his own home were means by which the stability of the Unitarian form were replaced by the new stability of "person and place."

CHAPTER VII

HOME WITH THE GOODS: STABILITY
OF PERSON AND PLACE

During 1834-38 Emerson engaged in a psychological process whereby his once severed "umbilical cord," which had symbolically tied him to the church, was re-connected to a particular person and to a particular place. This new joining together did not limit his vocational horizons. Instead, investing his energies in a particular person and in a particular place he could call his permanent home supplied the steadiness Emerson needed for setting to work. Moreover, the way this was accomplished was an "anti-climax," or his final renunciation of the pulpit. For now, focus will be on Emerson's personal propensities toward recovering in a new higher key, owing to his greater maturity, all he had been discovering about his psychological style during 1825-33. That is, about his attempts to mitigate the tension between illness and travel according to the playful visual pattern of expansion within diminishment. Two major dimensions of Emerson's recovery of the meaning of 1825-33 are evident. The first concerns Emerson's second wife, Lydia Jackson, and his relationship with her; the second pertains to his desire to locate a suitable residence for himself at first, and to purchase a house later on which he and his wife would, in fact, call their home until their deaths. Not coincidentally, both centers of Emerson's personal preoccupation got firmly established during 1835 and begat personal stability: he bought a house and married. But he settled down in these two ways primarily insofar as the configuration of "person and place" managed to contain the meaning of the psychological and geographical factors associated with the long cluster of events of 1825-33. Not coincidentally such closure on and containment of the past for use in the present and for his future occurred after Emerson received the first half of the Tucker legacy, and after he realized prospects for receiving the balance were bright ones.

Emerson pleased himself just before 1834 when he contemplated the "felicity" of his present situation.[1] It seemed to him he was "singularly free" and able to unite "every virtue" and to develop toward "great improvement."[2] When he journeyed through Plymouth, Massachusetts on his way to New Bedford in order to lecture during January, 1834 his mind lingered on his situation in that particular historic place. He reported he had "stood on the Rock" and had felt that it grew more important "by the growth of this nation" in the several minutes he stood there.[3] Whether or not that particular importance had been imparted to the Rock by itself or because Emerson stood on it remains ambiguous. However, at this time he was gathering together thoughts about the value of comparative biographical studies by which a "picture" of the life of a great man was to be taken "for a standard of Man."[4] There was a sense of personal strength expressed by the image of the fusion of Emerson and Plymouth Rock. Furthermore, he undoubtedly met Lydia Jackson, resident of Plymouth, during that month of January, 1834. For on 19 January, 1834 he wrote to Paulina and Joshua Nash that he desired to assure them of his "warm good will," perhaps sensing that insult might be added to injury if they got wind of his budding romance.[5] Certainly the financial factor was the close horizon, or the ostensible reason, which informed his letter to them. But it was not as urgent as

---

[1] Emerson, JMN, 4: 253. [2] Ibid. [3] Ibid., p. 261.

[4] Ibid., p. 256. [5] See Emerson, Letters, 1: 405-406.

communicating another assuring sentiment. He reported that he wrote because he had been reading through some "verses and scraps of Ellen" that heightened his "admiration and . . . sorrow" about her.[1] On the basis of the meaning of his more distant horizon, namely, his budding romance with Lydia Jackson, anxiety associated with receiving Ellen's share of her father's estate was being grappled with by the surviving husband. Anxiety, if not guilt, usually always is associated with survival, especially when one survives that from which a person they love dies. Emerson survived the tuberculosis from which Ellen perished.[2]

That his profession was on his mind most was clear from his letter to William of 18 January, 1834 in which he stated, "Pray do not ask me or cause me to be asked to come to New York for I have no disposition to go there. . . . I am just on the edge of another journey to New Bedford where I am to spend the month of February having been persuaded by their overkindness and zeal."[3] It was not that he thought his new sister-in-law (Susan Havens) unimportant to meet, just that other more important matters, as far as he

-----

[1]Ibid., p. 405.

[2]Several studies of survivors suggest this. A general study is, Robert Jay Lifton, Death in Life: Survivors of Hiroshima (New York: Vintage, 1969). In regard to Emerson's particular visual preoccupation, especially in light of the fact of the poem to Ellen called, "Thine Eyes Still Shine," written during his marriage to her, in which he senses himself lost without her, see, Joan M. Erikson, "Eye to Eye" in Gyorgy Kepes, ed., The Man-Made Object (New York: George Braziller, 1966). Emerson's poetic reference to "eyes" and "beads" of dew on foliage can be linked to the visual form of the sphere, which Erikson would attribute to the shape and function of the eye in human development. The "eye," she says, "is that ur-form which we apprehend and take in visually with our mother's milk" (p. 56). This form is impressed in the feelings and longings of mankind and expressed in the symbols and forms of religion, as the eye that both "bless and curses" (p. 52). Clearly, anxiety and guilt, as well as hope and trust, can be associated with vision. At least, the meaning of seeing Ellen's writings is psychologically ambiguous.

[3]Ibid.

weighed them, were on his mind—matters pertaining to his own aborted marital situation.

Not coincidentally, on 12 February, 1834 Emerson wrote in his journal that he looked back at his entries about Ellen as a "book of Promise."[1] "These last three years," he wrote in the next line, "are not a chasm—I could almost wish they were—so brilliantly sometimes the vision of Ellen's beauty and love and life come out of the darkness."[2] Besides the possibility that Emerson evidently enjoyed the nostalgia and hope of a life richly furnished with marital imagery, this entry also is important for other reasons. His professional and personal life were merging early during 1834 as the second line of his entry suggests. If the tenor of his relationship with Ellen oscillated between "reprieve" and "condemnation," from or to the Unitarian ministry, then clearly his new acquaintance with Lydia Jackson was begun and carried out on an altogether different plane, one which made marriage and vocation much more congruent with his new self-confidence.

Emerson continued to say in his journal entry of 12 February, 1834, "can you believe, Waldo Emerson, that you may relieve yourself of this perpetual perplexity of choosing? and by putting your ear close to the soul, learn always the true way."[3] Not only had his choice been between Ellen and profession during the past, but now "the choice of two roads" appeared to be between his memories of Ellen, the verses and scraps of letters she had left him, and another wife, whom he had met just prior to writing this particular journal entry. Not only would he thank his "jealous Daimon" for the godsent of Carlyle's August, 1834 letter. But he was thankful also for

---

[1]Emerson, JMN, 4: 263-64.   [2]Ibid.

[3]Ibid.

having chosen between his memories of Ellen and thoughts of a new wife,
which he believed would "agree with the Daimon of Socrates."[1] The railroad
from Carlyle now extended to the Plymouth station, and Emerson chose the
road that led to a second marriage early during the following year, 1835,
but not without pangs of conscience about having to "give up Ellen." In
fact, at one point he invited Lydia to peruse those pages of his journal
and Ellen's letters to him which depicted his "recent love wounds."[2] During
the later part of January, 1835 he would return to Concord from Plymouth
with "most agreeable recollections," that is, engaged to marry Lydia.[3]

Recall that Emerson's thumbnail sketch of the life of Thomas and Jane
Carlyle not only specified his "love" for his literary master and Teacher,
but also stated he thought Jane Carlyle was a "treasure" of a wife.[4] However,
according to biographer Froude, the Carlyle's marriage and domestic life
had been marked by "tensions and fierce outbursts" and that though the spirited
Jane Carlyle had been something of a martyr to her husband, she was "far
from an uncomplaining one."[5] The Carlyles' marriage and Emerson's own first
marriage were hardly alike, as one can readily surmise. Ellen Tucker Emerson
may have been a martyr of sorts, but she hardly was one to complain about
her life and fate. Ellen hardly was an adversary-like person like "spirited"
Jane Carlyle. One might imagine Ellen Emerson and Jane Carlyle on a trip
to the market: Ellen usually had help with her domestic chores, and probably
was not one to hold her own, so to speak, in the face of a hard bargain.
However, one is hard-pressed not to imagine Jane Carlyle getting her money's

---

[1] Ibid.

[2] Emerson, Letters, 1: 437.

[3] Emerson, JMN, 5: 14.

[4] Emerson, Letters, 1: 395.

[5] Altick, Lives and Letters, p. 234.

worth, since she appeared to be much stronger in body and in will when compared with Ellen. Perhaps it was because of her inner strength or sense of will, then, that Emerson thought Jane Carlyle to be a real "treasure," as well as a most agreeable and accomplished woman.

In Carlyle's marriage to Jane was born a pattern of relationship which came to be reflected curiously in Emerson's marriage to Lydia. The stability of "person" was a further mode of Emerson's identification with Carlyle. A brief theoretical interlude, which draws upon a popular school of psychotherapeutic thought, facilitates an understanding of the qualitative differences between Emerson's two marriages. Such an interlude will suggest how Carlyle served Emerson as a model even in the realm of relations between the sexes.

In his book, I'm OK--You're OK, Thomas A. Harris has suggested that every person evidences a "Parent" (P), a "Child" (C), and an "Adult" (A).[1] These three phenomenological realities become orchestrated in various ways, depending on the kinds of "transactions" in which persons find themselves engaging, e.g., marriage. The Parent is the "playback" of "recordings of external events" which a young person absorbed during the first five years or so of his life from his own parents and which gave him a "taught concept of life," e.g., "the only good Indian is a dead Indian."[2] The Child is the "playback" of the "recording of internal events" experienced during the first five years of life, affording one a "felt concept of life."[3] Finally, the Adult is the "playback" of the "recording of data acquired and computed through exploration and testing," that is, a "thought concept of life."[4]

---

[1]See Thomas A. Harris, I'm OK--You're OK (New York: Avon, 1969).

[2]Ibid., p. 52.   [3]Ibid.   [4]Ibid.

Parent, Child, and Adult ("P-A-C") can be expressed, each by itself, in the course of any transaction. The ideal is to free each aspect of one's individuality so that it can be cultivated in so-called "appropriate" ways. One needs not to go much further into Harris' theory, especially its psychotherapeutic implications, in order to make the point. Namely, that in contrast to the transaction of his first marriage, Emerson's second marriage, we shall soon see, was a more "appropriate" or Adult relationship. This can be explained, indicating why the "market place" image was an apt one for his understanding of the marital dimension of his identification with Carlyle.

During 1829-31 Emerson virtually suspended his Adult, allowing his Parent to trod on toward the Unitarian ministry, and his Child to bask securely in marriage. His vocational insecurity and his unwillingness to embrace whole-heartedly his ancestral calling became the pretext for projecting "higher aspirations." They, in turn, elicited from the young Ellen Tucker an attitude of "adoration." Emerson's Parent was his ancestry, its tacit mandate that he choose the ministry as his forefathers had for generations. His Child was dominant in marriage, since his relation to Ellen accentuated the "felt" component and gave vent to neither "taught" nor "thought" dimensions. These distinctions are not exclusive ones, just matters of emphasis. In any case, because Ruth Emerson was dominant within the family circle, her presence served to punctuate Emerson's Child in marriage. And because he was laboring under Aunt Mary's watchful eyes, she can be recognized to have served a similar function, namely, reinforcing Emerson's Parent. Generally, during 1829-31 Emerson was inhibited in giving birth to his Adult just as he had no children by Ellen, since the potential force of the Adult was contained domestically, that is, embodied in the daily-encountered expectations of both his mother and his aunt.

However, because Emerson severed the cord that held him tightly in that particular domestic transaction, insofar as it was symbolized by Second Church, and because out of a position of autonomy he initiated his legal suit "to enforce his rights" for part of the Tucker estate, Emerson retrieved his Adult and gave it birth, so to speak. He began to "explore and test" the lecturer's props. As the Adult came to the fore, the Parent of vocational "condemnation" and the Child of marital "reprieve" became somewhat segregated, put in their places by the Adult, their "proper" places.

Therefore, it was not insignificant that when he and Lydia were married during September, 1835 Emerson's mother departed shortly afterward for an eight-month-long stay in New York City with William and his wife.[1] She was now "blessing" the marriage of the son whose wedding she had refused to attend. Also, Aunt Mary soon became estranged from Emerson and Lydia on two counts: she did not get along with Lydia, and she worried about and admonished her nephew for his "transcendentalism."[2] If the first marriage was ruled by Emerson's Child and was largely a matter of feelings (Emerson's first love had been his "infatuation" over Martin Gay; and the pattern of that relationship was carried-over into his relationship with Ellen, also his younger peer), then the second marital relationship was ruled increasingly by his Adult which, itself, had been triggered and cultivated best by his conversion from the pulpit to the lecture platform during 1832-33. His Adult was not without expectations. Many of them were conditioned by the psychology of his most potent identification with Carlyle.

Therefore, it is revealing to note that when Emerson first married he

---

[1] See Emerson, Letters, 1: 454.

[2] Rusk, The Life of Ralph Waldo Emerson, p. 220.

was twenty-six years old. Ellen Tucker had just turned seventeen. This was not an unusual age spread, nor was Ellen's youthfulness thought to imply a lack of preparation for marriage. What is more interesting are the differences that appear between the partners' ages of that marriage and the ages of Emerson and Lydia Jackson when they were married. Emerson was thirty-two years old in 1835. Lydia, also thirty-two years old, was eight months Emerson's senior. In the first marriage there inhered a structural tendency toward an accentuation of the Child. Emerson had not yet grown free from his Parent and, thus, had been prone toward accepting a "reprieve" from his Adult, which only marriage to Ellen could assure him. In his second marriage such a structural arrangement did not exist or, at least, if it did it was hardly accentuated as it had been during the first marriage. The structural tendency of the second marriage was toward the Adult. Emerson freed himself from the expectations of his mother and his aunt (as symbolized in the Unitarian ministry) and, thus, from his Parent. He no longer feared the freedom of his Adult, since not only did he have his identification with Carlyle to support him, but also he was having successes of his own on the lecture platform. The matter of whether to seek "reprieve" or "condemnation" was not relevant to his life any longer. These issues shrank into the past and were contained by his 1835 marriage. If in Emerson's eyes Thomas and Jane Carlyle stood for the marriage of one Adult to another Adult, then Lydia came closer to the mark of Jane Carlyle than Ellen ever did or, for that matter, ever could.

In spite of the fact that at the beginning of her marriage Lydia turned away regretfully from "high discourse to Martha-like care of wine and custards" when her husband's transcendental visitors came to Concord, as the years went by she gradually ceased such behavior.[1] Her husband may have taken her for granted, but young Henry Thoreau did not. In fact, Thoreau so idealized his admiration for Lydia, fifteen years his senior, that after she read several letters sent to her by him early in the 1840's she felt a little ashamed to let anyone else see them: Thoreau "had exalted her by very undeserved praise."[2] Moreover, she wrote letters to Emerson during his second journey to England, during 1847-48, telling him in no uncertain terms she thought he avoided her and deliberately caused her loneliness.[3] A bit of a hypocondriac, Lydia would become ill usually when Emerson was away from home and especially while she waited in vain for "that unwritten letter always due, it seems, always unwritten."[4] When she was in her seventies she bloomed into an avid conversationalist. Not noticing the decline of her husband, she would trek off almost once or twice a week to meetings of the club initiated by Louisa May Alcott. There she found a world where her worth was more valued, it seems than it had been at home.[5] Therefore, Emerson's second marriage and its antecedent period of engagement was, he announced upon his engagement on 5 February, 1835, "a very different feeling from that with which I entered my first connexion. This is a very sober joy."[6] Though his heart was wrapped-up in memories of Ellen, the nostalgia of his Daimon chose to follow the path of mature thought and it embraced a future with Lydia, not an "ideal" peer, just an average one. Emerson was not to be "drunk" with love again, though he now valued the "permanency" of a commitment more, perhaps, than making the commitment

---

[1]Ibid. Quoted on page 255.

[2]Ibid. Quoted on pages 290-91.

[3]Ibid., p. 358.

[4]Ibid. Quoted on page 358.

[5]See ibid., p. 438.

[6]Emerson, Letters, 1: 436.

itself.

So it is reasonable to assume that marriage for a second time went hand-in-hand with Emerson's vocation and that it was to be worked-out upon a new plane of more mature relationships. That new plane was to be one of adulthood, free choice, exploration, testing. But most of all, Emerson was in control now just as his mother had been virtually in control of his first marriage. But he not only selected a mate who resembled his mother, insofar as she was co-equal to or the embodiment of all his mother meant to him during 1825-33, but he had other models in mind as well. In particular, a model of a marriage between the Carlyles. Like the marriage of his own parents, the Carlyle marriage was built upon sufficient distance or, in other words, a reasonable resolution of the psychosocial crisis of intimacy versus isolation specified by Erikson. To refer to Jane Carlyle as a "most agreeable accomplished woman" and a "treasure" worthy of adulation, was only a stone's-throw of an expression away from what he thought of Lydia: "This lady is a person of noble character whom to see is to respect. I find in her a quite unexpected community of sentiment and speculation and in Plymouth she is respected for her love and good works."[1] Certainly there was some note of panegyric in this description. There had been the same kind of panegyric in his description of Jane Carlyle, if one is to understand Froude's more balanced portrait of her to be true. However, like his description of Jane Carlyle, Emerson's description of Lydia was perfunctory. The comparable letter announcing his engagement to Ellen was was not only twice as long as his announcement about Lydia, but it contained much more detail about Ellen that the presently considered note did about

[1]Ibid., pp. 394-95, 436.

Lydia.[1] Moreover, the note was written to William and this implied he
did not want his mother and his aunt to interfere.

As immediate as the press of that extended identification may have
been, other factors also prompted Emerson to secure a wife in rather short
order. During August, 1834 he had received an offer to become a full-time
minister to the New Bedford congregation. However, as he told his step-
grandfather, Ezra Ripley, the senior minister of the church in Concord,
late in September, 1834 and after much conversation with the New Bedford
congregation, he "declined going there for the coming winter."[2] On 9 October,
1834 Emerson and his mother moved from Boston, and took up residence in the
Old Manse with the Ripley's in Concord as they had done long ago, during
1814.[3] Concord would be Emerson's permanent home ever afterward. One of
the reasons undoubtedly involved in the decision to move was Charles' imminent
engagement to Elizabeth Hoar, a daughter of Samuel Hoar, who was running
for Congress from the Concord district at the time. Charles would die in
1836 before he and Elizabeth could be married. But prior to his death,
Charles would be invited by Samuel Hoar to take the helm of his soon-to-be
father-in-law's thriving law practice in Concord. Being close to Charles
and Elizabeth attracted Emerson and his mother.

On 16 December, 1834 Emerson told William that Mr. Hoar was "undoubtedly
elected last Monday to Congress. Perhaps he will want Chas to take his
office here. I hope C. will be able to stay where he is."[4] That last line
was an odd comment--did Emerson imply Charles was unwanted in Concord? A

[1] See ibid., pp. 256, 436. [2] See ibid., pp. 419-20.

[3] Ibid., p. 421. [4] Ibid., p. 429.

combination of two major factors can be offered as an explanation. First, Edward had died in Puerto Rico on 1 October, 1834, and Emerson realized all too well that Charles himself was not only subject to "depressions," first noticed during his college years, but also that he suffered from the family's inheritance--tuberculosis.[1] Work on Court Street was demanding no doubt. But opening one's office alone in Concord could bring on further calamity at a time when the last youngest hope of the Emerson family grew brightest. On the other hand, Emerson may have begun to enjoy his Concord too much. He had become acquainted with Elizabeth Hoar himself, and their affection for each other resembled the affection he had known with the only other much younger woman in his life, Ellen. If Emerson was emotionally cold and disposed to be shy, as is often thought of him when the name, "Emerson," flashes before the public eye, then this type of person might be most happy with an immature or, at least, a younger person who will respect and adore him. As he once needed Ellen for such aggrandisement, so too he found young Elizabeth a convenient source of uplift when the world was too much with him, so to speak.[2] A closer look at this factor seems in order.

---

[1] See Rusk, The Life of Ralph Waldo Emerson, pp. 112-13. Charles' self-assessment is quoted: "There are moments of enthusiasm when I feel a nascent greatness within me, and then anon comes the hour of dejection and melancholy, when I mourn over my humble capacity; at college my classmates, I see none whom my vanity acknowledges as more intelligent than myself--but at home where they surely ought to know best, why they think but little of me. Balancing these contradictory results, I have come to the sad conclusion that I shall never blind the world with excess of light. . . . " If Emerson had not usurped the central place in that group of Emerson brothers during 1825-33, then it seems reasonable that Charles' psychological posture was hardly inclined to thrust itself into that spot. Charles was as psychologically distant from the Emerson household during 1825-36 as William and Edward (until 1834) were geographically.

[2] See Pommer, Emerson's First Marriage, pp. 96-97, 121, footnote No. 50.

On 8 February, 1836, exactly five years from the day of Ellen's death, for example, Emerson wrote about Charles. He reported how Charles had just come from "reading and talking with Elizabeth," and had asked, "Are we and shall we always be two persons?"[1] If a radical sense of intimacy is presupposed as a sense of being unable to be freely isolated from another person, then it is clear that Charles' relationship with Elizabeth Hoar was more like Emerson's relationship with Ellen than it was like that of Emerson and Lydia. For that matter, by recounting his brother's meeting with Elizabeth, Emerson brought to life once again pleasant memories of Ellen, now vicariously depicted by Elizabeth. After all, had not Emerson himself denied his own "reality" by dreaming of wanting to join Ellen in death, and by opening her coffin late in 1831 or thereabouts, hoping she was witness to his conviction about the soul's "immortality?"[2] Charles, Emerson reported, went on to say, "any strong emotion" between him and Elizabeth made the "surrounding parts of life to fall away and look death-like. One sometimes questions his own reality--it so blanches and shrivels in the flame of a thought, a relation, that swallows him up. If that lives, he lives."[3] Emerson seemed used to following this sort of psychological map, a pattern of response rooted in his marriage to Ellen.

After his own conversation with Elizabeth Hoar (not at all a vicarious interchange) during June, 1836 one month after Charles' death, Emerson thought the "presence or absence of friends" was immaterial to the "clear vision" of our "highest states of mind."[4] Not that one was isolated and alone in such states, but that, for example, he and Elizabeth sensed a significant

---

[1] Emerson, JMN, 6: 383-84. [2] Ibid., 3: 226-27; Ibid, 4: 7.

[3] Ibid., 6: pp. 383-84. [4] Ibid., 4: 170.

merging together, "into the communion" with God where "names and ceremonies and traditions are no longer known but the virtues are loved for their loveliness alone."[1] Though it would seem that in such states of communion "our dearest friends are strangers," the reality of the merging itself simply conveyed that fact of unification, of intimacy, namely, that "there is no personeity in it."[2] Erikson's definition of intimacy, of course, pertains to the act of psychological merging--"ego loss in situations which call for self-abandon."[3] And on the basis of these quotations, we get the feeling that Emerson could readily feel more intimate with Elizabeth Hoar, as he had with Ellen, than he did with Lydia as we shall soon sub-stantiate. We will note how he no longer was uncontrollably captive of intimacy alone. New isolation required that intimacy prove itself as the mark of adulthood. He was not, for example, prompted to follow Lydia to Philadelphia, as he was once with Ellen, for fear of losing her. Because he did not fear ego loss in experiences like the one he reported above, isolation and self-absorption were not in control of his outlook either. Generally, we will note that Emerson's second marriage was emblematic not only of his resolution of vocational ambivalence, but also of the young man's psychosocial crisis of intimacy versus isolation. Regardless of which was the more dominant factor (Charles' health or Emerson's attraction to and subsequent transcending of the Child of Elizabeth Hoar), with William married and with Charles' marriage not far off, Emerson sent out marital antennae of his own. On 30 January, 1835 he became engaged to Lydia Jackson. From this time on he would have her referred to not as Lydia but, signaling

---

[1] Ibid.   [2] Ibid.

[3] Erikson, _Childhood and Society_, p. 225.

his command of things, his preference, "Lidian."

The tenor of the relationship of the engaged couple can be presented in several ways, once it is agreed that there was at least some sort of significant similarity between Emerson's mother, Jane Carlyle, and Lidian, if only by dint of the fact that all persons considered were avowedly "Adults." Perhaps three ways are clearest: First, to offer for consideration Emerson's first extant letter to Lidian; second, to indicate that he was wont to place priority on his professional life rather than on his relationship with Lidian (which, incidentally, would portend what Erikson calls the psychosocial crisis of "generativity versus stagnation"), and this contrasted sharply with his priorities when Ellen was in his midst; and, third, to suggest that the birth of a son and, later, of two daughters were births which he regarded as his--less births of him and his wife together. This third way of depicting the tenor of the second marriage, at least, confirmed Emerson's progress of a psychological nature insofar as the balance was tipped in the direction of "isolation" more than it was toward "intimacy." That is, that the action of performing this emotional task had become stable and permanent. Emerson's second marriage was hardly a "rebound," hardly a recapitulation of the style, pattern, and tenor of his first marriage.

Just as he had been prepared to see other loves--Gay, Ellen, and Carlyle-- Emerson had been prepared (literally) to see Lidian early in January, 1835. While telling a story about the coy meeting of a "youth and a maid," he suggested that there "are some occult facts in human nature that are natural magic."[1] The chief of these, he believed, was vision: "the glance (oeillade)" or "the mysterious communion that is established across a house between two

---

[1]Emerson, JMN, 5: 8.

entire strangers, by this means, moves all the springs of wonder."[1] Without

being able to glance at Gay, or at Ellen, or at Carlyle (except by means

of photographs, only to be exchanged at a later date), Emerson had been,

nonetheless, fixing his sights on a particular "stranger" during 1834.

During 1835 he was planning on moving her to a particular "house." Let

us first consider that stranger, Lidian. Afterwards we will consider that

house, "Coolidge Castle," and the meaning Emerson invested in it. It

will be shown that, like a castle, it was his means of being in the world

but not a part of that world. It would become the buffer zone of an idealist.

On 1 February, 1835, just two days after their engagement, Emerson

wrote his first letter to Lidian. He had returned from lecturing in Plymouth

and wrote from Concord. Caught up in his preparations for his lectures on

biography, he relied on the line from Edmund Burke, "A wise man will speak

the truth with temperance that he may speak it the longer," in order to

contain "this new sentiment" which his "Lidian Queen" had awakened in him.[2]

The nature of that sentiment was its "quietness" which, though it might

be a scare to a more vigorous engaged young man, Emerson took as a "pledge

of permanence."[3] His psychosocial crisis was over. He went on to say about

his new engagement to Lidian that he found "a sort of grandeur" in the

"modulated expressions" of a love in which the "individuals, and what might

seem even reasonable personal expectations," were "steadily postponed to

to a regard for truth and the universal love."[4] But he cautioned his

fiancee not to think of him as "a metaphysical lover," since he sympathized

with the "homliest pleasures and attractions" and was gratified that between

---

[1]Ibid.

[2]Emerson, Letters, 1: 434.

[3]Ibid.

[4]Ibid.

them, he was sure, the "most permanent ties should be the first formed and thereon should grow whatever others human nature will."[1] In short, he felt that Lidian would establish a good home and bear his children, but male chauvanist that he now was, he granted her little else. On 4 March, 1835 he asked her not to address him as the "Rev."[2] Indeed, Emerson finally began to settle down to custard, so to speak.

From the time of his first letter to Lidian and throughout the rest of his years, Emerson granted the woman very little of his time. Perhaps she grew used to being neglected in this way. His pattern of touring and lecturing took him away from home more often than she would have preferred. Evidently, work and profession came first. Unlike his trip with Ellen to Philadelphia in 1830, he never again traveled with his new fiancee and wife. He wrote to Lidian on 1 February, 1835 saying that he would "come to Plymouth on Friday" in order to visit, but "if I do not succeed--do not attain unto the Idea of that man--I shall read of Luther Thursday and then I know not when I shall steal a visit. . . ."[3] Obviously he did not make it to Plymouth. For on 13 February, 1835 he wrote to her that, "Days have I not to give" because he was the "reverent slave" to the uncontrollable "moment of inspiration" which had not been up to par lately.[4] In the past, his loves had been his inspiration. Now things had changed. Knowledge of "very unfit preparation for my three last lectures made me say at Plymouth that I could not come again till they were done."[5] Early in March, 1835 the story was no different. On 2 March 1835, a Monday, he wrote that "Thursday night, if I am well, will release me from my present strings, and promises

---

[1] Ibid.   [2] Ibid., p. 441   [3] Ibid., p. 435.

[4] Ibid., pp. 436-37.   [5] Ibid., p. 437.

me the happiness of more of your company."[1] Again, he never got to Plymouth,

for on Wednesday night of that week he wrote telling Lidian he would be

unable to "stay next Friday," since on Saturday night he was to lecture at

Waltham and on Sunday "preach there on an old agreement, which abridges

my brief week."[2] Therefore, Emerson's professional commitments were pushing

aside whatever may have been his domestic inclinations. Thus, assurance

of marriage in September, 1835 was a harbinger of his professional develop-

ment.

But another major dimension of their relationship also came into play,

especially before their wedding day. Just prior to his 15 September, 1835

wedding day Emerson had gone away from Concord to Plymouth where the ceremony

would take place, evidently arriving a day or two ahead of time. After

the ceremony and the brief reception on their wedding day, he spirited Lidian

off, back to Concord. Thus, Emerson brought Lidian "home," to his ancestral

home: "Hail to the land of my fathers!" he declared late in 1834.[3] Sym-

bolically, Lidian was an "exile" from Plymouth, but after 15 September,

1835 she was an exile whom Emerson managed to gather in to himself and,

therefore, to bring "home." The action involved in these symbolic notions

of "exile" and "home" followed the pattern established earlier. Similar

action would come to condition his later lecture tours, namely, sweeping

"out," sweeping "back," in short, the telescopic ritual of expansion within

diminishment. Emerson's faith was working, not on his own behalf but on

the behalf of someone else; and in his marriage was prefigured his national

course for the future.

---

[1] Ibid., p. 439.

[2] Ibid., p. 440.

[3] Emerson, JMN, 4: 335.

Although the symbolic notion of "home" must be left suspended for the moment, that Lidian became an "exile" whom Emerson brought home, or better put, whom he gave a new home, was clear from the prolonged debate over living in Plymouth or living in Concord. Lidian was inclined, of course, to choose the former, but her fiance and later her husband insisted on the latter. He wrote that if Lidian were to visit him in Concord, "right welcome" she would be since it was the only way he could think to reconcile "this divided empire" of loyalty which Lidian in Plymouth, and his "inkstand" in Concord, both claimed of him.[1] His roots, he wrote during February, 1835 were "in this paternal soil" of Concord.[2] It was important that he choose Concord for even greater symbolic reasons: Concord, unlike Plymouth, was associated with national independence. Moreover, the Puritans who landed on Plymouth Rock were known as "non-separating" Puritans, loyal to the Church of England and believers that they themselves were merely reforming it in absentia.[3] Thus, where the minutemen held their own was where Emerson chose to live. Plymouth was out of the question.

He was quick to insert into his first letter to Lidian that "Concord is only one of a hundred towns" in which he might find natural beauty but "Plymouth," he feared, "is not one. Plymouth is streets; I live in the wide champaign."[4] It seemed more important to him not to live in Plymouth

---

[1] Emerson, Letters, 1: 437.   [2] Ibid.

[3] See Smith, Handy, and Loetscher, American Christianity, I: pp. 82-89. Distinguished here are the two major strains of Puritanism: The "non-separatists," or those who sought reform of the Church of England; and the "separatists," or those who were concerned not with reform but with being recognized as distinct, autonomous churches.

[4] Emerson, Letters, 1: 435.

than to live in Concord. One wonders if in-laws were a problem, for he

implied that no one, not even Lidian, attracted him to Plymouth. After

all, as far as he was concerned, "Plymouth's but a seabeach.   What can

you say for it?" he asked Lidian on 4 March, 1835, perhaps with some memory

of his dislike of St. Augustine, Florida, also a desolate "seabeach," far

from "brother barnacles," which was fit only for orange-rolling.[1] Also,

Lidian evidently had refused at first to venture to Concord during the

first months of their engagement. He wrote to her somewhat sarcastically

on 13 February, 1835, "as to your deliberate visit to Concord could you

not most wise Lidian defer it until December! I deny that it will take

any horse from the first of March to the first of May to go from Plymouth

to Concord. Really my dear friend we live several miles on this side the

Ohio."[2] The use of "we" implied he still thought of himself as the "family

man" of the Emerson clan. As he himself had found a new birth after 1833,

he confirmed it and offered it as well to Lidian, whom he brought "home"

shortly afterwards, doing so all by himself.

The last of three ways in which the tenor of his relationship with

Lidian comes into focus clearest is contained in two single remarks he

made in connection with the birth of two of his children, his first two

children. His second marriage produced the fruit of four children in all:

Waldo Emerson in 1836 (d. 1844), Ellen Tucker Emerson in 1839 (d. 1909),

Edith Emerson, after 1865 and marriage her last name became Forbes (d. 1929),

and Edward Waldo Emerson in 1844 (d. 1930). On 31 October, 1836 Emerson

wrote in his journal, "Last night at 11 o'clock a son was born to me," and

he added that "as the face of the sky is different every hour" so too Waldo

---

[1] Ibid., p. 440.   [2] Ibid., p. 437.

"presents a new aspect" each hour.[1] In regard to his first daughter he
wrote something similar in 1839: "24 February at 8 o'clock, a daughter
was born to me . . . Lidian, who magnanimously makes my gods her gods,
calls the babe Ellen. I can hardly ask more for thee, my babe, than that
name implies. Be that vision," he added, "and remain with us, and after
us."[2] The point is that in both cases--for the first-born male, and for
the first-born female--the children are thought of as being born "to me,"
to Emerson and, therefore, not "to me and Lidian." When he was on his
southern journey during 1826-27 he said he had all his "maladies" to "himself" and now it would appear that restitution had occurred. He had his
children all to himself as well. Such was the psychological meaning of
his first two children.

Ellen Emerson, his daughter, would become her father's constant companion and secretary who, unlike her quite able mother, would journey with
him when he toured during his later years. She was to be with him when
he made his last visit to Carlyle in England during 1872. Thus, her life
reflected the life of her namesake. Over-all, with a resolution of his
quite evident crisis of intimacy versus isolation weathered, Emerson, for
sure, was more concerned with the coming generation than with whatever may
have been his own difficulties at the time.

But what of the stability of "place?" Has not the symbolic notion of
"home" already been said to have been as important a personal center for
Emerson as "person?" Achieving stability of "place" went hand-in-hand with
his second marriage, and it had symbolic value for his life during 1835,

---

[1]Emerson, JMN, 5: 234. Emphasis added.

[2]Forbes-Emerson Edition of the Journals, 5:166-67. Emphasis added.

as well as for the success of his literary labor of later years. If in a general way the stability of "person" was emblematic of a neutralized psychosocial crisis of intimacy versus isolation, then in the same general way the stability of "place" was at the same time emblematic of a neutralized geographical crisis of intimacy versus isolation also. On the one hand, Emerson no longer had to worry about juggling marriage as either a "reprieve" from his vocation or as a "condemnation" to it. Likewise, he no longer needed to use "travel" as a means to ease his physical "ailments." In this sense, therefore, Emerson's character (i.e., the structure of expansion within diminishment) had been "formed" by 1835. As was his concern that children be generated, so too he became concerned to acquire property, real and financial, and to sink roots into it. Generally, if during 1825-33 psychological and geographical vicissitudes were joined together, by 1835 Emerson could give them form enough so as to foster their gradual differentiation.

Before, a connection was proposed between Ruth Emerson, Jane Carlyle, and Lidian Emerson on the basis of the psychological framework of Thomas Harris. Generally, though less can be said here about Jane Carlyle, the psychological similarity between Ruth Emerson and Lidian Emerson was suggested on the grounds that 1834-35 were capsule-like years in which the meaning of Emerson's personal growth during 1825-33 was contained symbolically in his quest for stability of "person and place." As his mother presided over his experience during the events of 1825-33, so too would Lidian preside over his domestics affairs after 1835. However, unlike the events of the earlier period, which Emerson conceived mostly in domestic terms, after 1835 that domestic conception shrank in size and in sway. This allowed his professional life to grow beyond familial and domestic parameters. One might say that his life came under the sway not only of maternal promptings, but also promptings more paternal in nature.

By moving beyond the domestic limitations toward the wide world of the American Lyceum, Emerson recapitulated what his own father had done more than three decades before. The Rev. William Emerson had moved from what he regarded as a provincial situation in Harvard, Massachusetts to one he regarded as more professional in Boston, insofar as it implied he was minister to a whole citizenry, not just to a tiny rural congregation. It was a "step up" in the world. However, Emerson altered the paternal pattern somewhat, though its basic meaning was retained. At the age of thirty years the Rev. William Emerson moved from the area of Concord (Harvard was just over the hills to the west) to Boston; and Emerson, at the age of thirty-two years, moved from Boston to Concord. On the surface of things it would appear that Emerson "dropped out" of the rising tides or urban life, but on a psychological level of consideration he was affirming the place of his origin in order to go beyond Boston, beyond New England, and even beyond America, at least from his viewpoint on the professional thrust of his life.

Emerson closely associated Concord with his father and with the inertial impact of a ministerial ancestry. Emerson was struggling under pressures of a harsh conscience, undoubtedly cast in paternal imagery, to bring a higher order of meaning to bear on his life, that is, to create a "projection" less child-like and more congruent with his new sense of maturity. He hoped such order might find fertile grounding in some sort of vocational identity. Travel, like Ellen's "reprieve," loosened the demands of conscience which, at its best, rocked between the adolescent-like "all or nothing" alternatives of either accepting the ancestral vocation or giving it up altogether as his brother William, among others, had demonstrated during

1825 (which Emerson himself could not easily have done). By considering

Emerson as he went about coping with pressures of a harsh conscience, new

sense can be made out of some most curious journal entries and letters

which appeared during June of 1835, just one month prior to his purchasing

of a permanent residence in Concord--Coolidge House.

Emerson was neither capitulating to a sense of the punitive side of

his conscience nor choosing a professional course for himself uninstructed

by such psychological pressures. He simply was understanding the tenuous

nature of his outlook, that is, his projections of meaning onto the world,

and preparing to transcend their harsher strictures. They were soon discovered

to be, as he put it, "optical deceptions." However, to be deceived and to

realize the deception were means of seeing through a harsh conscience--

expansion within diminishment. In this sense, Emerson was, to use the

notion of the psychologist of religion, Peter Homans, experiencing the

"collapse" of his "transference" to what his mother had led him to understand

as a vocational obligation, namely, to succeed in the ministry as his father

had.[1] Purchasing his house in Concord was symbolic of accepting that

obligation and its long tradition. Yet, Emerson was literally "seeing

through" it toward broader horizons. If "nature" was the "projection of

---

[1]See Peter Homans, Theology After Freud, Part Two (Indianapolis: Bobbs-Merrill Company, Inc., 1970). This book is about some of the psychological implications of the Protestant experience in America. As Emerson left the Unitarian church, so too did his transference relationship to it falter. His recovery of "visual" transcendence once again was a marker that for him denominational Protestantism had come to an end. Insofar as he was representative, and insofar as he was concerned a new transference relationship was recovered in terms of the idea of America, the nation had also experienced the end of a viable Protestant experience, though vestiges of it have lingered well into the twentieth century.

God" as he would say in June, 1836, then Concord was Emerson's altar.[1]

Let us go to the record. The purpose, of course, will be to depict this unique and fairly complex psychological complex, namely, his quest after a "higher order" of meaning. We have noted Emerson's understanding of the phrase "optical deceptions," which he referred to on 23 December, 1834 and, also, which he used earlier to interpret a social affront he experienced while on a date in Italy with one Mrs. Davey.[2] As he understood it, Emerson believed that disappointment was deception if it resulted from hearing another person utter the truth one had realized but had not himself voiced first. In effect, deception was preliminary to seeing the truth without the tarnishing effects of personal jealousies and prejudices. Emerson carried this a step further in a letter on 25 June, 1835, as well as two days later in his journals.

He wrote to Frederic Henry Hedge, one-time supplier of his pulpits and who, one year later would initiate the meetings of the group which came to be known as the "Transcendental Club." Emerson said that in his own experience "good society" was "such an optical illusion" that he thought it should be classed with Bacon's Idols of the Cave. Carlyle affirms that it is extinct."[3] Later, and in accord with his first thought he believed as well that "institutions are optical illusions."[4] Bacon, of course, was a scientist who thought his method of scientific investigation was obstructed by four sorts of "Idols": Idols of the Tribe, or racially "wishful" and anthropomorphic ways of thinking (e.g., an explanation by final causes);

---

[1] Emerson, JMN., 5: 184.   [2] See ibid., 4: 370-71

[3] Emerson, Letters, 1: 446; Emerson, JMN 5: 54.

[4] Ibid., 7: 177.

Idols of the Cave, or personal prejudices; Idols of the Market Place, or failure to define terms; and Idols of the Theatre, or blind acceptance of tradition or authority.[1] That Emerson mentioned only Idols of the Cave, not of the Tribe, Market Place, or the Theatre, was very significant. It was _personal_ deception out of which he was being jogged. Moreover, this entailed that he be jogged out of societal idolatry as well. Moving to Concord was a legitimate way of becoming "obscure" in terms of the Idols of the Cave, that is, in terms of ordinary Brahmin habits. He no longer would think very much of Boston's limelight. However, in terms of the achieved sense of clear, undeceived sight, the Idols of the Cave could be viewed from afar as deceptions indeed. Turning away from "society," toward Concordian "solitude" corrected Emerson's optics, so to speak. His limelight was where he made his home, and that was no longer synonymous with Boston. Furthermore, that he mentioned only the Cave meant that its idols could be accepted, seen through, and transcended. Plato's seer in the allegory of the cave does no less. The result was, as Peter Homans' work implies, a restored sense of sociality or, in other words, a sense that one's alienation from others (in this case, Emerson from his countrymen) is radically mitigated. In short, Emerson made his faith work.

So much for psychological theorizing. The importance of doing so has been to indicate, first, that for Emerson to reside in Concord was for him to re-work the meaning of his paternal heritage and, second, that he did so in terms which have carried through his life and which, at that time in 1835, were clearly and expressly visual. Moreover, they referred directly to a cave which was not at all dissimilar to the one portrayed by Plato,

---

[1]See Francis Bacon, _Novum Organum_, tr. Peter Shaw, 1 (London, 1818): 15ff.

because, like Plato's cave, Emerson gave expression to his own sense of
being in a cave. By appropriating Bacon's notion and using it at a particular time and in a particular way, Emerson merely lent confirmation to the
ritualization of expansion within diminishment.

However, in order to see all this theorizing in more of the biographical
data itself, it is necessary to start with Emerson's achievement of "solitude"
in Concord during 1834-35. If his first meeting with Carlyle was as important
as he seems to have thought it was for his own literary career, then Carlyle
served as a suggestive model not only for his marriage but for his place of
residence as well. Though Carlyle had found his "entire solitude tedious"
at Craigenputtock, Emerson thought it was conducive to his hero's craft;
and he hoped Carlyle would "not leave the moors," for it was best if a man
of letters could "nurse himself in seclusion."[1] Boston was hardly as far
from Concord as Craigenputtock was from London, and Emerson's solitude
would be hardly as "tedious" as that of Carlyle. This reference of August,
1833 was part of Emerson's identification with the Englishman. As such
it predisposed the young American to enshrine the meaning of the geographical
movement of 1825-33 in a stable "place" in Concord, a solitude all his own.

Emerson had lived in more residences than ever a good memory could
recall readily throughout his first thirty-two years of life. Even after
he returned from abroad late in 1833 he stayed with his friend, George
Sampson, in Boston, then moved to Newton where his mother boarded, then
into the residence of James Pelletier in Boston where Charles had been
boarding, and finally he moved to Concord with his mother late during 1834
(after many interruptions lecturing in New England). He turned down offers

----

[1]Emerson, Letters, 1: 395.

to be the minister in New Bedford and Waltham during 1834, largely for two reasons: First, because during May, Beza Tucker's closed coffers opened half-way; second, because during the fall he had commenced writing his transcendental manifesto, Nature, and had received his first encouraging letter from Carlyle. (The encouragement from this foreigner was not unlike the discouragement William had received about the ministry from Goethe, his foreigner.) Noted has been how his first glimpses of financial and professional success were conducive to the vista of marriage a second time around. The same glimpses were also instrumental in supplying him with funds sufficient for buying a house of his own during July, 1835, a house which his wife-to-be could call her home. But, of course, it was his house. To the degree it was, Ellen's legacy was to allow him to be independent of Lydia. In a sense, he was using Ellen to justify his lack of a more intimate, less "sober" commitment to Lydia. "I have dodged the doom of building and have bought the Coolidge House," he wrote to William on 27 July, 1835.[1] Though it cost only $3500, Emerson was inclined to think more about its market value in the past and as future equity. Likewise, he inclined at that same time to think more and more about the market value of "mileage" he might get out of his lectures.[2] He told William, "The seller alleges that it cost him 7000. I am quite sure it need not cost so much. I give about its value."[3] Having a house, especially in that particular town of the family's parentage, meant the entire Emerson family not only had been restored to its rightful place in the New World under freedom's firmament, but also that the family had recovered a center for their life together for the future. It had been long in the offing and only Emerson, not any of his brothers, brought it

---

[1]Ibid., p. 447.   [2]Ibid., pp. 447-48.   [3]Ibid., p. 448.

about. He could be the "family man" at last.

Four months after their wedding Lidian was pregnant with young Waldo, and she would suffer from dyspepsia most of 1836 as a result. However, that was the least of Emersons' problems, and perhaps it was even cause for joy in light of what soon happened to Charles. He was sick again with the signs of tuberculosis. Emerson wrote to Lidian in April, 1836, while lec-turing in South Brookfield, that Dr. Jackson said, "he cannot find that any thing is the matter with him more than a catarrh."[1] Such a slight inflamma-tion had been abated before. Charles had taken a short voyage to the West Indies from late 1831 to early 1832 and everyone thought that the result was sound health. During those last days of April, 1836 Emerson decided that even though Dr. Jackson said Charles' health must not be judged "by the first appearance which is more unfavorable that it should be" and that "he did not find the lungs diseased,"[2] his brother ought to go to New York for the heat. Perhaps the wiser for his years, Emerson cautioned William to get Charles to have a total physical examination in New York since, "owing to the faintness," he believed Dr. Jackson "was not able to make a thorough examination."[3] Evidently, Emerson had learned to side-step the physician as he had done during 1830-31. Only this time he actually helped Charles "leave home." This was clearly the case because both Emerson and his brother had mused just about one year before about how they and their wives, as well as William and his wife, could join their mother once again and live under one roof.[4]

Ruth Emerson had been in New York City visiting her eldest son, his wife, and her new grandson, Willie, who had been born on 18 June, 1835. It was into this setting that Charles arrived late in April or early in May, 1836. Ruth

---

[1] Ibid., 2: 12.

[2] Ibid., p. 15.

[3] Ibid.

[4] See ibid., 1: 438, ftnt. No. 28; 445.

Emerson had been their since shortly after Emerson and Lidian were married during September, 1835. Their mother's presence meant that New York City was a logical spot for Charles to go, that is, logical in terms of the psychological meaning Emerson had attached to his mother's presiding and seemingly curative presence in the past. Ostensibly, however, New York City was warmer than New England. At this point Emerson's sense of "home" was taking a decisive turn toward fission. He had his own home in Concord, where Lidian presided over the domestic machinery but when the chips were down in the case of Charles, he rushed him "home" to his mother. Ruth Emerson symbolized home in a way in which Coolidge House could not. Nonetheless, Emerson himself returned to Concord after seeing Charles off to New York City, and he awaited not only good news about his brother's health but also word that he and Charles could "bring mother home" to Concord shortly.[1] It is possible that Emerson sent Charles to New York City in order to pressure Ruth Emerson to return. After all, Lidian was four months pregnant and stricken with persistent dyspepsia, and undoubtedly he was reminded of the time he had another sick wife on his hands. When Emerson received William's note that Charles was on his last legs and seemed doomed, he and Charles' fiancee, Elizabeth Hoar set out for New York City together. They did so in vain for Charles died on the day they left Concord, 9 May, 1836. The funeral was on May 11th and Emerson, Elizabeth, and Ruth Emerson returned saddened to Concord on May 13th. A multitude of factors prompted Ruth Emerson to return to Boston, not the least of which was William's precarious financial circumstances, especially after funeral costs.

On 12 May, 1836 Emerson had written to Lidian from New York City that

[1] Ibid., 2: 14.

he had "determined to live in Concord" at first because Charles was thinking of making his residence there early in 1835, but now "that the immense promise of his maturity is destroyed," he felt "not only unfastened there and adrift but a sort of shame at living at all."[1] His last sentences were cast in visual terms: "How much I saw through his eyes. I feel as if my own were very dim."[2] He wrote this in New York City and had come to feel "unfastened" from his home, as he had felt separated from Ellen, as well as alienated from Second Church several years before. However, he made his way back to Concord according to his old pattern of "travel" as a means of mitigating "illness" (i.e., the loss of Charles) and "commitment" (i.e., to Concord). On 19 May, 1836 he searched for a "just view" once again according to the legacy of his past meanings of Charles: "I find myself slowly after this helpless mourning. I remember states of mind that perhaps I had long lost that before this grief, the native mountains whose tops reappear after we have traversed many a mile of weary region from home. Then shall I ever revisit?"[3] He would. But he did not realize when he described Coolidge House to William on 27 July, 1835 just after buying it how prophetic his description would be. For, indeed, he came to re-fasten himself to that hallowed presence: "It is a mean place and cannot be fine until trees and flowers give it a character of its own. But we shall crowd so many books and papers, and, if possible, wise friends, into it that it shall have as much wit as it can carry."[4] This was precisely what happened during 1836-37--the next phase of the cluster of events of 1834-38.

Emerson had written these lines just prior to purchasing his house:

---

[1] Ibid., p. 20.

[2] Ibid.

[3] Emerson, JMN, 5: 160.

[4] Emerson, Letters, 1: 447.

"The advantage in Education is always with those children who slip up into life without being objects of notice. Happy those then who are members of large families."[1] Evidently he had spent a good deal of his past "praying without ceasing," for during 1836 he was not only taking notice of increasing stability of "person and place" but others were taking notice of him too. He was "seeing" and "being seen" after years of comparative obscurity. Though the pattern of the game of "peek-a-boo" is associated with childhood, it also can be the plan according to which cultural creativity occurs. During 1836-37 Emerson was pulling-out all the stops on whatever professional inhibitions thwarted his success as an American literary laborer. During this period his personal life was rounded-out and prepared for staging a wider, social retraction of "optical deceptions." In the final chapter to follow, we will present a scenario along this line. Then Emerson's "staging" of his retraction of the "optical deception" of a Unitarian commitment made in 1836, and his renunciation of it during 1838 will be described as ritual behavior with cultural significance. For now, however, we may note three ways in which the stability of "person and place" began giving rise to beacons of professional success for Emerson. First, let us say a word about Emerson's initial successes.

Within the short time from 9 September, 1836 to 30 October, 1836 Emerson had his book, Nature, published (September 9th); attended the very first meeting of Hedge's Club, or the Transcendental Club (September 19th); and was given a son (October 30th). Also, he began speculating with his money, investing in real estate on Staten Island, New York with the broker-like aid of William who, what with the imminent financial depression of 1837, was close to poverty again. Emerson's financial speculations were entered into

---

[1] Emerson, JMN, 5: 52.

shortly after his income was enhanced by taking administrative charge of the Unitarian church in East Lexington.[1] He was as busy as ever, able to talk well and make good money at it. Here, then, within the many works of a busy young man, three marks of new-found professional prominence loom into view.

Elizabeth Hoar was no mean companionship for Emerson during 1836, since Lidian, pregnant with Waldo, suffered day in and day out with dyspepsia which by mid-summer confined her most of the time to her chamber.[2] According to a letter of 30 May, 1836, Emerson reported, Elizabeth "is staying with us" in Coolidge House in order to "compare notes of pleasure and pain" after losing Charles, and, he said, she found "sincere comfort in the memory of her friends councels and opinions and purposes."[3] Elizabeth probably received reports of some comforting experiences from the man who called her "sister."[4] Emerson had written in 1835 that when Ellen died, despite his grief, "the air was still sweet, the sun was not taken down from my firmament, and however sore was that particular loss," he still felt it was "particular, that the Universe remained to us both."[5] What he meant by this was that the "Universe abode in its light and in its power to replenish the heart with hope. Distress never, trifles nevers abate my trust."[6] After Charles' death,

---

[1]Though this will be the involvement to be considered in the last chapter, suffice it to say here that taking charge of the church at this time in his career as a lecturer was merely construed according to the pattern of his character, namely, expansion within diminishment. Administering that particular pulpit was a context from within which he might "speculate" beyond its meagre financial return. So too, it became an appropriate stage upon which he would renounce the pulpit finally, upon which he never again would act.

[2]See Emerson, Letters, 2: 35, 37, 41, 42, 177.

[3]Ibid., p. 25.   [4]Ibid., p. 44.

[5]Emerson, JMN, 5: 19-20.   [6]Ibid.

however, he "groped" as did Elizabeth "in greater darkness and with less heed. Night rests," he believed on 30 May, 1836, "on all sides upon the facts of our being, tho', we must own, our upper nature lies aways in the Day. But we cannot stand still, and Hope is behind all the changes even the last. We shall soon know all."[1] The simple fact that Elizabeth stayed with the Emersons, as well as the fact that she and Emerson consoled themselves together over Charles' death, was enough to raise in each the sense that, as he recorded it in 1835, together they were "wistful and babe-like."[2] His next thought was potentiated by the geographical setting in which he and Elizabeth found themselves in Concord: ". . . we cannot help thinking that a correspondent sentiment of paternal pleasantry must exist over us in the bosom of God."[3] He could now trust his wife and his home to such a degree that whatever caught his glance was charged, as it were, with "intense light."[4]

Emerson had compared Nature to Sampson Reed's, On the Growth of the Mind-- a "work of genius," during the middle of 1836.[5] By doing so he placed it beside Plato's Dialogues, Carlyle's Characteristics, and Frisbie's professorial chair at Harvard.[6] On 28 June, 1836 he said that his "little book is nearly done" and that its contents would not be any bulkier than Reeds' tome.[7] Almost two weeks later he told William he had inquired about a publisher and found out it would cost "a little more than a hundred dollars to make a handsome little book."[8] He added that from the first edition he expected "no profit," and if "it attained to a second the success should be profit enow."[9] Not

---

[1] Emerson, Letters, 2: 25.
[2] Emerson, JMN, 5: 19-20.
[3] Ibid.
[4] See ibid., 4: 376.
[5] See ibid., 5: 232.
[6] Emerson, Letters, 1: 176.
[7] Ibid., 2: 26. [8] Ibid., p. 28. [9] Ibid.

only had he been supported by earnings from Ellen's estate and from lecturing, but also he had received some of the balance from Charles' estate at this time. Furthermore, that he worried only about professional success and not about making a lot of money from Nature was evidenced by a new, heightened awareness of financial dealings, that is, of ways to make money by means other than the risky business of writing and publishing. In a postscript to a letter of 7 July, 1836 he wrote the following, what became increasingly characteristic of his leisurely preoccupations henceforward: "I learn from F.A. & Co. that C.C.E. (Charles) had 1 July $357.00 in their hands beside some interest. Of this sum 100. is property of M.M.E. (Aunt Mary) about 75. of Mrs. R.E. (mother). They advise me not to sell my Mill Dam shares as they are estimated at 15.00 but will only sell for 10.25."[1] From Charles' estate he had money in excess with which to pay for the first edition of his "handsome little book."

Evidently Emerson had received an invitation from Frederic Henry Hedge late in June, 1836 to share some of the ideas that would be contained in that book. But it was not until after an unusually lengthy delay after receiving the "welcome letter a month ago," that Emerson accepted "with much contrition."[2] He apologized for tardiness by saying he "ought to have testified" his "hearty good will to the project of the symposium," since he believed such a meeting would certainly "make the earth a more tolerable lodging even if it should not directly increase the wit of the compotators--rather say, co-operators."[3] It was not Emerson's intention to debate "men of strong understanding," whom he regarded as "a menacing rapid trenchant race" who "cut me short--they drive me into a corner--I must not suggest, I must define--

---

[1] Ibid. [2] Ibid., p. 29. [3] Ibid.

and they hold me responsible for a demonstration of every sentiment I endorse."[1]
He was not one to have the exclusivity of his most potent inspirations impinged
upon by inappropriate inquires. He was not committed to Bacon's method.
But if he refused to debate, then he agreed to converse.

Emerson thought his "power of conversation" was sufficient to convey
his meaning "in calm times and quiet places" when it was allowed to "stretch
out all its slovenly length" and by "many fragments of thought to dot out
the whole curve."[2] Less than one month later, after being visited by Amos
Bronson Alcott and Margaret Fuller, he was disposed to suggest it "always
a great refreshment" to see a "very intelligent person," for it was like
"being set in a large place. You stretch your limbs and dilate to your
utmost size."[3] Underlying this imagery was the psychological sense that
not only was his life "expanding," but also that as it did, strength-of-self
would be derived from the wider horizon of vocation stretching beyond his
marriage and beyond his home. Emerson's identity was being animated by the
growing sense that the dots of American national consciousness were then
defining the whole curve. When Hedge's Club met for the first time at George
Ripley's house in Boston on 19 September, 1836--in honor of "Plato . . ."[4]
it, as Nature, was telescopic. The club expanded Emerson's world beyond
the past, beyond his present, and lifted the curtain hiding his "transcendental
vision." A new firmament in sight, however, owed its greatest debt to Emerson's
capacity to find mature ways of giving vent to his own maternal instincts,
at least, to an envy of the mother-infant relationship.

---

[1]Ibid.

[2]Ibid.

[3]Ibid., p. 32.

[4]Rusk, The Life of Ralph Waldo Emerson, p. 243.

The last and final capstone of Emerson's personal forward rush toward
his cultural labor was the birth of his son, Waldo, on 30 October, 1836.
If Lidian was impregnated during January of 1836, then by October it was clear
that in a symbolic way he made her, as he put it on 23 October, 1836 to
William, "a prisoner to her chamber," chained by the sickness of child-bearing.[1]
When his own period of incubation ended after 1833, when the "umbilical cord"
connecting him to Second Church had been severed by his journey abroad, Emerson
sensed himself undergoing a symbolic rebirth. Now, as Waldo, his son, had
his cord severed, Emerson, in effect, freed Lidian, an "exile," from her prison,
from the cave of her borning-room chamber. She too was symbolically reborn.

Indeed, the universe looked "friendly" to Emerson because the birth went
well.[2] However, the action to which he responded was also a bearer of a
symbolic dimension. The birth was a recapitulation of his own vocational
"birth trauma," as well as a reminder of the hope which he inhaled with the
first breath of "blithe air" which uplifted his head "into the infinite space"
of a civil ministry.[3] Therefore, it was not coincidental that the first one
to receive the news of his son's birth, beside those in direct attendance
of Lidian, was Elizabeth Hoar, not William, his only surviving brother and
not Aunt Mary, the other most important person in his life.[4] Elizabeth Hoar
played the unique position of being not quite a member of the Emerson family,
but, at the same time, not quite a stranger to it either. That was precisely
how Emerson felt now that his birth from "domesticity" into "civility" had
been corroborated symbolically by Waldo's birth. Before Charles died, Emerson

[1] Emerson, Letters, 2: 42.   [2] Emerson, JMN, 5: 234.

[3] Ibid., pp. 18-19. Later this quotation was embellished with the image of a "transparent eyeball" and included in the first introductory lines of Nature.

[4] See Emerson, Letters, 2: 44.

had planned to build two new rooms into the "L" of his house in order to accommodate the newlyweds, his brother and Elizabeth.[1]   With Charles gone and her father off in Congress, it was easy for Elizabeth to associate with the Emersons. And, too, that the precedent of "taking in" Charles and Elizabeth had been set, being close to Elizabeth afforded Emerson relief from memories of Ellen. Elizabeth Hoar would join the Transcendental Club later on and, insofar as was implied by announcing Waldo's birth to her first, she, though like Ellen in many ways, differed in that she also played party to the future.

On 7 May, 1838 Waldo was baptized by the Rev. Ezra Ripley and was dressed for the occasion in Charles' very own baptismal robe. "Lidian," wrote Emerson, had "a group of departed spirits in her eye who hovered around the patriarch and the babe."[2] Contained symbolically therein was Emerson's past and his future, his ancestors and his progeny. The thrust of his professional labor would run continuously between them. However, before it would, first a final "ritual severance" of the cord which lingered to bind him to the pulpit was necessary. This would be an act of cultural speciation, action which would point toward a level of cultural awareness transcending factional and denominational bickering among both religious and less than religious Americans.[3] By creating a situation and using it to renounce the pulpit, Emerson not only drew attention to the Unitarian tradition (and the colonial ethos of which it was a part), but he also and more importantly drew attention to the broader and deeper unity of the American tradition for his generation the world over. For the proper stage and adequate actors he turned toward three places: the

---

[1] Rusk, The Life of Ralph Waldo Emerson, p. 230.

[2] Emerson, JMN, 5: 324.

[3] Erikson, Gandhi's Truth, pp. 395-440 passim.

church in East Lexington, his grandfather's church in Concord, and the Harvard Divinity School.

CHAPTER VIII

INVESTING IN THE FUTURE: RITUAL
RENUNCIATION OF THE PULPIT

During November, 1836 Emerson was persuaded to take charge of the pulpit
at the church in East Lexington, Massachusetts. He probably took it because,
as Ralph Rusk suggested, his income from all sources was "hardly enough
to turn the wheels of the domestic machinery that Lidian quickly built up."[1]
Meanwhile, he was preoccupied by the lectures he was to give on the "Philosophy
of History" in Boston from 15 December, 1836 through 2 March, 1837.[2] He made
shares of stock available to William during December because his brother
had written and had requested financial help. However, he offered the stock
under terms of "punctual payment of interest of $2900, at 6 per cent," since
"it is my living and I depend on this income 1 April and 1 October."[3] Moreover, Emerson entered into real estate speculation when, in spite of his
alleged "great ignorance of business," he told William to put some Staten
Island property up as collateral or "landed security" for the sake of Lidian
and Waldo.[4] Emerson was put out by the request for support from his brother
whom he thought "a very naughty boy."[5] But this family obligation encouraged
him to make an even greater investment in his professional future by commiting
himself to supply the parish in East Lexington.

Unlike the kind of supply preaching which Emerson had known in the past,
East Lexington was of a different sort of arrangement. It seems as though

---

[1]Rusk, The Life of Ralph Waldo Emerson, p. 251

[2]See Emerson, Letters, 2: 48.   [3]Ibid., p. 50.

[4]Ibid.   [5]Ibid.

one Ambrose Morill wrote to Emerson on 11 October, 1836. Morill told him
money had been raised and that it seemed an amount sufficient to cover the
costs of holding public worship. He added that the congregation was ready
to spend their money in this way if Emerson would take the charge.[1] Emerson
was not to be the actual supply preacher. Instead, he was simply to be the
administrator of the pulpit, the person who would arrange for other preachers
to fill the pulpit each Sunday: "Mr. Morill receives the ministers and I
am accountable for the supply."[2] The job hardly was as tedious as supplying
the pulpit oneself and being pressed into making doctrinal statements.
Evidently Emerson was relieved not to be the one always expected to rise to
the occasion each and every Sunday, though he would preach there from time
to time. Coincidentally, however, some of his behavior at this time of
making the commitment to East Lexington resembled his behavior during the
period 1825-33. On 8 June, 1837 he reported that he had been "sick for a
week and more" and was "very weak and imbecile now."[3] He stated his sickness
would be a good excuse for visiting William in New York City but that he
was too obligated with church duties to do so.[4] What he implied in his statement seemed clear. Namely, that again he found the psychological ploy of
illness a way to appear committed to the church without actually giving as
much as he possibly could to a charge.

Two weeks later he was still troubled by a "somewhat increased inflammation on the lungs," and he considered making a "long journey or a voyage"
while explaining to his brother that this was why he did "not wish to make

---

[1] Ibid., p. 79, footnote No. 97.   [2] Ibid.

[3] Ibid., p. 80.   [4] Ibid.

any new engagement" either to supply a pulpit or to lecture.[1] Slightly over

a month after the appearance of his spring-time lung inflammation he reported

on 30 June, 1837 that he was now "very well" and not in need of travel.[2]

Not needing to travel was a major psychological accomplishment for him in

the light of similar circumstances and behavior during 1825-33. However,

he added shrewdly in his letter of June 30th a mention about a trip which

had already been planned. Since he was "idle on system" he thought it

"good economy" to pay a visit to "wifes friends at Plymouth which has been

promised so long it has almost become a bug bear."[3] However, he said he

preferred to stay at home, not to do his pulpit administration but simply

to behold his home: "I hate to go abroad so much that even the immortal

Rock on which those Ancients 'The famed fountains of our freedom laid' looks

hostile seen afar from my peavines and strawberry beds."[4]

"Seen afar" indeed. During May, 1837 Emerson declared, "Our age is

ocular," and referred to himself in a fashion which was very congruent with

matured ritualized vision.[5] Emerson referred to himself as a "seer of

Unity."[6] For example, his garden of peavines and strawberry beds prompted

his visual admiration, and that sort of style of regard had long characterized

precisely what he thought constituted the essence of the ministerial office

(in the broadest sense): "I behold; I bask in beauty; I await; I wonder;

where is my Godhead now? This is the Male and Female principle in Nature.

One Man, male and female created him. Hard as it is to describe God, it is

harder to describe the Individual . . . this is the habitual posture of

the mind-beholding. But whenever the day dawns, the great day (of) truth

---

[1]See ibid., pp. 81, 83.

[2]Ibid., p. 84.

[3]Ibid.

[4]Ibid.

[5]Emerson, JMN, 5::328, 337.

[6]Ibid.

on the soul, it comes with awful invitation to me to accept it, to blend with its aurora."[1] Emerson sensed the firmament of meaning of his phenomenal world to be reaching down and touching him sympathetically, or at least he thought a blessing was brought to him in this way. More was in store for him. When he returned from the Plymouth visit early during July, 1837 he stopped in Boston before going on out to Concord. After conferring there with one Mr. Sohier, a financier, he found out that within days he not only would be called to "blend with the aurora" of his peavines and strawberry beds in Concord, but also would be able to take into his purse the second and final installment from Beza Tucker's long-awaited estate.

With his annual income now assured at over $1200 a year, Emerson could turn his mind to staging a final act of severing his connection with all pulpits ever after, and plan to find "America" as his rightful source of succour and inspiration. Therefore, the "umbilical cord" of his "conscience" was readied to leave a narrow ministry in favor of commitment to a much broader one. This involves two major symbolic steps. The first is tied to Emerson's opinion of scholarship in America. The second is associated with the meaning of religious commitment. Emerson's literary successes have already been mentioned or alluded to: his friendship and publishing help which Carlyle accepted, the starts on the lecture platform, and the formation of Hedge's Club which gathered together all the literary liberals Emerson would ever have wanted to meet (and some he could do without!). Moreover, due to the manifesto-like quality of Nature he soon reigned in the center of the transcendental group.[2] But perhaps this native son's first step toward renouncing the pulpit completely, apart from all these literary successes,

---

[1]Ibid., p. 337.   [2]See ibid., p. 194.

came in the form of the "Oration" or the "American Scholar Address," which
was delivered before the Phi Beta Kappa Society at Harvard on 31 August, 1837.

The original invitation went to the Rev. Dr. Wainwright, but he declined
quickly.[1] Probably because he realized he was something of a stop-gap choice,
Emerson only slowly abided by the request from Cornelius Conway Felton of
22 June, 1837, on behalf of the Society, to address the group on their anniversary. However, the source of Emerson's trepidation seems to have been more
complex that that. His worries involved factors less conscious than the act
of accepting or rejecting an invitation. On 21 August, 1837 he reported
that he had experienced a nightmare, in particular, "a dream of a duel."[2]
It foreshadowed the message he was about to present in his address. Namely,
that the American scholar should no longer be timid, imitative, or too deferen-
tial to European and English literary precedents. Rather, the American
scholar should be independent and self-reliant. Once done, Emerson assured
the audience, "the huge world will come round to him," to the American scholar.[3]
He was implying not only that he had dueled with "Mother England," but also
that now triumph was his. In this sense, Emerson had "defeated" Carlyle
in something of a literary duel. At least, the fact that Emerson was the
only means Carlyle had to have his work published in America was a mark
of successful "control" which Emerson could readily cherish. In this way
Emerson symbolized that he no longer was subject to "optical deceptions of
the mind." The "Idols of the Cave" had been smashed or, at least, demoted.
If he could exercise some control over Carlyle, then Emerson could understand

---

[1]See Emerson, Letters, 2: 94, footnote No. 150.

[2]Emerson, JMN, 5: 371.

[3]Rusk, The Life of Ralph Waldo Emerson. Quoted on page 264.

himself to be able to control the institution of English literature the man represented. As he had awakened from his nightmare, so too did Emerson's eyes turn from cultural dependence on England to the bright light of national cultural independence. Indeed, in anticipation of William James and John Dewey he concluded his "Oration" to Phi Beta Kappa by saying that although "action is with the scholar subordinate," it was nonetheless "essential." Without action the scholar "is not yet man. Without it thought can never ripen into Truth. . . . Only so much do I know, as I have lived. Instantly we know whose words are loaded with life, and whose not."[1] Though he had playfully "locked antlers" with England through association with Carlyle, and though he had declared himself to be an American scholar, Emerson's duel funnelled-down into a second step, or final act of ritual severance from the consciousness of scholarly and religious colonialism.

According to Ralph Rusk, the over-all theme of the "American Scholar Address" was "self-trust, self-realization."[2] This theme, now come to a full-blown head, was the meaning or accomplishment of 1825-33. Like that hard-won meaning, Emerson brought his duel closer to his personal life. He did so by way of going beyond "person and place" into prominence in a national cultural and religious role. Up to the point of 1 September, 1837 he had preached and lectured but had not yet been recognized solely and exclusively as a lecturer. This recognition was of fundamental importance to him because it would thrust him finally away from diminishing, narrow denominational commitments to the Unitarians and towards expanding, broad civil commitments to the people of his homeland. Emerson's second step toward renouncing

---

[1] Ibid. Quoted on pages 264-65.

[2] Ibid., p. 265.

the pulpit consisted finally of <u>renouncing the pulpit</u> in a seemingly uneventful, matter-of-fact way. Ritualization would succeed in allowing him a sense of ego-mastery which was free from conventions of his past.

The stage had begun being prepared during 1834-38 when on 28 December, 1834 Emerson declared in his journals, "Rather let me 'a pagan suckled in a creed outworn' thou cowardly deny or conceal one particle of my debt to Greek art or poetry or virtue."[1] There is no way of knowing just what Greek sources he had in mind, but he was convinced by the implied meaning that the ancient teat was far sweeter than all the others he was wont to suck for personal and intellectual nurturance. On 15 July, 1837 that line about the pagan would be delivered as a part of the text of his "Divinity School Address," except then he would distinctly substitute that ancient teat for the corruptions of historical Christianity, especially the Unitarian strain of supernatural rationalism. He would say that historical Christianity "corrupts all attempts to communicate religion" in that it exaggerates the importance "about the person of <u>Jesus</u>" and prevents the soul from expanding "to the full circle of the Universe."[2] Even prior to that particular journal entry of December 28th Emerson displayed a disaffection with the office of the Unitarian ministry during the early months of the period of 1834-38. To the degree he did, he prepared to culminate his renunciation in terms of some hard-won but rather ordinary realizations during the early part of 1838.

On 20 October, 1833, after having attended a "Sabbath in the country" (Newton), Emerson felt quite beyond it all.[3] "Mr. Bates," he said, was a

---

[1] Emerson, <u>JMN</u>, 4: 380.

[2] Emerson, "The Divinity School Address," p. 73.

[3] Emerson, <u>JMN</u>, 4: 91.

plain and serious Calvinist who was "not winning but not repelling: one of
the useful police which God makes out of the ignorance and superstition of
the youth of the world."[1] When he wondered, "When is religious truth to
be distinctly uttered--what it is, not what it resembles?" he yearned after
the major human strength of youthful identity quests, namely, the virtue
of "fidelity."[2] As long as the "youth of the world" offended against "their
conscience" they would not be happy.[3] Only when attached to "religious truth"
would happiness be theirs.[4] In this sense, Emerson was suggesting that the
youth of the world follow his lead and work to bring together their close
and distant horizons, not wait for the coming age of eternal "damnation"
or "salvation."

The virtue of fidelity entailed that all pretensions and appearances
be jettisoned in favor of pure truth. Emerson had assumed an attitude devoid
of most pretension about the ministry on several instances. Characteristic
of his attitude was his self-description of 15 January, 1833: "I . . . .
am a dull scholar . . . I am content to belong to the great all, and look
on and see what better men can do, and by my admiration realize a property
in their worth."[5] He did not feel cast into the supposed Unitarian mold,
a mold which for him entailed much pretentiousness. Moreover, on 2 June,
1834 he was giving up "appearances" also. The day before he "preached at
Waltham," and he worried in retrospect about "when some trenchant Iarno"
would come across him and read him "such a lesson."[6] Iarno, of course,

---

[1]Ibid.   [2]Ibid.   [3]Ibid.   [4]Ibid.

[5]Ibid., pp. 110-11; also, see ibid., 3: 152, 225. The ministry was
defined as "seeing creation with a new eye . . . to behold," and the minister
was thought to be merely a "Spectator."

[6]Ibid., 4: 294.

was the character in Goethe's <u>Wilhelm Meister,</u> who warned Wilhelm to be himself without fearing appearances. Emerson did not offend his conscience.
Narrow social expectations were thwarted by Iarno's initiatives: "Is the
preacher one to make a fool of himself for the entertainment of other people?
. . . When there is any difference of level felt in the foot board of the
pulpit and the floor of the parlor, you have not said that which you should
say."[1] Emerson already pictured his foot coming down off the pulpit and
it poised, ready for the mounting. Such elevation did not imply theological
condecension, but it pointed the way toward national fidelity. Like his
foot, his affections were drawn away from the pulpit as well. Having gone
to Harvard Divinity School on the morning of 15 July, 1835, he heard a sermon
which was alleged to have been "the best performance."[2] But Emerson found
it to have been "founded on nothing," and he wondered "at the patience of
the people" who listened to it.[3] He asked himself, "Why do I still go to
pasture where I never find grass, to these actors without a purpose unless
a poor mechanical one, these talkers without method, and reasoners without
an idea?"[4] He wondered this exactly three years to the day before he would
deliver the "Divinity School Address" at the same place.

If Emerson was also an actor, his purpose was coming to the foreground
of the drama he would soon stage. During 1836 the pastures of moral edification
were not any grassier, but his turf, at least, was becoming much more greener
in more ways than one. On the one hand, he cultivated his muse more than he
tended to sermon-making. On the other hand, he was doing business as a lecturer
and as a novice financial broker. He was making money at these occupations

---

[1]Ibid.

[2]Ibid., 5: 58.

[3]Ibid.

[4]Ibid.

during a year of considerable financial depression all along the Atlantic coast. He described himself often in conflict over this curious coincidence of preoccupations when he wrote to William on 21 July, 1837. He thought of himself as a "scholar floundering for the first time in a quagmire of business with all the dwarf brevity of a broker, as if it were enough to suggest one to know a sum and date and could forsee and transpierce all the rest."[1] There is a bit of false deference here, given William's financial difficulties: He requested William's advice about how to make the best deals trading stock, implying that although he enjoyed dabbling in "a little business," doing so tended to spoil "a great deal of time for the muses."[2] In general, Emerson seemed quite removed from the possibility that he might ever again be conflicted over commitments to the Unitarians. Other more interesting things were on his mind.

Emerson's increased concern for the "market place" of Muses and money during 1834-38 was a mark of psychological growth. This is related to the differentiation and integration of mastery, which stems from the exercises of play. Emerson's preoccupation with finances signals the "payoff" in money and self-confidence of successful ritualized vision. During the period from his childhood to about 1826 or 1827 his standard mode of handling money was simply to "take in" all he could, usually because his family needed every spare penney members could earn. Such a manner of handling money was a "retentive" one, associated with the alimentary function of retaining feces and controling their expulsion at will. However, this mode of money management grew out of that mode of functioning which occurs first in human development, namely, the more fundamental, more infantile mode of "incorporation."

---

[1] Emerson, Letters, 2: 89. [2] Ibid., p. 90.

This, of course, is a function associated with ingestion, as in taking in the nipple and a mother's milk and warmth. Together, retention and incorporation can become styles of adult preoccupation, especially when money is involved.

During July of 1837, however, Emerson handled money differently. He displayed much more tenacity in his freedom either to "hold onto" money or, for that matter, to "let go" of it. He was freer to give up the treasures of money and the treasure of dependency upon external sources of authority, be they literary ones, like Carlyle, or religious ones, like the pulpit. Investing was a risky business but Emerson seems to have felt free enough not to hold onto the little money he had. If any return could be realized, then he would be able to "hold onto" even more. Just what may have brought on this new tenacity of financial freedom and, hence, psychosocial mastery probably was a mixed ball-of-wax. It might have sprung from the unique combination, on the one hand, of Emerson's psychological style of expansion within diminishment and, on the other hand, his earnings from, first, his lectures and occasional sermons and, second, the fact that he received the full and final balance of the Tucker estate early during July, 1837. Regardless of the sources of his mastery, he seemed quite able to handle the conflict between "mammon and Muses" as he implied in his conclusion to William on 21 July, 1837: "I will not try to elevate this letter so base and mercantile by a single word of better matters. But do not I beseech you let care carve one wrinkle in the sublime brow. Other men have had losses and lived to laugh at them; and every loss is somehow a gain."[1] Emerson's attempts

[1] Ibid.

at bringing psychological closure to bear on the vocational issues which gripped him tightly during 1825-33, met with success during 1832-33. Now that same vocational closure became the pretext for a new personal recentering at a higher level of differentiation and integration. This time Emerson's center would no longer draw him into the throes of personal ambivalence, as well as into the task of resolving that ambivalence around issues related to vocation. The new focus for his attentions would expand into the broader and deeper cultural ambivalence of his country, as well as into a way of bringing that ambivalence to a reasonable degree of resolution. Therefore, such a shift of centers marks the nexus of whatever psychohistorical impact Emerson had on American life during the nineteenth century.

Before such a wider context of meaning for his professional fruition could emerge, it was first necessary that professional closure be carried full course. This Emerson did in terms of the experiences he pondered after attending several church services and after hearing the preaching of the Rev. Ezra Ripley's assistant, the Rev. Barzillai Frost of the Concord church. Within the person of Frost Emerson concentrated all the personal negative thoughts and feelings he had about the Unitarian ministry. In doing so, he employed the young Concord preacher as a foil against which he might see in a positive light an act of final defection from the Unitarian ministry. Emerson invited himself to regard himself _not_ as one who had merely abandoned the ministry but, rather, as one away from whom the Unitarian ministry itself had slipped! He could have rejected the Unitarians as he had done during 1832. However, for reasons connected with his identity-needs as a lecturer to Americans, he needed to believe that the Unitarians (the ministers), not he, munched on pastures like docile, dependent cattle. As such, it was they who had failed to attain to the heights of consciousness Emerson believed he had attained.

This whole study began with the scene of the death of Emerson's father, and the study can be wound-down with the depiction of another "scene," one which also illustrates the pattern of expansion within diminishment. Emerson had moved from Boston to rural Concord during 1834 and by that time he had undoubtedly become acquainted with the Rev. Barzillai Frost, the new young assistant of the Concord church.[1] Frost had come to Concord as a colleague of Ripley, Emerson's paternal step-grandfather. Later, Frost took Ripley's place. During all but about forty-three of Concord's two-hundred year or so long existence, the preachers in the town's pulpit had been Emerson's ancestors, about seven generations of Emersons.[2] Therefore, Frost was an exception to the general rule of succession, and Emerson probably felt some tinges of regret about this fact. Undoubtedly he allowed it to punctuate the fissure he needed to feel between the ministry in the broad sense (which he associated with his patriotic ancestors of minutemen stature) and that of the Unitarians, ministry in the narrow sense. The "scene" Emerson painted around Frost was to set the stage upon which the last act of ritual severance from the Unitarian pulpit would be carried out.

Though a conscientious pastor to his flock, Frost's ministry was mediocre at best.[3] The fact was that Frost's monotonal and pedantic style of preaching inspired very few parishioners, especially Emerson who was becoming known in New England for his superb eloquence. On 7 May, 1837 he wrote, reacting

---

[1]Ibid., p. 112.

[2]See Rusk, The Life of Ralph Waldo Emerson, pp. 43-53.

[3]See Conrad Wright, The Liberal Christians (Boston: Beacon Press, 1970) p. 44.

to hearing Frost preach, that he could not "hear the young men whose theological instruction is exclusively owed to Cambridge and to public institution without feeling how much happier" was his "star which rained," on him "influences of ancestral religion."[1] "The young preacher," Emerson recorded on 1 October, 1837, "preached from his ears and his memory, and never a word from his soul."[2] Incidentally, Emerson added that he believed all preaching in the land was the "reverberation" of a handfull of men who did preach from their soul, and they were "five or six seers and sayers."[3] Furthermore, his ancestral religion lived on not only in the person of his step-grandfather with whom he could identify readily as a man of great strength of character, but also in Ripley's son, Samuel: "I could not help remarking at church how much humanity was in the preaching of my good Uncle S. Ripley (preacher at Waltham). The rough farmers had their hands at their eyes repeatedly. But the old hardened sinners, the arid educated men, ministers and others, were dry as stones."[4] Plymouth Rock had been declared an arid stone as well, at least Emerson found it more of a strain to consider living near it than he did to consider the greater merits of living in Concord. Therefore, his ancestry, insofar as he embraced it as his very own, was a warm backdrop against which Barzillai Frost contrasted distinctly.

It was significant that the women in his life were not close by as he considered resigning his East Lexington charge early during 1838. Lidian had gone to Plymouth for a visit during February, 1838 and Ruth Emerson was

[1] Emerson, JMN, 5: 323.

[2] Ibid., p. 380.

[3] Ibid.

[4] Ibid., p. 445.

in New York City on another lengthy visit with William, Susan, and young
Willie. During 1832, when he left Second Church his first wife had left him
alone, taken away from him by death. During that time Emerson seemed also
to have paid his debt to his mother with the price of Ellen's death, and he
had grown beyond much of her sway. Now during February, 1838 he wrote to
Lidian, telling her of his desultory daily life during her absence: "Nobody,"
he wrote, "has been here but Mr. Frost since I came home and no letters of
importance."[1] On 18 February, 1838 Emerson "went to Lexington and told the
Committee there" that he wished to be "put off" his charge and, if possible,
"commit it to Mr. Dwight."[2] The next day he wrote to Lidian telling her
of his action: The Society, he said, consented, "provided I engage to supply,
and then send Mr. D., rather than put it on them to engage him; as they think
the first course will give the people more satisfaction. It is a trifle and
I submit, astonished to arrive at the dignity of patronage."[3] As would
a respected father, Emerson got the matters straightened out to the satisfaction of all.

Though dignified by patronage from the congregation, Emerson also conveyed more infantile fears and yearnings. These were clearly cast in mother-
son terms. With language once again reminiscent of the theme of the umbilical
cord, he asked somewhat teasingly of his more religiously orthodox wife,
"But does not the eastern Lidian my Palestine mourn to see the froward man
cutting the last threads that bind him to that prized gown and band the
symbols black and white of old and distant Judah?"[4] Though during 1832 he
wrote that his "umbilical cord" to the Unitarian church had been severed,

---

[1] Emerson, Letters, 2: 112. [2] Ibid., p. 113.

[3] Ibid. [4] Ibid., pp. 113-14.

some "threads" had remained attached. However, during the month of February, 1838 they had been finally and completely "unfastened." Writing to his mother toward the end of the month after his resignation, his conviction about the quality of his own eloquence as a lecturer was firm: ". . . henceforth I shall live by lecturing which promises to be good bread. I have relinquished my ecclesiastical charge at E. Lexington and shall not preach more except from the Lyceum."[1] With these lines he affirmed the tenacity of his new-found sense of personal strength and freedom as well as his course toward carrying his ministry and his preaching to a higher level. Moreover, his independence assured him the blessings of his wife and mother.

Not even Ezra Ripley's failing health, with more frequent minor strokes, pulled Emerson off his course.[2] The step-grandson's attendance at church services in Concord since February of 1837 was brought to a poignant peak on March 4th of the next year, after his East Lexington charge had been ended: "Let the clergy beware when the well-disposed scholar begins to say, 'I cannot go to Church, time is too precious.'"[3] The sense of another duel was in the air. He pointed out his belief that the "best and worse men in the parish meet one day as fellows in one house, the eminent and the plain men," and that such classless socializing had become the "paramount motive" for attending church.[4] Emerson disavowed that one "should not shun the one opportunity of equal meeting with all citizens that is left!"[5] However, he had little time to suffer the Rev. Frost, let alone all those other "arid" souls. On the next day, Monday, 5 March, 1838, he made reference

---

[1] Ibid., p. 120.

[2] See ibid., p. 114.

[3] Emerson, JMN, 5: 456.

[4] Ibid.

[5] Ibid.

to the day before, a Sunday, a beautiful day indeed, and implied the nature
of the better use of his precious time: ". . . mild, calm, and though the
earth is covered with snow, somewhereas two feet deep, yet the day and the
night moonlit were as good for thought, if the man were rested and peaceful, as any in the year. The meteorology of thought I like to note."[1]
Not dwelling on the sermon which he heard in church the day before, he proceeded to distill out of that morning the natural beauty of the day. Such
beauty affirmed his sense of a hallowed presence, the personal numinosity
he felt while sitting in the midst of the small congregation avoiding hearing
Frost's message.

Numinosity came to the foreground of his awareness two weeks later as
he reflected upon the time he had spent listening once again to the painful
preaching of Mr. Frost. Sunday, 18 March, 1838 was stormy and snowy. It
was a day during which the "meteorology of thought" influenced all judgment.
That evening Emerson wrote: "At Church all day but almost tempted to say I
would go no more. Men go where they are wont to go else had no soul gone
this afternoon. The snowstorm was real, the preacher merely spectral.
<u>Vast contrast to look at him and then out of the window.</u> . . I think it
shows. . . that there is commanding attraction in the moral sentiment that
can lend a faint tint of light to such dullness and ignorance as this coming
in its place and name."[2] Emerson was inclined to peer out of windows as if
they were mouths of caves inside which he was confined. On 25 February, 1834
he had procured "solitude" by going "to the window" and by gazing "at the
stars."[3] Moreover, he gazed at himself. He was the "beyond" in contrast

---

[1]Ibid., p. 457.   [2]Ibid., pp. 463-64. Emphasis added.
[3]Ibid., 4: 267.

to the spectral preacher who, he said, had no fault but who seemed to be merely "one of the large class of sincere persons based on shams; sincere persons who are bred and live in shams."[1] From within the world diminished by his circumstances in church, Emerson projected horizons which expanded toward the shamless Infinite. The action of looking, for example, at Frost and "then out of the window" was a consumation of ritualized vision, won after years of difficult visual play, which was buffetted by life's events. Once again, "seeing" his way out of those Sunday morning circumstances further articulated his ritualization of vision. Moreover, just several days after creating this scene in his journals he received an invitation to present what would be referred to later as the "Divinity School Address." Like the Concord church, it supplied him another stage for exercising ritualized vision.

This ending of the scene inside the church served to indicate two things which already have emerged in this study. These are the fact that "Nature" was believed to be the outward expression of the abiding sense of numinosity Emerson felt deep within himself, and that the movement implicit in his struggle to make a connection between his personal life and his cultural context occurred according to a pattern of ritualized vision, the pattern of expansion within diminishment. Therefore, a suggestion is that snow stood as a symbol of "Nature," and that the description of the meaning of snow which Emerson wrote in his journal of 18 March, 1838 derived fundamentally from the ritualized visual pattern.

Both snow and numinosity bear the same characteristics of brightness, softness, and the capacity to soothe; especially, perhaps, Emerson's jangled

---

[1] Ibid., 5: 463-64.

sensibilities while listening to Frost preach. Emerson understood the snow
as something more than a mere inconvenience in getting to church that afternoon, more than crystallized water. Indeed, snow expressed Nature's highest
eloquence and bore with her eloquence a transcendence-inducing sense of a
hallowed presence. In this sense, snow was emblematic of a recovered sense
of hope. Snow became the object of Emerson's ritualized vision when he
shifted his gaze from Frost in the pulpit and the congregation around him,
toward the bright snowstorm outside, through the window. What Emerson
managed to do was to set the "scene" within the church into a much wider
and expansive visual context, snow extricating his gaze from the diminished
scene inside the church.

If ritualized vision meant a recovery of the sense of hope, then Emerson
could successfully regress in the service of his ego. That is, he could
touch well-springs of trust first engendered in infancy, when the primary
relationship fostering all feeling is the exclusive bond of mutuality between
the infant and the mother--"Madonna and Child." By going back in thought,
feeling, and fantasy, Emerson could "diminish" his purview in the present
so as later to "expand" beyond it with a renewed sense of independence and
self-confidence. Such regression in the service of his ego is well depicted
in a journal entry of 18 March, 1838. As a virtual summary of thirty-five
years of personal testing and forging, Emerson unwittingly casts his entry
in imagery related to mothers and expanding beyond mothers from within the
hope they foster. He had learned many lessons, but none was as important
to him during the early months of 1838 as what he wrote about in that particular entry:

> The men I have spoken of above--sincere persons who live in
> shams, are those who accept another man's Consciousness for
> their own, and are in the state of a son who should always

suck at his mother's teat. I think Swedenborg ought so to
represent them or still more properly, as permanent embryos
which received all their nourishment through the umbilical
cord and never arrive at a conscious and independent existence
. . . Once leave your own knowledge of God not to mention all
the subsequent history of Europe and America. But he is not
his own man but the hapless bondman of Time with these continents and aeons of prejudice to carry on his back. It is now
grown so bad that he cannot carry the mountain any longer and
be a man. There must be a Revolution. Let the revolution
come and let One come breathing free into the earth to walk
by hope alone. It were a new World and perhaps the Ideal would
seem possible. But now it seems to me they are cheated out
of themselves, and live on another's sleeve.[1]

Ruth Emerson's son had given up many teats in his life, not the least of

which had been her own, in practical effect during his infancy and in sym-

bolic effect during 1829-33.

Emerson would preach his last sermon during January of 1839, but the

"cut threads" were only unravelled as loose ends further at that occasion.

What really finalized the breach was the "Divinity School Address." He

received the invitation to deliver the address from the graduating class of

the Harvard Divinity School just several days after he created the "scene"

of his visual ritualization in March, 1838. Like the time just prior to

delivering the "American Scholar Address," he also had a disturbing dream

while putting the final touches on the "Divinity School Address" on 20 April,

1838. He mentioned only that the "ill dream" was significant because it

seemed to "counteract my inclination."[2] At any rate, at the Phi Beta Kappa

anniversary a year before he had had the scholars of Harvard in their own

stronghold. Now he could come to grips with the preachers in theirs.

The rupturous message of the address was straightforward: "When the

mind opens and reveals the laws which traverse the universe and make things

what they are, then shrinks the great world at once into a mere illustration

---

[1]Ibid., 5: 465-66.   [2]Ibid., p. 475.

and fable of this mind."[1] This sentiment was nothing more than an intuition, and it needed not to be sensed "second hand." Jesus recognized the intuition himself, and it was only the "noxious exaggeration about the person of Jesus" by historical Christianity that made Jesus into a "mediator" of this intuition between God and man.[2] Emerson suggested this situation could be remedied only if men dared to love God without any sort of mediator, be it a Jesus, a church, or a preacher like the Rev. Frost and all the other "sincere men." All-in-all, though Emerson raised the hackles of the Unitarian professors at Harvard, the students were gratified. However, for all the factors which led up to the address, he was more gratified than anyone else.[3] His ritual severance from the pulpit had been affected in final fashion, personally and now intellectually. Having brought about the shift of identity centers from church to country, the psychohistorical impact of that shift could be embraced by future generations.

Though the ritual engagement between Emerson and the Unitarians might be regarded to have come to a head on that day of 15 July, 1838 when the address was given, the crux of the psychohistorical significance of that address had its sharpest cutting-edge in the personal meaning Emerson invested in it. For that one must emphasize the ritualized vision effected four months before, during March of 1838. Unlike Emerson's contemporary, John Henry Newman, for example, whose break with the Church of England came to its highest consummation in institutional allegiance to the Catholic Church,

[1] Emerson, Nature, p. 67.

[2] Ibid., p. 73.

[3] See Rusk, The Life of Ralph Waldo Emerson, p. 272. Rusk suggests that Emerson's poem, "Uriel," was a "sublimation" of the circumstances surrounding the "Divinity School Address."

Emerson consummated his break with the Unitarians by paying allegiance to his non-institutionalized pattern of expansion within diminishment or, if you will, "cultural peek-a-boo." However, what Newman and Emerson did share was the common element of sanctity in the ritual act of breaking away itself. Emerson thought of institutions as being merely "optical illusions," and not deserving of "confrontations."[1] To do battle was not his style. Yet, he did effectively break away. His propensity throughout his early life was to rely on "seeing" beyond present circumstances which did, in fact, often involve institutional commitments as we have seen. During the month of March, 1838 his ritualized vision seems to have been most animated, just as his psychological and geographical propensities had been during 1825-33. During that winter month of 1838, the die had been cast. A young man's life was coming to an end, and, as good Christians welcomed Easter, that young man was turning into a leader who believed in a promised land.

---

[1]See Emerson, JMN, 7: 177.

APPENDIX: SHORT CHRONOLOGY OF EMERSON"S EARLY LIFE

Year	Age	Events
1803	-	Born, May 25th, second son of the Rev. William Emerson, minister of First Church, Boston; and Ruth Haskins Emerson, daughter of a prestigious Boston merchant.
1806	3	Attends remedial reading class "again" because he is unable to read well according to his father; endures serious illness afterwards, which is blamed on worms.
1811	8	Father dies; financial pressure mounts and loss of parsonage is imminent.
1812	9	Enters Boston Latin School, excelling in poetic compositions; War of 1812 commences.
1814	11	Use of parsonage ends, and British threaten to cut off supplies to Boston; family moves into the home of paternal relatives, the Rev. and Mrs. Ezra Ripley, in Concord, the Emerson's ancestral town.
1815	12	Family moves back to Boston, and commences running boarding house business; several changes of residence.
1817-1818	15	Enters Harvard College; refrains from participating in the annual sophomore riots in the fall; family financial situation critical.
1819	16	Eldest brother William founds School for Young Ladies in Boston as hedge against family poverty; Emerson excels in literary studies in college.
1820	17	Commences keeping what would become voluminous journals; idolizes literature teacher, Levi Frisbie; first mention of relationship with Martin Gay (last would appear in journals in 1822).
1821	18	Graduates 30th out of 59; resigns himself to assisting brother at School for Young Ladies, having failed to be appointed usher at the Latin School.
1822	19	Increases theological correspondence with Aunt Mary Emerson (who helped family after her brother's death).
1823	20	Becomes in full charge of the School; relies on mother for disciplining refractory girls.
1824	21	Edward graduates from Harvard, and Ralph anticipates financial conditions favorable for taking up ministerial training at Harvard Divinity School; writes "letter to Plato;" closes school.
1825	22	Attends biblical theology courses given by Boston's "Unitarian Pope," Andrews Norton; goes blind; withdraws to the country; family problems fall upon his shoulders (Edward's breakdown; Charles' depressions; Bulkeley's derangement; William's abandonment of ministerial plans).

1826	23	Returns to Harvard as graduate resident; gets rheumatism; depressions--seeks the respect of "one Plato;" sight returns; prepares approbation sermon, and is approbated to preach in October; notices signs of tuberculosis afterward; sails to South for his health.
1827	24	Returns to Boston in June; hedges taking any permanent ministerial post, using health as an excuse; preaches as "supply" in various posts; meets Ellen Tucker in New Hampshire at Christmas.
1828	25	Commits himself to three concerns as the year unfolds--Edward's health (he would be forced to enter an asylum); Ellen (they would become engaged to marry at Christmastime); and Second Church, Boston (which he would supply for several months at the end of the year, and be called to fill permanently during the next).
1829	26	Ellen's first bleeding attack (she was severely tubercular); ordination in March ("execution day"); Ellen's second bleeding attack; takes full charge of Second Church; travels in country, forsaking church duties, for Ellen's health; marriage in Sept.; lameness forces him to sit while preaching.
1830	27	Travels to Philadelphia and New Hampshire for Ellen's health, avoiding parish duties; Ellen's third and last attack in August; Doctor Jackson offers advice which falls on deaf ears; Edward contracts serious TB, and Ruth Emerson reacts to him differently than she does to Ellen, who is worse; to move south or not?
1831	28	Ellen dies in February, leaving Emerson "alone and strangely happy;" Charles joins Edward who is in St. Croix for his health.
1832	29	Begins making himself unacceptable to Second Church in June, recommending the society find someone else to offer the sacrament of the Lord's Supper; retreats to the mountains to consider his request; society says "no" to his request; tenders resignation in September; praises anonymous author (who turns out to be Thomas Carlyle); resignation accepted by society after 62 ballots, and after Emerson's summer-long bout with diarrhea subsided; likens the church to a mother whose child's umbilical cord he had severed; sails for Europe and England on Christmas Day.
1833	30	From Italy to England; visit with Carlyle was a "white day" in his years; returns to United States in autumn; first lecture at Masonic Temple, Boston (on natural history).
1834	31	Lectures in New England; receives first advance on Ellen's estate; Edward dies of TB in Puerto Rico; begins lecturing on biography and "representative men." Presumably meets Lydia Jackson of Plymouth, Mass. while lecturing there.

1835	32	Engaged to Lydia Jackson in January (thereafter refers to her as "Lydian"); purchases house in ancestral town of Concord; marries and carries Lydian away from Plymouth to Concord, much to her regret; continues to lecture, realizing that travelling increases the market value of each lecture.
1836	33	Charles anticipates legal career in Concord and marriage to Elizabeth Hoar, but grows sick with TB while in New York City visiting William, who is an attorney there; Charles dies in New York in May; the transcendentalist "manifesto," Nature, published in September; first meeting of "Hedge's Club" ten days later; born, son Waldo, in October; Emerson takes administrative charge of East Lexington church temporarily.
1837	34	Settles into life in Concord; continues lecturing; takes on much of the financial burden incurred by William, who is speculating in real estate on Staten Island in New York during a year of economic depression; delivers "American Scholar" address before Phi Beta Kappa Society at Harvard in June; "Divinity School Address" in July; receives second and final balance of monies from Ellen's estate; mother ferried between the Emersons in Concord and those in New York City.
1838	35	Asks East Lexington church to dismiss him; records impressions about the minister in Concord, Barzillai Frost, in journals ("negative identity"); final renunciation of the Unitarian ministry in the ritual of "seeing" out the window of the Concord parish meeting house; devotes the rest of his days to lecturing to the American public--core of his message is the personally hard-won reality of "self reliance."

1847	44	Lectures in England
1850	47	Lectures in Chicago and St. Louis
1853	50	Again
1867	64	Again
1871	68	Lectures in California
1873	70	Lectures in England
1882	79	Dies

SELECTED BIBLIOGRAPHY

Biographical Process

Altick, Richard D. Lives and Letters: A History of Literary Biography in England and America. New York: Alfred Knopf, 1965.

Altman, Leon. "'West' as a Symbol of Death." Psychoanalytic Quarterly. 28(1959): 236-241.

Arnheim, Rudolf. Art and Visual Perception. Berkeley: University of California Press, 1971.

_____. Visual Thinking. Berkeley: University of California Press, 1969.

Asch, Solomon E. "Gestalt Theory." International Encyclopedia of Social Sciences, vol. 7. Edited by David L. Sills.

Bailey, Greg. "The Significance of the Divine Eye as a Means of Spiritual Vision in Ancient Indian Religion." Journal of Studies in Mysticism 2/2 (Spring, 1979): 86-94.

Banks, Robert. "Religion as Projection: A Re-Appraisal of Freud's Theory." Religious Studies 9 (1973): 401-426.

Barbu, Zevedei. Problems of Historical Pschology. New York: Grove Press, 1960.

Barzun, Jacques. "History: Her Muse and Her Doctors." Journal of History, 1972, 77: 36-64.

Berger, Peter and Luckmann, Thomas. The Social Construction of Reality. New York: Anchor Books, 1966.

Black, Max. Models and Metaphors. Ithaca, New York: Cornell University Press, 1962.

Bloch, Marc. The Historian's Craft. Translated by Peter Putnam. New York: Princeton University Press, 1953.

Buckle, Henry T. History of Civilization in England. London, 1891.

Burridge, Kenelm. Someone, No One: An Essay on Individuality. Princeton: Princeton University Press, 1979.

Campbell, Joseph. The Hero with a Thousand Faces. New York: Pantheon, 1949.

_____. The Masks of God: Occidental Mythology. New York: The Viking Press, Compass Edition, 1970.

Capps, Donald E. "John Henry Newman: A Study of Vocational Identity."
    Journal for the Scientific Study of Religion, 9 (Spring, 1970): 33-51.

_____. "Orestes Brownson: The Psychology of Religious Affiliation."
    Journal for the Scientific Study of Religion, 9/1 (1968): 197-209.

Capps, Donald E. and Reynolds, Frank, eds. The Biographical Process.
    The Hague: Mouton, 1976.

Clifford, James L. Biography as an Art. New York: Oxford University
    Press, 1962.

_____. From Puzzles to Portraits. Chapel Hill, North Carolina: University
    of North Carolina Press, 1970.

Chapman, Hester W. "Notes on Historical Biography." Times Literary Supple-
    ment, August 8, 1959.

Coles, Robert. Erik H. Erikson: The Growth of His Work. Boston: Little,
    Brown, and Co., 1970.

Dilthey, Wilhelm. Pattern and Meaning in History. Edited by H.P. Rickman.
    New York: Harper and Row, 1961.

Edel, Leon. "Biography: A Manifesto." Biography: An Interdisciplinary
    Quarterly 1/1 (1978): 1-4.

_____. Literary Biography. London: Rupert Hart-Davis, 1957.

Ehrenzweig, Anton. The Psychoanalysis of Artistic Vision and Hearing. New
    York: George Braziller, 1956.

Erikson, Erik H. Childhood and Society. New York: W.W. Norton, 1963.

_____. "The Development of Ritualization." The Religious Situation:
    1968. Edited by Donald E. Cutler. Boston: Beacon Press, 1968.

_____. Dimensions of a New Identity. New York: W.W. Norton, 1974.

_____. Gandhi's Truth. New York: W.W. Norton, 1969.

_____. "Identity and the Life Cycle." Psychological Issues, Vol. 1,
    No. 1. New York: International Universities Press, 1959.

_____. Identity, Youth, and Crisis. New York: W.W. Norton, 1968.

_____. Insight and Responsibility. New York: W.W. Norton, 1964.

_____. Jefferson Lectures, 1973. As reported in The Congressional Record,
    May 2, 1973, p. s8122.

Erikson, Erik H. "Ontogeny of Ritualization." Psychoanalysis: A General Psychology. Edited by R.M. Lowenstein. New York: International Universities Press, 1966.

_____. "Play and Actuality." Explorations in Psychohistory. Edited by Erik H. Erikson and Eric Olson. New York: Simon and Schuster, 1974.

_____. Young Man Luther. New York: W.W. Norton, 1958.

Erikson, Joan M. "Eye to Eye." The Man-Made Object. Edited by Gyorgy Kepes. New York: George Braziller, 1966.

Focht, Mildred. What is Gestalt Theory? New York: Columbia University, 1935.

Freud, Sigmund. Jokes and Their Relation to the Unconscious. Translated and edited by James Strachey. New York: W.W. Norton, 1963.

_____. Leonardo Da Vinci: A Study in Psychosexuality. Translated by A.A. Brill. New York: Random House, Vintage Books, 1947.

_____. "Slips of the Pen," The Psychopathology of Everyday Life. The Standard Edition of the Complete Works of Sigmund Freud. 24 Vols. Edited by James Strachey. London: Hogarth Press, 1960, VI.

Garraty, John A. "The Interrelations of Psychology and Biography." Psychological Bulletin 51, No. 6 (1954): 569-82.

_____. The Nature of Biography. London: Jonathan Cape, 1958.

Geertz, Clifford. "Religion as a Cultural System." Anthropological Approaches to the Study of Religion. Edited by Michael Banton. New York: Praeger, 1966.

George, Alexander L. and George, Juliette L. Woodrow Wilson and Colonel House: A Personality Study. New York: Dover Publications, 1956 and 1964.

Gifford, Edward S., Jr. The Evil Eye: Studies in the Folklore of Vision. New York: Macmillan, 1958.

Gobar, Ash. Philosophic Foundations of Genetic Psychology and Gestalt Psychology. The Hague: Martinus Nijhoff, 1968.

Goldmeier, Erich. Similarity in Visually Perceived Forms. New York: International Universities Press, 1972.

Gorman, Herbert. A Victorian American: Henry Wadsworth Longfellow. New York: George Doran, 1926.

Greenacre, Phyllis. "The Eye Motif in Delusion and Fantasy." American Journal of Psychiatry 25(1938): 297-334.

Hadas, Moses and Smith, Morton. Heroes and Gods: Spiritual Biographies
     in Antiquity. New York: Harper and Row, 1965.

Harris, Thomas. I'm OK--You're OK. New York: Avon, 1969.

Hart, Henry. "The Eye in Symbol and Symptom." The Psychoanalytic Review
     36(1949): 1-21.

Henle, Mary, ed. The Selected Papers of Wolfgang Kohler. New York: Liveright,
     1971.

Hodges, H.A. The Philosophy of Wilhelm Dilthey. London: Routledge and
     Kegan Paul, 1952.

Holland, Norman N. The Dynamics of Literary Response. New York: Oxford
     University Press, 1964.

Homans, Peter. Theology After Freud. Indianapolis: Bobbs-Merrill, 1970.

Hughes, H. Stuart. History as Art and as Science. New York: Harper and
     Row, 1964.

Huizinga, Johan. Homo Ludens. Boston, 1955.

Hutch, Richard A. "Emerson and Incest." Psychoanalytic Review, 1975,
     Summer: 320-332.

_____. "Helena Blavatsky Unveiled." Journal of Religious History, 11/2
     (December, 1980): 320-341.

Jensen, Adolf. Myth and Cult Among Primitive Peoples. Chicago: University
     Chicago Press, 1963.

Johnson, Allen and Malone, Dumas, eds. Dictionary of American Biography,
     20 Vols. New York: Charles Scribner's, 1930+.

Johnson, Samuel. Idler 84 (November 24, 1795).

Kallich, Martin. "Psychoanalysis, Sexuality, and Lytton Strachey's Theory
     of Biography." American Imago 15, No. 4 (Winter 1958): 331-370.

_____. The Psychological Milieux of Lytton Strachey. New York:
     Bookman Associates, 1961.

Kleeman, James A. "The Peek-A-Boo Game." The Psychoanalytic Study of the
     Child, 22 (1967): 239-273.

Koffka, Kurt. Principles of Gestalt Psychology. New York: Harcourt, 1935.

Kris, Ernst. "The Image of the Artist." Psychoanalytic Explorations in
     Art. New York: International Universities Press, 1952. Pp. 64-84.

Lane, Michael. Structuralism. London: Jonathan Cape, 1970.

Luckmann, Thomas. The Invisible Religion. New York: Macmillan, 1967.

Martz, Louis L. The Poem of The Mind. New York: Oxford University Press, 1966.

_____. The Poetry of Meditation. rev.ed. New Haven: Yale University Press, 1962.

Maurer, Adah. "The Game of Peek-a-boo." Diseases of the Nervous System. 28 (1967): 118-121.

Mazlish, Bruce, ed. Psychoanalysis and History. New York: Grosset and Dunlap, 1971.

Merrill, Dana K. American Biography: Its Theory and Practice. Portland, Me.: Bowker Press, 1957.

Meyer, Leonard. Emotion and Meaning in Music. Chicago: University of Chicago Press, 1956.

Moraitis, George and Pletsch, Carl. "A Psychoanalytic Contribution to Method in Biography." The Psychohistory Review 8/1-2 (Summer-Fall, 1979), 72-74.

Mucchielli, Roger. An Introduction to Structural Psychology. Translated by Charles Lam Markmann. New York: Funk and Wagnalls, 1970.

Muller-Vomer, Kurt. Towards a Phenomenological Theory of Literature: A Study of Wilhem Dilthey's "Poetik." The Hague: Mouton Press, 1963.

Murray, Henry A. Explorations in Personality. New York: Oxford University Press, 1938.

_____. Manual of the Thematic Apperception Test. Cambridge: Harvard University Press, 1943.

_____. "What Should Psychologists do About Psychoanalysis?" Journal of Abnormal and Social Psychology 35 (1940): 152-53.

Murray, Henry A. and Kluckhohn, C. "Outline of a Conception of Personality." Personality in Nature, Society, and Culture. Edited by H.A. Murray, D. Schneider, and C. Kluckhohn. New York: Knopf, 1953.

Olney, James, ed. Autobiography: Essays Theoretical and Critical. Princeton: Princeton University Press, 1980.

_____. Metaphors of Self: The Meaning of Autobiography. Princeton: Princeton University Press, 1972.

Petermann, Bruno. The Gestalt Theory and the Problem of Configuration.
      London: Routledge and Kegan Paul, 1932.

Rickman, H.P. "Wilhelm Dilthey and Biography." Biography: An Interdisciplinary
      Quarterly 2/3 (1979): 218-229.

Schachtel, Ernest G. Experiential Foundations of Roschach's Test. New
      York: Basic Books, 1966.

_____. Metamorphosis. New York: Basic Books, 1959.

Smith, Jonathan Z. "The Bare Facts of Ritual." History of Religions, 20/1+2
      (August-November, 1980): 112-127.

Smith, Page. The Historian and History. New York: Vintage, Random, 1964.

Stanfield, James. An Essay on the Study and Composition of Biography.
      Sunderland, England, 1813.

Strauss, Anselm L. Mirrors and Masks: The Search for Identity. Berkeley:
      The Sociology Press of the University of California, 1969.

Strout, Cushing. "The Pluralistic Identity of William James: A Psychohistorical
      Reading of The Varieties of Religious Experience." American Quarterly
      XXIII/2 (May, 1971): 135-152.

Strumpf, Carl. Frscheinunger und psychische Funktionen. Berlin: Abhdlg.
      preuss, 1906.

Turner, Victor. The Ritual Process: Structure and Anti-Structure. Chicago:
      Aldine, 1969.

Von Laue, Theodore H. Leopold Ranke: The Formative Years, Princeton:
      Princeton University Press, 1950.

Wach, Joachim. The Sociology of Religion. Chicago: University of Chicago
      Press, 1962.

Wertheimer, Max. "Gestalt Theory." Social Research 11 (1925): 78-99.

_____. "Unterschungen zur Lehre von der Gestalt: I Prinzipielle Bemerkungen."
      Psychologische Forschung 1 (1922): 47-58.

White, Robert W. Lives in Progress. New York: Holt, Rinehart, Winston, 1966.

White, Robert W. ed. The Study of Lives. Chicago: Aldine-Atherton Press,
      1963.

Study of Emerson

Ahlstrom Sydney. A Religious History of the American People. New Haven:
      Yale University Press, 1972.

Ahlstrom, Sydney, ed. <u>Theology in America: The Major Protestant Voices from Puritanism to Neo-Orthodoxy</u>. Indianapolis: Bobbs-Merrill, 1967.

Aries, Philippe. <u>Centuries of Childhood: A Social History of Family Life</u>. Translated by Robert Baldick. New York: Knopf, 1962.

Bacon, Francis. <u>Novum Organum</u>. Translated by Peter Shaw. London, 1818.

Bishop, Jonathan. <u>Emerson on the Soul</u>. Cambridge: Harvard University Press, 1964.

Bloom, Harold. "The Native Strain." <u>Literary Theory and Structure</u>. Edited by Frank Brady, John Palmer, and Martin Price. New Haven: Yale University Press, 1973.

Bode, Carl. <u>The American Lyceum: Town Meeting of the Mind</u>. New York: Oxford University Press, 1956.

Boornstin, Daniel J. <u>The Americans: The National Experience</u>. New York: Vintage Books, 1965.

Bowen, Francis. "The Spirit of Reform." Commencement Oration, Harvard University, August 28, 1833, Harvard University, Archives.

Brodie, Fawn M. <u>Thomas Jefferson: An Intimate History</u>. New York: W.W. Norton, 1974.

Burke, Kenneth. "I, Eye, Aye--Emerson's Early Essay 'Nature': Thoughts on the Machinery of Transcendence." <u>Transcendentalism and its Legacy</u>. Edited by Myron Simon and T.H. Parsons. Ann Arbor, Mich.: University of Michigan Press, 1966.

Bushman, Richard L. <u>From Puritan to Yankee: Character and Social Order in Connecticut, 1690-1765</u>. New York: W.W. Norton, 1967.

_____. "Jonathan Edwards as Great Man: Identity, Conversion, and Leadership in the Great Awakening." <u>Soundings</u> 52, No. 1 (Spring 1969): 15-46.

Busst, A.J.L. "The Image of the Androgyne in the Nineteenth Century." <u>Romantic Mythologies</u>. Edited by Ian Fletcher. New York: Barnes and Noble, 1967.

Cabot, James Elliot. <u>A Memoir of Ralph Waldo Emerson</u>. 2 vols. Boston: Houghton, Mifflin, and Co. 1887.

Carpenter, Frederic I. <u>Emerson Handbook</u>. 6 vols. New York: Hendricks House, 1953.

Channing, William E. "Unitarian Christianity." <u>Works</u>. 1st Complete American Ed. Boston: J. Munroe, 1841-43, 3: 59-103.

<u>Christian Disciple</u>, New Series, 2 (1820) and 5 (1823).

Christian Examiner 4 (1827).

Christian Spectator 4 (1822).

Columbian Centenial, September 19, October 10, 1812.

Cross, Barbara, ed. The Autobiography of Lyman Beecher. 2 vols. Cambridge:
       The Belknap Press of the Harvard University Press, 1961.

_____. The Educated Woman in America: Selected Writings of Catharine
       Beecher, Margaret Fuller, and M. Carey Thomas. New York: Teachers'
       College Press, Columbia University Press, 1965.

Demos, John. A Little Commonwealth: Family Life in Plymouth Colony. New
       York: Oxford University Press, 1970.

Demos, John, ed. Remarkable Providence, 1600-1750. New York: George
       Braziller, 1972.

Dodds, E.R. The Greeks and the Irrational. Berkeley: University of California
       Press, 1964.

Donald, David. "The Folklore Lincoln." Lincoln Reconsidered: Essays on
       the Civil War Era. New York: Vintage Books, 1961.

Dwight, Theodore. Summer Tours; or, Notes of a Traveller. 2nd ed. New
       York: Houghton, Mifflin, 1934. First edition, 1847.

Dwight, Timothy. A Discourse on Some Events of the Last Century, delivered
       in the Brick Church in New Haven on Wednesday, January 7, 1801.
       New Haven, 1801.

Edinburgh Review, Vol. 46, No. 91 (June, 1827).

Emerson, Charles. "Friendship." Harvard Register. (January 1828), pp. 333-36.

Emerson, Ralph Waldo. The Early Lectures of Ralph Waldo Emerson. Edited
       by Stephen Whicher and Robert Spiller. Cambridge: Harvard University
       Press, 1959.

_____. Emerson's Journals. Edited by Edward Waldo Emerson and Waldo
       Emerson Forbes. 10 vols. Boston: Houghton, Mifflin, 1909-1914.

_____. The Journals and Miscellaneous Notebooks of Ralph Waldo Emerson.
       Edited by William H. Gilman, Alfred R. Ferguson, George P. Clark,
       and Merrell R. Davis. 16 vols. Cambridge: The Belknap press of
       the Harvard University Press, 1960 +.

_____. Nature (1836). The Selected Works of Ralph Waldo Emerson. Edited
       by Brooks Atkinson. New York: Modern Library, 1964.

Emerson, Ralph Waldo. Poems. Household Edition. Edited by Edward Emerson. Boston: Houghton, Mifflin, 1904.

_____. Young Emerson Speaks. Edited by Arthur C. McGiffert, Jr. Port Washington, N.Y.: Kennikat Press, 1938.

_____. Works. Edited by Edward Waldo Emerson. 12 Vols. Centenary Edition. Boston: Houghton, Mifflin, 1903-1904.

Emerson, the Reverend William. A Historical Sketch of the First Church of Boston from its Foundation to the Present Period to which are added two Sermons, one on leaving the old, and the other on entering the new house of worship. Boston: Munroe and Francis, 1812.

Emerson, William. The Diaries and Letters of William Emerson, 1743-1776.

Faust, Clarence H. "The Background of Unitarian Opposition to Transcendentalism." Modern Philology 25 (1838): 297-334.

Fischer, Eric. The Passing of the European Age. Rev. ed. Cambridge: Harvard University Press, 1948.

Francis, R.L. "Architectonics of Emerson's Nature." American Quarterly 19 (Spring, 1967): 39-52.

Frothingham, O.B. Transcendentalism in New England: A History. Boston: American Unitarian Association, 1914.

Gaustad, Edwin. The Great Awakening in New England. Quadrangle Books. New York: Harper and Row, 1968.

Gay, Robert. Emerson: A Study of the Poet as Seer. New York: Doubleday, Doran and Co., 1928.

Gould, Joseph. The Chautauqua Movement. New York: New York State University of New York, 1956.

Gregg, Edith, ed. One First Love: The Letters of Ellen Louisa Tucker to Ralph Waldo Emerson. Cambridge: The Belknap Press of the Harvard University Press, 1962.

Greven, Philip, Jr., ed. Child-Rearing Concepts, 1628-1861. Itasca, Illinois: F.E. Peacock Publishers, Inc. 1973.

Harris, Kenneth. Carlyle and Emerson: Their Long Debate. Cambridge, Massachusetts: Harvard University Press, 1978.

Harris, Neil. The Artist in American Society. New York: George Braziller, 1966.

Harrison, John S. The Teachers of Emerson. New York: Haskell House, 1966.

Hopkins, Samuel. The System of Doctrines Contained in Divine Revelation Explained and Defended 2 Vols. 2nd. ed. Boston, 1811.

Hopkins, Vivian C. Spires of Form: A Study of Emerson's Aesthetic Theory. Cambridge, Massachusetts: Harvard University Press, 1951.

Howe, Daniel Walker. The Unitarian Conscience: Harvard Moral Philosophy, 1805-1861. Cambridge: Harvard University Press, 1970.

Hutchison, William R. The Transcendentalist Ministers: Church Reform in the New England Renaissance. New Haven: Yale University, 1959.

LaRosa, R.C. "Emerson's Search for Literary Form: The Early Journals." Modern Philology 69 (August, 1971): 25-35.

Levin, David. History as Romantic Art. New York: Harcourt, Brace, and World, 1959.

_____. In Defense of Historical Literature. New York: Hill and Wang, 1967.

Lewis, R.W.B. The American Adam: Innocence, Tragedy, and Tradition in the Nineteenth Century. Chicago: University of Chicago Press, 1968.

McLoughlin, William, ed. The American Evangelicals, 1800-1900. New York: Harper and Row, 1968.

Marty, Martin E. The Righteous Empire. New York: Dial, 1970.

Marx, Leo. The Machine in the Garden: Technology and the Pastoral Ideal in America. New York: Oxford University Press, 1964.

Matthiesen, F.O. The American Renaissance. New York: Oxford University Press, 1944.

Mead, Sidney. The Lively Experiment. New York: Harper and Row, 1963.

Merritt, Richard L. Symbols of American Community, 1735-1775. New Haven: Yale University Press, 1966.

Miller, Perry. The Life of the Mind in America. New York: Harcourt, Brace, and World, 1965.

Morrison, Theodore. Chautauqua: A Center for Education, Religion, and the Arts in America. Chicago: University of Chicago Press, 1974.

Obuchowski, P.A. "Emerson, Evolution, and The Problem of Evil." Harvard Theological Review 72 (January-April, 1979): 150-156.

O'Neil, Edward H. A History of American Biography, 1800-1935. Philadelphia: University of Pennsylvania Press, 1935.

Pastore, Nicholas. Selective History of Theories of Visual Perception: 1650-1950. New York: Oxford University Press, 1971.

Paul, Sherman. Emerson's Angle of Vision. Cambridge: Harvard University Press, 1952.

Perry, Bliss. "Emerson's Savings Bank." Praise of Folly and Other Papers. Boston: Houghton, Mifflin, 1923.

Plato. The Republic. Translated by Bejamin Jowett. Vol. 7 of Great Books of the Western World. Edited by Encyclopedia Britannica 54 Vols. Chicago: Encyclopedia Britannica, 1952.

_____. "Theaetetus." The Dialogues of Plato. Translated by Bejamin Jowett. Vol. 7 of Great Books of the Western World. Edited by Encyclopedia Britannica. Chicago: Encyclopedia Britannica, 1952.

Pommer, Henry. Emerson's First Marriage. Carbondale: Southern Illinois University Press, 1967.

Porte, Joel. Representative Man: Ralph Waldo Emerson in his Time. New York: Oxford University Press, 1979.

Ricoeur, Paul. Symbolism of Evil. Translated by Emerson Buchanan. Boston: Beacon Books, 1967.

Riepe, D. "Emerson and Indian Philosophy." Journal of the History of Ideas 28 (January, 1967): 115-122.

Rovit, E. "American Literary Ego: An Essay in Psychohistory." The Southern Review: A Literary and Critical Quarterly Magazine 14 (July, 1978): 409-427.

Rusk, Ralph L. The Life of Ralph Waldo Emerson. New York: Colu bia University Press, 1949.

Slater, Joseph, ed. The Correspondence of Emerson and Carlyle. New York: Columbia University Press, 1964.

Smith, Henry Nash. "Emerson's Problem of Vocation." Emerson: A Collection of Critical Essays. Edited by Milton Konvitz and Stephen Whicher. Englewood Cliffs: Prentice-Hall, 1962.

Smith, H. Shelton, Handy, Robert T., and Loetscher, Lefferts A., eds. American Christianity 2 Vols. New York: Scribner's, 1963.

Sprague, William B. Lectures on Revivals of Religion. New York: D. Appelton and Co., 1833.

Sweet, William W. Religion in the Development of American Culture, 1765-1840. Gloucester, Mass.: Peter Smith, 1963.

Thistlethwaite, Frank. The Anglo-American Connection in the Early Nineteenth Century. Philadelphia: University of Pennsylvania Press, 1959.

_____. The Great Experiment: An Introduction to the American People. Cambridge, England: Cambridge University Press, 1955.

Thundyil, Z. "Emerson and the Problem of Evil: Paradox and Solution." Harvard Theological Review 62 (January, 1969): 51-61.

Tuckerman, Joseph. Principles and Results of the Ministry-at-Large in Boston. Boston, 1838.

Tuveson, Ernest L. Redeemer Nation: The Idea of America's Millennial Role. Chicago: University of Chicago Press, 1968.

The Twenty-Eighth Report of the American Unitarian Society. Boston, 1853.

Tyack, Joseph. George Ticknor and the Boston Brahmins. Cambridge: Harvard University Press, 1967.

Tyler, Alice F. Freedom's Ferment. New York: Harper and Row, 1944.

Wagenknecht, Edward. Ralph Waldo Emerson: Portrait of a Balanced Soul. New York: Oxford University Press, 1974.

Ware, Henry, Jr. Letters Addressed to Trinitarians and Calvinists. Cambridge, 1820.

Ware, Henry, Sr. A Sermon Delivered at Hingham, Lord's Day, May 5, 1805. Boston, 1805.

Whicher, Stephen. Freedom and Fate: An Inner Life of Ralph Waldo Emerson. Philadelphia: University of Pennsylvania Press, 1953.

Wright, Conrad. The Beginnings of Unitarianism in America. Boston: Beacon, 1966.

_____. "The Early Period (1811-1840)." The Harvard Divinity School. Edited by George H. Williams. Boston: Harvard University Press, 1954.

INDEX

Thoreau, Henry D., 299
Transcendental Club, 315, 322, 326, 328, 333
transcendentalism, 96, 119, 188, 216-217, 278, 297, 298, 318, 326, 333
travel, 117, 121, 126, 128, 132, 136, 164, 246, 251-252, 249-254 (and health), 256, 258-259, 261, 311, 321, 332
tuberculosis, 16, 52, 56, 84, 98-99, 112-113, 129, 132-133, 149-150, 159, 162, 163, 166, 178, 192f, 197-198, 201, 213, 219, 233, 237, 254, 288, 292, 302, 319, 331, 332
Tucker, Beza, 206, 239, 284, 286, 288, 318, 333
Tucker, Ellen, 53, 86, 155, 157-158, 163, 164, 165, 168, 169, 170, 171, 175, 176, 179, 182, 183, 184, 185, 187, 191-248, 220-234 (death), 254, 261, 264, 275, 284, 286, 287, 288, 292, 293, 294-305, 306, 313, 318, 321, 323, 328, 344
Tucker, Margaret, 210, 243, 285, 286
Tucker estate, 255-256, 284-288 (probate), 291, 292, 297, 333, 340

Umbilical cord, 58, 82, 242-243, 245, 247, 287, 289, 290, 297, 326, 328, 333, 344-345, 349
unitarians, 5, 7, 16, 92, 96, 98, 105, 107-138 passim, 139, 155, 165, 171, 204, 212, 234, 241, 243, 250f, 253, 271, 284, 328, 335, 336, 339, 341-351

Vincent, John H., 279
vision, 11, 13, 21, 40, 68, 87, 96, 101, 150, 189, 198, 241-242, 244, 246, 251-252, 270, 274, 293, 303, 305-306, 311, 314, 324, 332, 339f, 347-351
visual patterning and imagery, 10-12, 18, 19, 26, 44-46, 50, 72-87 passim, 101, 141, 209, 216-218, 255, 267, 268, 314, 316, 321, 326, 332, 339f, 347-351

War of 1812, 57
Ware, Henry Jr., 157, 164, 167, 172, 176, 179, 181, 185, 186, 251
Webb, Rufus, 58
Webster, Daniel, 125, 273, 280
Winthrope, Governor John, 48

withholding, 234, 277, 339-341; see "anal retention and elimination"
women (Emerson's relation to), 20-21, 294-301, 312-313, 343-345
worms, 28, 250
writings, 1803-1838 (of personal significance)
(a) "American Scholar Address" (1837): 334-336, 349;
(b) "Divinity School Address" (1837): 336, 338, 347, 349;
(c) "Initial, Daemonic, and Celestial Love": 199, 242;
(d) "Letter on Hope" (1817): 62-70;
(e) "Letter to Plato" (1824): 100-105, 109, 127-128, 155, 267'
(f) Nature (1836): 1, 5, 12, 19, 134 (n.1), 248, 318, 322, 324-325, 326;
(g) "The Magician" (1821): 78-81, 90, 93, 238;
(h) "The Pleasures of Hope": 62;
(i) "Pray Without Ceasing" (1826): 122, 140-143, 167;
(j) "Thine Eyes Still Shine": 198, 233, 242;
(k) "Turkey Passage" (1827): 147

Zoroastrians, 130f, 141, 218